THE SPRINGBOKS AND THE HOLY GRAIL

BEHIND THE SCENES AT THE RUGBY WORLD CUP, 1995–2007

THE SPRINGBOKS AND THE

HOLY GRAIL

BEHIND THE SCENES AT THE RUGBY WORLD CUP, 1995–2007

DAN RETIEF

Published by Zebra Press
an imprint of Random House Struik (Pty) Ltd
Company Reg. No. 1966/003153/07
80 McKenzie Street, Cape Town, 8001
PO Box 1144, Cape Town, 8000, South Africa

www.zebrapress.co.za

First published 2011
Reprinted in 2011

3 5 7 9 10 8 6 4 2

Publication © Zebra Press
Text © Dan Retief 2011

Cover image © Getty Images

'World in Union'. Traditional, arranged by Charlie Skarbek
and published by Bucks Music Group Ltd. All Rights Reserved.

'Hymn of the Big Wheel'. Words and music by Robert Del Naja, Grantley Marshall,
Andrew Vowles, Neneh Cherry and Horace Hinds © 1991 Universal/Island
Music Ltd (90%)/Universal Music Publishing MGB Ltd (5%). Used by permission
of Music Sales Ltd. All Rights Reserved. International Copyright Secured.

PUBLISHER: Marlene Fryer
MANAGING EDITOR: Ronel Richter-Herbert
PROOFREADER: Thea Grobbelaar
COVER DESIGNER: Sean Robertson
TEXT DESIGNER: Monique Oberholzer
TYPESETTER: Monique van den Berg
PRODUCTION MANAGER: Valerie Kömmer

Set in 11 pt on 14.5 pt Adobe Garamond

Printed and bound by CPI Group (UK) Ltd, Croydon, CR0 4YY

ISBN 978 1 77022 147 5 (print)
ISBN 978 1 77022 213 7 (ePub)
ISBN 978 1 77022 214 4 (PDF)

Over 50 000 unique African images available to purchase
from our image bank at www.imagesofafrica.co.za

Contents

Acknowledgements

To the bearers of the many names that appear in this book, especially those who added a thread to the tapestry of the Rugby World Cup, thank you for what you have meant to me in my life as a sports journalist. You have been the currency of my career. Particular thanks to James Small, Louis Luyt, Joel Stransky, Gary Teichmann, André Joubert, Fourie du Preez, Merle (McKenna) McLintock, Laurie Kay, André Watson, Naas Botha and Rudolf Straeuli for giving of their time and adding intimate details that enhance the story.

There might not have been a book had it not been for old-fashioned courtesy. I had an idea for a tale about the World Cups and asked a couple of writer friends for the contact numbers of publishers with whom they had worked. I made a few calls, left some messages, and Marlene Fryer, publisher at Zebra Press, returned my call. Fortunately Marlene liked my proposal and gave it the thumbs-up. I thank her sincerely for turning an idea into the pages you hold in your hands.

And if those pages make some sense, it's down to Ronel Richter-Herbert, my editor at Zebra Press, who applied great care and an eagle eye to smooth out the bad habits of writing unedited on a website for 10 years... and for her patience as the words mounted, additional perspectives accumulated and pressing deadlines loomed. In Ronel I was privileged to work with someone who gave meaning to the word 'edit'.

Zebra Press's professionalism and attention to detail never failed to impress me, and I am indebted to Monique Oberholzer for the design of the book and Monique van den Berg for the typesetting. I am very proud of *The Springboks and the Holy Grail*, and I could not have done it without the team at Zebra Press. Also, thank you to Christopher Bjornestad, who made sure I had my facts straight, Sanet le Roux, who indexed the book, and Sean Robertson, who designed the cover.

A picture is worth a thousand words and this book would have been incomplete were it not for the many fine photographs supplied by Gallo Images. A special thank you to Andrew Pittaway and Paul Sales for putting together an excellent lightbox. (It was a new term for me!) It is particularly pleasing to me that this book contains some of the work of outstanding photographers such as Duif du Toit, Tertius Pickard, Grant Leversha and Wessel Oosthuizen.

None of this would have come about had it not been for the *Sunday Times* and SuperSport appointing me to report on the World Cups and providing the financial support that made the tournaments wonderful experiences. A big thank you to both for helping me to achieve whatever status I hold as a journalist.

Finally, to the mentors, colleagues and friends who helped shape my career – the likes of AC Parker, George Parker, Brian Ross-Adams, Philip Gardner, Edward Griffiths, Colin Bryden, Rodney Hartman, Clinton van der Berg and David Williams – and to the rugby people, especially the players of this rough-and-tumble game we love so much, who provided the raw material that enabled me to achieve some repute and, yes, some notoriety in a career that has been great fun and cannot, in all seriousness, be classified as work.

So this book is dedicated to you... the people who are there for me, the people who play the game and the people who make it all worthwhile.

Preface: A voice in the crowd

Central Sydney has that rundown, tatty feeling that most city locations in the surrounds of a major railway station acquire. Named after the Central Railway Station, the largest in Australia, it does not feature in travel guides. It's at the wrong end of George Street, a long way from Sydney's picture-postcard harbour.

This was where I found myself, in a somewhat seedy hotel, for the last two weeks of the 2003 Rugby World Cup, feeling a little down about my life, cut off from the vibe of the tournament and with the Springboks having already flown home.

Then, through a series of extraordinary events, everything changed. In Melbourne I had met up with my old friend from ITC Sports, Richard Nurse, who was leading a group of English fans on their travels through Australia. During a get-together in a pub at The Rocks in Sydney, he offered me a room that was unoccupied at the plush Four Seasons Hotel near the hub of Sydney's famous ferries, Circular Quay, the Opera House and The Rocks, and that had glimpses of Harbour Bridge.

The new address meant that, when returning from Telstra Stadium after the third-place play-off between New Zealand and France, I was in the middle of the Rugby World Cup festivities and able to join Liam del Carme (then of *This Day*) for a drink at one of the many pubs close by. We were edging through the throng when a voice called, 'Dan!' It turned out to be Linda, a former colleague of mine at the *Sunday Times*.

That chance meeting provided me with someone who was to become my friend, partner and soul mate. If I had not moved to downtown Sydney, if I had not decided to stroll into The Rocks, if there had been a delay of mere seconds at any time during the night's journey, I might have missed Linda's call. I think it's called serendipity – my World Cup prize.

I dedicate this book to Linda, whose success in her career, infectious determination and support of the decisions I have made have given me the freedom to do it.

To family, distant and near, but especially to Kate and Jess, this is a chance to simply say: Love you, Dad.

Finally, to all my friends, who put up with the cranks of this old loner, who laugh with me, put me in my place, play golf with me and drink beer and wine with me: you mean more to me than you will ever know.

Throughout this tale of my experiences of covering the Springboks and the World Cup, I was conscious that I did not want to make it my story, but an account of a sporting tournament that has provided such extraordinary moments in South Africa's history that they have been woven into the national psyche. Throughout the process I was aware of not imposing my ego and of being fair to those who contributed to the storyline, but of still being true to myself, of telling it as I saw it.

I was constantly aware that there are more important things in the world than 15 oafs chasing a rugby ball, especially in a country as fraught as ours. But nothing I ever experience will match the elation and pride I felt at Ellis Park on 24 June 1995 and at the Stade de France on 20 October 2007 – unless, of course, there's something to surpass it at Eden Park in Auckland on 23 October 2011!

DAN RETIEF
JOHANNESBURG
APRIL 2011

1

Jonah has a Small problem

James Small, the earphones of his Walkman fixed firmly in place, feels he is having an out-of-body experience as the coach in which he's travelling turns into the little road that runs straight towards the main entrance gates of Ellis Park. A strange calmness comes over him as, outside the window, the surging crowd seems to be moving in slow motion, the brightly coloured South African flags a blur, like a dream sequence in a movie. Moments earlier – indeed for the hours, minutes and sleepless nights of the entire preceding week – he had been terrified of what lay ahead, but now he is suddenly calm. He is ready to do what has to be done.

And what James Small has to do is go out and confront, man to man, the most terrifying figure the world of rugby has ever seen. And not just in any old game, but in the final of the Rugby World Cup.

It is 24 June 1995 at Ellis Park Stadium in Johannesburg and, against all odds, South Africa is about to take on New Zealand for the rugby championship of the world.

Watching the scene from my vantage point high above, leaning on the cold concrete of one of the vast stadium's balustrades, away from the humdrum of the spacious pressroom that had been fitted into the massive reception hall, I find my attention drawn to one green-clad figure in the tableau of crawling buses, swarming masses and swirling flags below – James Small.

The jaw of the Springboks' firebrand wing is clenched, and even at this distance I can see that he is not making any eye contact as he stoops to haul his kitbag out of the bus's hold. I notice the earphones plugged into his ears. What could he possibly be listening to at this time?

Moments earlier, the All Blacks, South Africa's keenest rugby foes, had arrived at the stadium. And there he was … Jonah Lomu, the human juggernaut, the most feared rugby player on the planet who, a week earlier, had figuratively and physically trampled England into the dirt of Newlands, thus ensuring that South African–born Mike Catt would always be seen as road kill left behind by the lugs of his giant boots. My God, he's *huge*, I thought.

Lomu's earphones could not be missed. In keeping with the size of the man who would one day turn his car into a sound bomb, the big Kiwi, as he towered above the throng, had on a giant pair of ear mufflers of the kind normally worn by disc jockeys.

The media and the public, as well as those who recognised his pulling power and that he would soon change the face of rugby forever, were enraptured by Lomu. All the talk centred round what it would take to stop him in his tracks. Back in the present, I heard shouts of 'Go, James!' from the milling crowd below, and I thought how terrifying it must feel to be at the centre of such huge expectation.

But what followed was an occasion like no other. It was an event of so many unforgettable images and deeply etched emotions, of such tension and joy – perhaps it was even the greatest day in South Africa's sporting history. And always the image of James Small getting off the bus stayed with me. What had he been listening to?

I decided that it was a question I had to have answered when I started chronicling the incredible drama of the Springboks and the Rugby World Cup that had played out before my front-row seat in the press box.

When we met for coffee in the trendy Johannesburg suburb of Parkhurst, where Small has turned his hand to supervising the building of upmarket homes, he knew exactly what song had been spinning the windmills of his mind, and how apt it would turn out to be.

'Massive Attack. "Hymn of the Big Wheel",' he said without hesitation.

The big wheel keeps on turning
On a simple line day by day
The earth spins on its axis
One man struggles while another relaxes

Those of us who watch from afar have no idea of the strain involved in an occasion like the Rugby World Cup final. Yes, we may be tense, and of course we jump up and down and shout and sometimes shed a tear, but it cannot compare to actually being involved in the game itself.

Fifteen years later, the emotion is still as raw as ever for James Small when he recalls how he had been the one tasked with stopping Lomu. He was, he says, terrified before the game: 'Shitting myself.'

'You play it over and over in your mind and you pray that you don't make a fool of yourself. The fear just gnaws at you. Not so much of Lomu, but of the occasion. But then suddenly this calmness came over me as we got near the stadium. I have no recollection of getting out of the bus, of going into the stadium and of Nelson Mandela coming into our dressing room. I did not even know he had been there. It was only afterwards, when we were already out on the field, that the lights came back on again and I started to take it all in.

'It probably had something to do with the noise on the field and suddenly being confronted by the All Blacks. Facing the Haka. Up until that moment, I had not seen Jonah up close, and all I could think was, "My God, he's a big ****."

'As I said, I was totally unaware of Madiba having come into the dressing room. My recollections started on the field. We had first met Madiba at Silvermine while training in the Cape, but I was overwhelmed when he spoke to me on the pitch of Ellis Park. He said, "My son has a picture of you on his wall. You are his hero. You have a very big job to do today, but my son says you can do it."'

He blinked back the tears at the memory.

Small's major concern – how to stop Lomu – had not been assuaged by the Springboks' crusty coach, Kitch Christie. At a press conference earlier in the week, Christie was asked, 'Do you have a plan to stop Jonah Lomu?' He replied: 'Don't ask me. That's James's problem.' Some fans picked up on what Christie had said, and at the final they unfurled a banner that read: 'Lomu has a Small problem!'

But there was, in fact, a plan – devised by Hennie le Roux. Small recalled: 'We agreed that I would stand wide and force Lomu inside, which made me very nervous and uncomfortable. It was not the way I was accustomed to defending. I liked to think the touchline was my ally; I would give the guy the outside and trust my pace to get to him and force him into touch. I wasn't that scared of Lomu. He was big and fast, but I felt that I would always be able to get hold of him. I had a picture in my mind of a leopard stalking [its prey]; they go in low and get a grip, and they don't let go!

'To tell you the truth, I was more nervous of Inga Tuigamala, whom we'd met in 1992. He was only 5'10", but he was also built like a brick shithouse and he would come straight at you with his knees churning – it was much harder to get a grip on him. As it turned out, though, the plan worked, because Lomu did tend to go inside, only to be nailed by the cover defence. Funnily enough, Japie Mulder hit him a really good one when he was on the outside.'

In retrospect, Small's fixation on a turning wheel was extremely apt in relation to the game of rugby, the Springboks and the World Cup, for through the years there have been more plots, sub-plots, intrigues and storylines than one can realistically keep track of. From the axis of the symbolic wheel, the spokes, or subjects, fan out, blur into a haze, slow down and become distinguishable again, somehow connected but all separate, as the outer rim, the game, keeps on spinning.

The big wheel had brought the Springboks to this point – just one more game to win the World Cup – but what a road had been travelled for South Africa: not only to be presenting the World Cup, but to have actually reached the final.

South Africa had not been part of the first two World Cups – in New Zealand in 1987 and England in 1991 – but had played a crucial part in establishing a tournament that a great many members of the rugby establishment had been dead against.

Hard as it is to believe now, this tournament, which is now the third or fourth biggest in world sport (audience figures have a way of fluctuating from source to source) after the Summer Olympics, the FIFA World Cup and the World Championships in Athletics, did not find universal favour when it was first proposed.

It took a few visionaries from the southern hemisphere to put forward the idea of bringing together the great and the good of the game in a single competition, but some administrators – especially those of the four Home Unions (England, Wales, Scotland and Ireland), memorably tagged as the 'old farts' by Will Carling – were far from convinced that it was a good idea.

The concept of a World Cup of rugby was raised for the first time at an AGM of the International Rugby Board (IRB) in 1979. This was two years before South Africa's contentious 'flour-bomb tour' to New Zealand, which effectively made it impossible for the Springboks to tour overseas. New Zealand delegates Ces Blazey and Bob Stuart tabled a motion to discuss the idea 'in principle'.

'The idea found no support,' read the minutes, but the notion was bubbling under, and in 1982 the IRB received proposals from sports marketing companies to stage a World Cup. Member unions were also becoming more receptive, and when France and New Zealand put forward proposals in 1984, the board finally agreed that a feasibility study should be undertaken.

It fell to Australia and New Zealand to put this together, and they appointed a highly respected pair, Sir Nicholas Shehadie, a former Wallaby captain and Lord Mayor of Sydney, who had toured South Africa and become friendly with Dr Danie Craven in 1953, and the highly respected Kiwi administrator, Dick Littlejohn – or 'Dick and Nick' as they came to be known while peddling the concept of a World Cup to rugby's doubting Thomases – to undertake the task.

What is often not appreciated is that just eight countries – England, Wales, Ireland, Scotland, France, New Zealand, Australia and South Africa, the founding members – controlled rugby. However, it was not as simple as forcing a 5-3 vote in favour of a World Cup, as each union was repre-sented by two delegates, who would not necessarily vote the same.

New Zealand and Australia were obviously in favour; France, represented by Craven's great friend and ally Albert Ferrasse, was for; England was split; Wales also went both ways; but Scotland and Ireland were unanimously against, which meant that South Africa, by now in deep isolation, would hold the swing vote by way of its delegates, Dr Danie Craven and Prof. Fritz Eloff.

In the end, Craven, holding out hope that his beloved Springboks might still be included in the tournament, voted in favour of staging a World Cup, but the honourable gentlemen of the IRB would nevertheless have their hands forced by a phenomenon they feared above all else – professionalism.

At the time, an Australian entrepreneur, David Lord, sent paroxysms of indignation rippling through the corridors of power by casting attractive financial hooks at top players (and getting some serious nibbles) to establish a professional tournament, which the worthies of the IRB huffily dismissed as a 'circus'. But, as Keith Rowlands, who at the time represented Wales and later headed his country's presentation of the 1999 tournament, explained: 'It wasn't the proposal itself and its commercial value, which was pretty non-existent, [that held sway]. It was the fear that if the [IRB] didn't establish [a World Cup], then somebody else might.' That is to say, someone might come along and do to rugby what Kerry Packer had done to cricket.*

So it came to pass that on 20 March 1985, one year short of the IRB's centenary, on the first day of the AGM, in Paris, at the end of a marathon

---

* *In 1977, Australian television mogul Kerry Packer revolutionised cricket by launching a made-for-TV 'World Series' in which players, kitted out in bright outfits, were remunerated much better than they had previously been – it was the catalyst for the game going fully professional.*

four-hour discussion of 'Dick and Nick's' feasibility study, the chairman of the board, Australia's long-serving administrator Dr Roger Vanderfield, was compelled to put the proposal to the vote. The result was minuted thus: 'The Board considered the feasibility study entitled "World Cup Rugby" and resolved to accept the principle of an International Tournament as outlined, but subject to it being under the control of the International Board.' It was decided that what turned out to be the inaugural tournament in 1987 would be staged jointly by New Zealand and Australia, with the bulk of the matches scheduled to be played in the two islands of the former.

It would have been a difficult time for Dr Craven, as the fallout from the 1981 tour to New Zealand, plagued by anti-apartheid demonstrators, was still fresh in everyone's mind. As a result, it had become obvious that the Springboks would not be taking part in any World Cup, and South Africa's status as outcasts would soon become even more entrenched with the advent of the 'rebel' tour by the New Zealand Cavaliers, the All Blacks in all but name, in 1986.

However, had Craven and Eloff voted *against* a tournament in which they knew South Africa would not be able to participate, there might never have been a Rugby World Cup. It has been suggested that South Africa might have abstained from voting in the hope of finding a way back in, in the event of the anti-apartheid boycott being repealed, but there is little doubt that without the support of Craven, the *éminence grise* of world rugby, others might have been swayed to vote against it.

The vote having been passed – to stage just *one* World Cup tournament – it was down to Sydney Hospital director Dr Vanderfield to provide the necessary prescriptions to get the ball rolling, as there was a momentary feeling of, 'now that we have voted for a Rugby World Cup, what do we do about it?'

An organising committee was, of course, required, and the highly respected and skilled Englishman John Kendall-Carpenter, a great advocate of the tournament, stood out as the ideal man to chair the tournament committee, along with a key supporter in Wales's Keith Rowlands. Vanderfield also had the vision to bring in one of the naysayers, former Irish international and British Lions player Ronnie Dawson.

The committee obviously also had to have a New Zealander and an Australian on board. Former All Black skipper Bob Stuart, the man who had endured an arduous time as the Springboks' liaison manager during the 1981 tour, was an obvious choice to represent the Kiwis, and Australia was represented by the former Wallaby prop Ross Turnbull – a man who would turn up in a completely different guise during the 1995 Rugby World Cup tournament in South Africa and be the catalyst for the enormous sea change that would herald the dawn of an officially authorised, professional rugby union.

So, now there was finally a Rugby World Cup, but one which, staggeringly – such was the naivety of the time – was scheduled to be held in May and June in New Zealand and Australia: right in the middle of New Zealand's coldest and wettest months!

The Cavaliers tour to South Africa in 1986, by a New Zealand team that contained all but two of the All Blacks who would have been on the aborted tour of 1985, caused immense international controversy. It unleashed a furore not least because of the poorly kept secret that the players were being handsomely paid for their part in breaking South Africa's sports isolation. In retrospect, however, the Cavaliers tour probably motivated rugby minds to start organising the first World Cup, to take place the following year, in an effort to deflect attention from the ill-conceived tour and restore rugby's tarnished image.

In their planning, the realisation soon dawned that if one is to host a tournament called the 'World Cup', you have to have a cup! You would think the IRB would have called for designs to be tendered and then commissioned a gold- or silversmith to manufacture the trophy, but because time was tight and also, perhaps, because administrators were not convinced that a World Cup tournament would stick, John Kendall-Carpenter, as the chairman of the inaugural tournament committee, and Air Commodore Bob Weighill, the secretary of the IRB, former England forwards both, took themselves off to an exclusive establishment in the City of London to see a man about a cup.

Their destination was Garrard, the crown jeweller in fashionable Regent Street, where Richard Jarvis, the managing director of the company, brought a cup down from the vault and showed it to the two men. The cup had been crafted in the Garrard workshop in 1906, a Victorian version of a cup fashioned in 1740 by the gold- and silversmith Paul de Lamerie (1688–1751), whose Huguenot parents had fled to London and set up shop in Soho.

'Hmmm,' the gentlemen of the IRB probably murmured as they handled the golden pitcher. What they had in their hands was a cup fashioned in silver and gilded in gold, 38 centimetres tall, with two cast scroll handles.

On one handle perches the head of a satyr, on the other the head of a nymph – and, as one description put it, with the nymph, beautiful spirit of nature, forever safe from the randy aspirations of the goat-man. The terminals are a bearded mask, a lion mask and a vine, while the lid is topped by something that looks like a pineapple, and the whole thing is rather quite ornate and unrugbylike.

However, Kendall-Carpenter and Weighill liked what they saw, showed it to their fellow office bearers, and eventually Ronnie Dawson of Ireland, Keith Rowlands of Wales, Bob Stuart and Dick Littlejohn of New Zealand, and the Australians Nick Shehadie and Ross Turnbull approved their choice. They named it the 'Webb Ellis Cup' – note: no 'William'; and 'Cup', not 'Trophy'.

Garrard dates back to the first half of the 18th century, with royal connections from its beginning. In 1792, Robert Garrard, originally an apprentice at the company, became a partner, and then took control of the business. In 1843, Queen Victoria appointed Garrard the Crown Jeweller, which they still remain today. One of their stressful tasks was re-cutting the Koh-i-Noor diamond, and their first famous sporting trophy was the Royal Yacht Squadron's Cup, presented in 1848 by the Marquess of Anglesey. It is better known as the America's Cup, from the first winner of the race in 1851, the yacht *America*.

Interestingly, the officials charged with finding a trophy chose to pre-serve a legend as old as the game itself: that of William Webb Ellis who, at Rugby School in the English Midlands, was supposed to have picked up the ball 'with a fine disregard for the rules of football' and run with it. Subsequent research has provided little proof of the legend or that it was indeed Webb Ellis who was responsible for starting the rough-and-tumble game that would bear the name of the school he attended.

Nevertheless, now there was a cup, and attention invariably switched to which country might become the first to have its name engraved on the plinth and provide the first captain to hold it aloft in victory.

In South Africa, feigned disinterest masked envy as the 16 invited nations descended on New Zealand, the seven standing members of the IRB (minus South Africa) – New Zealand, Australia, England, Wales, Scotland, Ireland and France – being joined by nine others. Some choices were obvious: Italy, Romania and Argentina had respectable records against the major teams, while Canada, the United States, Japan, Fiji and Tonga had a history of playing the game. Canada, the USA and Japan also offered the potential of reasonable television markets. The 16th spot went to Zimbabwe, which, as Rhodesia, had once been a 'province' of the old South African Rugby Board. The Rhodesian players had also been eligible for Springbok selection.

The Cavaliers tour to South Africa and the strident accusations that the players who had taken part – David Kirk and John Kirwan were notable absentees – had sold out the All Black jersey were quickly forgotten as the New Zealand Rugby Football Union (NZRFU) pieced together its squad. The 'rebels' had been let off quite lightly, being banned for just two Tests, and most were quickly brought back into the World Cup squad thereafter alongside the 'Baby Blacks', so called because New Zealand had had to field sides with numerous new caps in the absence of the Cavaliers players. Among them was a promising player who would become an All Black legend: Sean Fitzpatrick.

Alison Kervin, former editor of *Rugby World* magazine, described the opening ceremony of the 1987 Rugby World Cup thus: 'The limitations of time and money showed rather ferociously as schoolgirl go-go dancers and young gymnasts cavorted across the pitch, looking tired and fed up in the drizzling rain. It was too damp even to attempt to light the rather feeble-looking clump of fireworks that sat alongside the young dancers, so it was left to a few strips of bunting and a cluster of national flags to announce [that] the World Cup had arrived.'

By all accounts, the first World Cup was – to use a great South African expression – a *jôl*. The British and Irish slopped around from one piss-up to another, the French sometimes did credit to their formidable line-up, the rest got whipped and the All Blacks were so dominant that, in the words of former Wallaby forward-turned-journalist, Peter FitzSimons, 'no one else was third'.

The first Rugby World Cup match took place between New Zealand and Italy, in Pool 3, at Eden Park in Auckland on 22 May 1987 in front of 20 000 spectators. New Zealand won the match 70-6, scoring 12 four-point tries, with flanker Michael Jones staking a special mention in rugby annals by scoring the first-ever RWC try – although, ironically, the first *actual* 'try' was a penalty try awarded by Australian referee Bob Fordham. Jones, nicknamed 'The Ice Man', would add an even better codicil to his record by also scoring the first try in the next tournament, when he crossed the line, against England, in the opening game of the 1991 RWC.

Despite New Zealand sweeping all before them and John Kirwan scoring a wonder try in the opening match, the early rounds of the tournament were marked by concern over mismatches and complaints about 'cricket' scores, and the tournament really came alive only in the semi-finals, when France and Australia, playing at the Concorde Oval in Sydney, produced one of the all-time classics.

With only a couple of minutes' play remaining, and the scores locked at 24-all, both sides were in all-out attack, desperately looking for the points to take them to the final. France attacked down the right through Denis Charvet, before swinging play back left. Patrice Lagisquet made ground, before Laurent Rodriguez fed fullback Serge Blanco, who outpaced four defenders to score in the corner. Didier Camberabero converted from the touchline to make it 30-24 and cap a sensational finish to a match that arguably secured the future of World Cup rugby.

The final, played in bright sunshine at Eden Park in Auckland on 20 June in front of 46 000 spectators, was refereed by Kerry Fitzgerald of Australia and won 29-9 by New Zealand. Michael Jones, David Kirk and Kirwan scored tries, with Grant Fox kicking one conversion, four penalties and a drop goal for the All Blacks. For France, Didier Camberabero kicked a penalty and converted Pierre Berbizier's try. The victory meant that scrumhalf Kirk, captaining the side in hooker Andy Dalton's injury-enforced absence, lifted the Webb Ellis Cup for New Zealand for the first and, so far, only time.

The World Cup was declared to have been a great success. Legends were born, a platform was created for the making of future legends, a whole new treasure trove of folklore was generated, and the Webb Ellis Cup would soon be seen as the Holy Grail of Rugby.

Franck Mesnel, the flamboyant centre from Racing Club de Paris, who had spurred his teammates on to outrageous acts, such as wearing pink bow ties in French championship matches, played flyhalf for *Les Tricolores* that day. He toyed with wearing the necktie in the final, but fearing punitive action by the IRB, is said to have stuffed the pink bow tie into his shorts. A few years later, when he launched his own line of clothing in a chain of chic stores, he named his business Eden Park and adopted a pink bow tie as his logo.

2

Apartheid's last outpost

Arguments concerning team selection are almost as old as the Springbok jersey itself, but some say that, at the time of the inaugural 1987 Rugby World Cup, Naas Botha was in charge of the best Springbok backline ever.

The year before, the Boks had beaten the New Zealand Cavaliers, the All Blacks in all but name and official sanction, 3-1 in a hotly contested and controversial series. Many aficionados rated the backline of Garth Wright, Naas Botha, Michael du Plessis, Danie Gerber, Jaco Reinach, Carel du Plessis and Johan Heunis as the best ever.

But some would say that the best line-up never actually played – for that you'd have had to put in Divan Serfontein for Wright at scrumhalf and Ray Mordt for the South African 400m record-holder Reinach on the right wing – but Botha has no doubt that his team, with a formidable and massive pack consisting of Piet Kruger, Uli Schmidt, Frans 'Domkrag' Erasmus, Louis Moolman, Schalk Burger, Wahl Bartmann, Gert Smal and Jannie Breedt (how good a set of forwards is that?), would have been extremely competitive and might even have won the 1987 World Cup, had they been allowed to compete.

That they didn't compete could be attributed to the apartheid policies of South Africa's then National Party government. Botha's recollection about missing out on the inaugural RWC is typical of many, but not all, of his teammates at the time. On the one hand, he was a highly trained, highly focused, highly determined sportsman denied an opportunity to compete on the highest stage, but on the other he accepts that the system he inadvertently represented was indefensible – after all, he had been in New Zealand in 1981 and had experienced how deep the world's abhorrence of racial discrimination ran.

Even so, not having been part of a tournament that might have crowned an already impressive career is not something Botha dwells on. He does, though, proffer a perceptive view of the role the Springboks played in helping the All Blacks win the Webb Ellis Cup.

'We had a very good series against the Cavaliers,' he says. 'They had top players such as Grant Fox, Dave Loveridge, Murray Mexted, Buck

Shelford, Jock Hobbs, Mark Shaw, Andy Haden, Gary Knight, Hika Reid and John Ashworth, and had set themselves the target of becoming the first New Zealand team to win a series in South Africa [something that was not achieved until 1996, under Sean Fitzpatrick].

'We had a very good side, with good depth, but even though we watched the World Cup games on TV and wished we were there, there is no point pondering on what might have been – certainly I don't. The reality is that we were not there, and you can't change that, but it's ironic that we probably played an important role in the All Blacks going on to win the World Cup for the first time.

'They [the sports administrators of the New Zealand Rugby Union] quickly forgave the Cavaliers, which meant they went into the tournament with a team forged in the heat of the fire the year before in South Africa. You can't underestimate how important that was. Plus, the fact that we played four Tests on four successive Saturdays for the first time ever also helped to hone the All Blacks for the tournament.'

As it turned out, Botha's potentially golden generation would not play in the next World Cup either, in England in 1991, as the steel door of isolation slammed shut.

But South African rugby administrators remained hopeful that their futile keep-politics-out-of-sport mantra would bring about a miraculous change of heart and allow the Boks back into the international game. In 1989, during the centenary celebrations of the South African Rugby Board (SARB), Prof. Fritz Eloff caused something of a stir when he announced at a function at his beloved Loftus Versfeld that South Africa would be applying to stage the 1995 Rugby World Cup.

South Africa's position as a founder member of the IRB, albeit a non-competing member, was entrenched, but some critics felt that Prof. Eloff, in his capacity as chairman of the IRB, had rather overstepped the mark.

After the tour by the Cavaliers in 1986, the Springboks had not played a single Test in the two following years, but by 1989 some of the anger had subsided and progressive murmurings from South Africa's Nationalist government persuaded the international community to permit a World XV, made up of Englishmen, Welshmen, Irishmen, Scotsmen, Australians and Frenchmen, but containing no New Zealanders, to play two Tests in South Africa to mark the SARB's centenary.

The ravages of isolation were already starting to show, however, and the Springboks battled to score a close 20-19 victory over a pretty useful World side at Newlands, while also scraping home 22-16 at Ellis Park in a match that could have gone either way.

The World XV was managed by Willie John McBride, coached by Bob Templeton and contained the likes of Australia's Greg Martin (now a familiar voice on Fox TV's rugby broadcasts), Rod McCall, Bill Campbell and Tom Lawton (who would help Natal to win their historic first Currie Cup the following season); France's Philippe Sella, Denis Charvet, Franck Mesnel, Pierre Berbizier, Laurent Rodriguez and Marc Cecillon; and England's Peter Winterbottom, Mike Teague, Jeff Probyn and Paul Rendall. For the Springboks, a significant new name turned up – André Joubert, who made his debut when subbing for Johan Heunis at Newlands.

Craven had long feared that the standard of local rugby would drop if international contact was lost, and composite sides had become a way for administrators, coaxed by him, to provide competition for the Springboks. But there was a great disparity in how seriously the teams approached these games.

I witnessed an amusing but telling incident that took place at the President Hotel in Sea Point, Cape Town, which spoke volumes about these contrasting attitudes. It occurred after a 'World XV', known as the Western Province Centenary Team, put together to mark the union's centenary in 1983, had played a South African XV (the Springboks in all but name) at Newlands. One of the players in the World XV was Irish hard man and rascal (funny how the two traits normally go together) Willie Duggan. The tough loose forward's impossibly white legs revealed why Afrikaans rugby old-timers often referred to teams from the Misty Isles as the *bleekbene* (pale legs). Duggan was a lazy trainer and approaching his swansong for Ireland. He was in South Africa for what his countrymen call the 'craic' (fun).

But Duggan played hard (while he had the breath!), was excellent company and easily approachable. In fact, he was so approachable that when an inebriated fan, hanging around the hotel foyer, asked him for a memento, Duggan ripped off his tour tie and gave it to him. Then, for good measure, he also shook off his WP Centenary XV blazer and hurled it at the man, waving a grand farewell and smiling broadly as the lift doors closed!

Although the World invitation sides often gave an excellent account of themselves – the 1989 team, for instance, could have won both Tests with a bit more luck and more of the desperation that marked the play of the Springboks – their trips were basically out-of-season holidays for the players and, even in those amateur days, I would not be surprised if it were to emerge that they were recompensed for their trouble. But while they were having a good time, the South Africans were fighting for their lives.

So, while the Springboks did not play any Tests in 1987, the rest of the world contested the first World Cup. In 1988, there were again no Tests, and in 1989 the Boks got two Tests against an 'invitation' squad (South Africa awarded full caps), but then did not play any internationals in 1990, nor in 1991, the year of the second Rugby World Cup.

In this period, their keenest rivals, the All Blacks, played 36 Tests. By the time the mantle of isolation was lifted in August 1992, when the two nations met at Ellis Park, New Zealand had played in 44 internationals versus the two of South Africa.

However, these were momentous times, and there is a danger, given this book's narrow focus on rugby and the World Cup, to trivialise or discount the massive tectonic shifts that were taking place in South Africa. This would be a mistake, as at the time I worked for so-called liberal newspapers such as the *Rand Daily Mail* and the *Sunday Times* and was acutely aware of the sea change taking place in society. In fact, I was often amused by popular suggestion that rugby could be separated from politics when the game had so often been tarnished by political interference ... and still is, it must be said.

I feel to this day that rugby, in some small part, played a role in changing deeply entrenched attitudes, eventually leading to the unbanning of anti-government organisations and the release of Nelson Mandela and other struggle leaders. These events, in turn, resulted in the lifting of the sports sanctions that had kept a generation of South African athletes out of international competition.

The protest-ridden tours by the Springboks to the UK and Ireland in 1969/70 and to Australia in 1971 had taken place before South Africa had television, but the 1981 tour to New Zealand was televised and South Africans could see for themselves how the rest of the world felt about apartheid (the Boks were also hounded and pilloried in America) and the lengths to which they were prepared to go to make their views known.

And so, when in March 1982 Nelson Mandela, as well as other senior ANC leaders such as Walter Sisulu and Ahmed Kathrada, were transferred from Robben Island to Pollsmoor Prison, it was purportedly in order to remove their influence on the new generation of young black activists being incarcerated on the island. Later it would be revealed that it might have been orchestrated to facilitate discreet contact between the ANC leaders and the South African government.

In 1985, a proposed tour by the All Blacks to South Africa was aborted after two Auckland lawyers, Philip Recordon and Paddy Finnegan, managed to obtain a High Court injunction against the NZRFU to stop the tour. That same year, President PW Botha offered Nelson Mandela his freedom, but only if he 'unconditionally rejected violence as a political weapon'. Mandela spurned the offer, but the cancellation of the tour sent another strong message that there would be no international rugby for the Springboks unless the South African government's policies changed drastically.

The great New Zealand rugby writer Terry McLean (later Sir Terry) wrote that the case to have the tour abandoned was 'masterfully handled by a Queen's Counsel, EW "Ted" Thomas', who called 'a special witness, a member of the Xhosa peoples of the Ciskei homeland and chaplain of the black University of Fort Hare, who recounted the simple, painful tale of the injustices of South African society'. His name? The Reverend Arnold Stofile, later to revert to his given name, Makhenkhesi, and to become South Africa's Minister of Sport in the new democracy.

The injunction, granted by Judge Casey of the New Zealand High Court, caused a flutter in my working life. Former Springbok captain Wynand Claassen and I had been working on his autobiography, principally chronicling his experiences in New Zealand in 1981, timed to be released to coincide with the tour. Our publisher, the late Hans Strijdom, a deputy editor of the *Sunday Times* and author of a controversial book on the Broederbond, *The Super-Afrikaners*, received a tip-off that the NZRFU would ignore the High Court ruling, as well as admonishments not to tour by New Zealand's Privy Council and Prime Minister David Lange, and that the All Black team would secretly sneak out of their country and turn up for the tour.

Pretty far-fetched, but Strijdom was panicked into rushing Claassen's autobiography, *More Than Just Rugby*, into print. One day I received a phone call from him. 'Come and fetch a copy of your book!' he exclaimed.

'What do you mean?' I said.

'It's here with me; I've just received the advance copies. It looks fantastic!' Fantastic indeed. Lying on my desk was a manuscript full of corrections in red ink, and he was telling me that the book had already been printed!

The book was a frank account of a turbulent time in Springbok rugby and caused quite a stir – unsurprisingly, the short chapter on any influence the Broederbond might have had on Springbok rugby and Claassen's career was seized upon, sometimes by people who had not read a word of it! The former captain had tried so hard – with no help from the touring team's officials, I might add – to reach out to the New Zealand people and explain the complexities of the South African situation. But he was to find that sport and politics were definitely indivisible when he was summarily axed from the Springbok selection panel to which he had been elected after his retirement from rugby.

Like Claassen, there were other rugby people who refused to bury their heads in the sand. Former Springbok captain Tommy Bedford was forever famous or notorious, depending on your point of view, for coining the phrase 'The Last Outpost of the British Empire' to describe Natal when he gave the finger to the national selectors of his day. With his liberal convictions (which made him hugely unpopular in certain circles), he had been in touch with the ANC in exile.

Bedford persuaded Dr Craven and other administrators to attend an exploratory meeting with members of the ANC in London in 1987, but in the end the only person who attended was none other than everyone's so-called arch-Afrikaner, Louis Luyt. Luyt, who was, ironically, not a member of the Nationalist Party or the Broederbond and who, in his edifying autobiography, *Walking Proud*, revealed that he was often snubbed by the Afrikaner establishment, reported back to Craven, and two months later he flew to another meeting, this time in Frankfurt. And this time Thabo Mbeki was present.

Dr Luyt got in touch with Foreign Minister Pik Botha, and his account of subsequent events revealed staggering indifference – or was it arrogance? – from the government of the time. But the great wheel was turning inexorably, and Luyt soon received word from Craven, again via Bedford and former All Black scrumhalf Chris Laidlaw, who was then New Zealand's first resident High Commissioner to Zimbabwe, that the ANC wanted another meeting, in Harare, where the full executive board would be present.

Laidlaw, who came to South Africa as an All Black tourist in 1970, when he was on the receiving end of a crunching tackle by Frik du Preez and Albie Bates (see Wessel Oosthuizen's famous photograph), was a strident critic of South Africa's race laws. Laidlaw was a Rhodes Scholar to Oxford, a diplomat and an MP, an author and New Zealand's Race Relations Conciliator, and he and Bedford were intellectual and emotional allies who had first met at Oxford. Their dual efforts, a Springbok and an All Black, helped to restore rugby's greatest rivalry in August 1992, a fact that is often overlooked.

Craven, Luyt and Bedford flew to Harare in the latter's private jet and were met by a group of ANC heavyweights, including Mbeki, Alfred Nzo, Barbara Masekela, the Pahad brothers Essop and Aziz, and a man who in the not-too-distant future would play an enormous role in the shaping of post-apartheid sport, Steve Tshwete. Ebrahim Patel represented the South African Rugby Football Union (SARFU), which, under the banner of the National Sports Council, had embraced the slogan 'No Normal Sport in an Abnormal Society' and supported, and was supported by, the ANC.

The ANC had long understood that rugby exerted a powerful influence on the psyche of the Nationalists, and their plan was to turn the meeting with South Africa's Mr Rugby into a media opportunity, as well as to issue a strong statement of intent at the end of it.

Delegates afforded Craven great respect, apparently referring to him as 'Oom Danie' or 'Oom Doc'. However, it was the clinically minded Luyt who helped draft a joint statement of intent, the main thrust of which was the formation of a single, non-racial controlling body for South African rugby through the unification of the SARB and SARFU.

The television images of this meeting between South Africa's leading rugby officials and the so-called 'terrorists' of the ANC caused a storm in the Republic, with rugby officials hastening to distance themselves from Craven and Luyt. The duo was roundly castigated by government – particularly by Minister of Education FW de Klerk. However, within a year of having succeeded PW Botha as president, De Klerk would be singing from a different psalm book when he lifted the ban on the ANC and the Pan Africanist Congress (PAC), setting in motion the negotiations that would result in Nelson Mandela's release from prison on 11 February 1990. Few recalled or acknowledged that Craven, Luyt and the game of rugby had played a massive part in hastening the process.

Following his release from prison, Mandela returned to the leadership of the ANC and, between 1990 and 1994, led the party in the multiparty negotiations that would result in the country's first multiracial elections on 27 April 1994. In the end, the long, patiently shuffling queues of people voted for Mandela to be inaugurated as the country's first black president on 10 May 1994.

Against this tableau of history in the making, it is easy to see how the second Rugby World Cup, staged by England in 1991, passed by almost unnoticed in South Africa. Rugby administrators from both sides of the apartheid divide had their hands full negotiating a unified body, and some were dragged kicking and screaming into the new arrangement when Craven and Patel were elected as joint presidents of the unified South African Rugby Football Union in Kimberley on 23 March 1992. Kimberley had been chosen as the venue for the meeting, as this was where the South African Rugby Football Board was established in 1889 and the SA Coloured Rugby Board in 1896. And, of course, it was to Griqualand West that Sir Donald Currie's golden cup, which bore his name and which would inspire generations of South African provincial players, was presented during the first-ever tour by WE 'Bill' Maclagen's British Isles team in 1891.

A symbolic mixed-race match was held to mark the occasion at De Beers Stadium. Naas Botha, captaining one of the sides, was partnered at half-back by Allister Coetzee, who would later become one of Jake White's assistant coaches at the 2007 Rugby World Cup and, shortly thereafter, the highly successful coach of the Stormers in the Super 14 and Western Province in the Currie Cup competition.

The merging of the two bodies resulted in the formation of the South African Rugby Football Union (SARFU), with the added and rather wonderful consequence of being readmitted to international rugby. Craven decreed that the 'outcoming' Test would be against the All Blacks at Ellis Park on 15 August 1992, followed by a Test against the newly crowned world champion Wallabies a week later at Newlands, and then a tour to play France (twice) and England. The years of isolation had clearly not diminished the arrogance of which South African rugby had often been accused – these just happened to be the four strongest teams in the world!

An upshot of South Africa's isolation had been intensified competition between New Zealand and their near-neighbours Australia, which had resulted in the Wallabies becoming increasingly competitive. A golden generation of players had thus emerged who were no longer prepared to stand back for the All Blacks and who would end up winning the second RWC tournament in 1991, beating England at Twickenham in the final.

South African rugby's miraculous transition from skunks of the world to the flavour of the month unfolded as other nations, who had missed the drawing power of the Springboks, clamoured to re-engage with them. This should have resulted in a period of magnanimous co-operation and harmony, but instead there was only controversy and turmoil, which would set the tone for the next decade and a half – and it started with the Test that marked the Springboks' re-emergence into international rugby.

Instead of humbly drawing back the isolation curtain and gingerly re-entering the international game, the Springboks arrived in a blare of amplified sound that reverberated throughout the country and the rest of the world when Louis Luyt declared that the old national anthem, 'Die Stem', would be played ahead of the game. The moment itself was awe-inspiring, largely because the song was sung with such defiance that I later described the fervour and bellicosity of the crowd as similar to a display at a Nazi youth rally. In addition, most of the spectators had ignored a request from Nelson Mandela himself to observe a minute's silence in memory of those who had died during the country's unrest and were waving old South African flags in a show of blatant rebelliousness.

Louis Luyt was unrepentant about his decision, and is to this day, writing in his autobiography, *Walking Proud*:

> For weeks leading up to the test, a debate raged in the press and over radio as to whether it would be appropriate to play 'Die Stem' at Ellis Park before the game. I disagreed with newspaper pundits who strongly opposed the playing of our national anthem on this occasion while raising no objection to 'Nkosi Sikilel' iAfrika' being played at soccer matches. After all, 'Die Stem' was still our official anthem. And even without the overwhelming support of the rugby public, I would still have pressed ahead. This was, in my view, an issue of principle. I was not about to deny the existence of a national anthem merely to please the ANC or any of the wimps who wished to roll over and play dead.

The ANC were quite understandably furious, and South Africa's guests none too impressed that they had been caught up in such an imbroglio, especially their next opponents, Australia. Be that as it may, the Test match that followed the singing of the anthem was an epic, with the All Blacks just hanging on to get home 27-24 in a match that showcased the sublime skills of Danie Gerber, but which left James Small in a state of depression over a pass he knocked on when it seemed he was certain to score. Interestingly, only four players – Naas Botha, Jannie Breedt (who had relinquished the captaincy to Botha), Adolf Malan and Heinrich Rodgers – had managed to straddle the three-year gap between the last pre-isolation Test, against the World XV in 1989, and the 1992 Test against New Zealand.

The Springboks' next opponents were the Wallabies, who had already arrived in the country. They had played Western Transvaal on the Tuesday and Northern Transvaal on the Friday, and they attended the Test match against the All Blacks at Ellis Park – and they did not like what they heard and saw!

The Wallabies' next game was against Eastern Province in Port Elizabeth on the following Tuesday – an occasion that provided me with a 'scoop' that I could not write. We were staying at the Holiday Inn next to the Humewood Golf Course and, returning from a late dinner on the Sunday night, I decided I needed a Coke from the vending machine at the end of the corridor. As I turned to walk back to my room, Nick Farr-Jones, the Wallaby captain with whom I'd conducted a good interview for the *Sunday Times*, came hurriedly towards me in a T-shirt, shorts and bare feet. 'We're out of here, mate,' he said. 'We're going home tomorrow!'

Sunday night! No paper to write for! Farr-Jones was on his way to a meeting in the room of the president of the Australian Rugby Football Union (ARFU), Joe French, coach Bob Dwyer, team manager John Breen and the old sage of Aussie rugby, Bob Templeton. They were none too pleased to see a pressman, but the affable Joe French, confirming that they were indeed intent on packing for Perth, asked me to keep the story under my hat in exchange for a full backgrounder for the *Sunday Times* at the weekend.

As it turned out, though, I never did get to write my story. During the night the telephones must have rung red hot, because by the next morning French called me aside and said that the situation had been resolved thanks to the intervention of Steve Tshwete and the team would not be flying home. They had received an apology from SARFU and an undertaking that no anthem would be played before their Test at Newlands.

The euphoria of the miraculous re-emergence of the Springboks had been somewhat sullied, and worse was to follow when the Wallabies rubbed in South Africa's disappointment by running up a record 26-3 victory over the Boks at Newlands – Naas Botha suffering the indignity of slipping and ending up on his bum in the mud while taking a goal kick!

Craven and Luyt, who was always the Doc's troubleshooter in tricky situations, felt that they held the moral high ground because of their meetings with the ANC, but the fact that both their personalities contained a strong element of 'I will not be dictated to' could be unhelpful at times.

The Boks were back, there was a tour in the offing to France and England at the end of the year, tours were scheduled to Australia and Argentina in 1993, and then there was the ultimate: a full-scale tour to New Zealand in 1994. And quite staggeringly, on top of all this, given South Africa's pariah status of just months before, the Republic had been assigned the responsibility of staging the third Rugby World Cup, in 1995.

The announcement had been made in Wellington in 1992, during the NZRFU's centenary celebrations. It happened in the wake of Nelson Mandela's release and the referendum in which white South Africans, in the last whites-only vote, were asked to express support for the reforms begun by FW de Klerk two years before, when he had proposed the scrapping of apartheid and the institution of a one-man, one-vote democratic system. The result, a clear affirmation for reform, was all rugby's 'old school' needed to invite the Springboks back into the club. Not only would they be allowed to play again, but they were also awarded the biggest prize in the game.

Although Natal administrator and former England international Nic Labuschagne had lost the presidency of the Natal Rugby Union to Keith Parkinson, he continued to represent South Africa on the board of Rugby World Cup Limited (RWCL), and he and Prof. Fritz Eloff played a key role in convincing the four Home Unions, as well as France, New Zealand and Australia, that South Africa was the ideal place to stage the tournament.

However, the World Cup might never have come to South Africa had it not been for the status and foresight of Dr Craven. Luyt, in the course of a long interview conducted in his magnificent penthouse with its unimpeded sea view on the top floor of an apartment block he built in Ballito, north of Durban, revealed that the tournament had been awarded to South Africa because Doc was owed a favour by New Zealand and Australia. 'South Africa got the World Cup in 1995 as a foregone conclusion,' Luyt recalled. 'When the first World Cup was staged in 1987, New Zealand and Australia were struggling to guarantee financial backing, and Doc arranged for $100 000 to be put up to help them get it off the ground.

'In the end, though, the tournament was a success and the money wasn't needed. However, Joe French of Australia never forgot that Craven had helped them, and he made it clear that he would go with South Africa when the time came to award the 1995 World Cup to a country. Eddie Tonks of New Zealand was less of a supporter but he was pretty much beholden, so we held a strong hand. We had it, but it still had to go to the IRB. But they were all pro-South Africa. Nick [Labuschagne] did a great job for us. And Fritz Eloff. In a way, they [the IRB] owed it to us. Craven was a cagey old bastard – the most clever man I've ever met.'

So the World Cup was South Africa's and, as always, Craven turned to Luyt to take on the daunting task of organising the country's first World Cup tournament. Sadly, Doc Craven, in ill health and perhaps feeling that his work was done once he had seen his beloved Springboks cross swords with the All Blacks, Wallabies, France and England once more, passed away in January 1993, and thus did not share in the glorious events that would unfold in 1995.

South Africa's re-emergence would set in motion a crazy merry-go-round of coaches: John Williams, Gerrie Sonnekus, Ian McIntosh, Kitch Christie, André Markgraaff, Carel du Plessis, Nick Mallett, Harry Viljoen and Rudolf Straeuli all held the post briefly up till 2003. Sanity eventually prevailed and Jake White retained the poisoned chalice from 2004 until South Africa's second World Cup victory, in 2007 ... But he, too, would be jettisoned at a time when one would have thought he was at the zenith of his expertise.

Boardroom battles would rage, Louis Luyt would pick a fight he could not win with President Nelson Mandela over a point of law and be pushed out of office, and attempts would be made to get rid of the Springbok as the symbol of South African rugby. This, in turn, would set in motion a ridiculous and petty cycle of political points-scoring that was to rear its head sporadically for years to come in spite of Nelson Mandela's symbolic validation of its importance when he wore the No. 6 jersey onto the field at the 1995 RWC final.

The Springboks' record on the field would be pretty scrappy, and they would constantly – and often unfairly – fall foul of a burgeoning disciplinary process that was enveloping the game.

But all this was still in the future. For now, Luyt was determined that not only would South Africa present the best World Cup to date, but that the Springboks would win it. He imposed his will on the process, and the man he chose to knock the Springboks into shape and secure the Webb Ellis Cup was a taciturn English-speaker of Scots descent who had not been a Springbok himself: Kitch Christie.

At the time, Christie said that he had been chosen to do an 'ambulance job', but as Churchill might have said: 'Some ambulance, some job!'

3

The winds of change

The area surrounding the Eastern Boulevard Holiday Inn, sandwiched between two highways at the foot of Devil's Peak in Cape Town, is not the best territory for jogging. The land slopes sharply, the roads are narrow and cobbled, and the route towards the city takes you into the windswept wasteland that used to be the vibrant District Six, where an entire community was uprooted and resettled in the name of apartheid – a scar on our collective conscience that always elicits feelings of guilt and discomfort.

These were my thoughts as I plodded back up the hill and started to do some stretches in the hotel's car park. It was early on Sunday morning, 30 April 1995, and I was staying at the hotel because the Springbok squad was billeted there. That evening, the 26-man team who would take part in the Rugby World Cup tournament, scheduled to kick off on 25 May, would be named in a live SABC TV broadcast from one of the hotel's conference rooms.

It being a Sunday, there was no *Sunday Times* to write for, but my sports editor, Colin Bryden, had decreed that he wanted me 'on tour', 'living' the World Cup, getting close to the team and providing in-depth coverage every Sunday of the run-up and beyond.

We reporters had all speculated on the make-up of Kitch Christie's squad, and I was wondering what impact a fractious and furiously fought match the day before at Newlands between François Pienaar's Bok squad and a Western Province team, led by Tiaan Strauss, would have on the make-up of the final team. In fact, the national team had been loudly booed before eking out a 25-23 win (significantly, thanks to a last-gasp drop goal from Joel Stransky). Now the moment of truth was upon us.

And that's when I saw him. Tiaan Strauss, striding out of the front entrance of the hotel, his face like thunder. He opened the boot of his car, hurled in his kitbag, slammed the boot shut, jerked open the driver's door, got in, slammed the door and revved the engine hard as he pulled away at speed.

It meant only one thing: Christie had not included the hero of Western Province, a man known as the Lion of the Kalahari, in his Springbok squad. And he had clearly just been informed of the fact. One can only begin to imagine his disappointment. And when I walked into the foyer of the hotel, there was further confirmation that the World Cup squad had been settled and that the players were aware of who was 'in' and who was 'out'. Transvaal teammates Ian MacDonald (flank) and Pieter Hendriks (wing), for whom fate would decree an unexpected return to international rugby in the forthcoming tournament, Natal No. 8 Gary Teichmann and Free State prop Ollie le Roux, grimly checking out. At times like these, you don't make eye contact – what do you say to someone who's just had the dream of a lifetime shattered?

I quickly made my way to my room to piece together who was left in the hotel and which players would have their names read out that evening. Strauss gone, MacDonald, Teichmann ... three loose forwards, so it could only mean that the big shock of the World Cup squad was going to be the inclusion of Western Province's Robby Brink ahead of his charismatic captain. The tall University of Cape Town student had played outstandingly in the Super 10 tournament, but his elevation above his much-admired provincial skipper was nevertheless a massive shock.

Later Christie would explain that he had decided to leave out Strauss because he felt the presence of such a strong character would counter-balance, perhaps even compete with, the influence of his chosen captain, François Pienaar. In a team packed full of Transvaal players, the situation would be untenable and could split a team that would depend on unity to see them through the toughest rugby tournament in the world.

Certainly, Christie had a point. Whereas Pienaar could appear smug and aloof, Strauss was earthy and charismatic. Christie never revealed whether he had discussed the potential clash of personalities with Pienaar, but it was nevertheless a strange decision, given that the two had played together in the loose trio in a number of Tests, against France, Argentina, Australia and New Zealand, while Strauss had taken over the captaincy when Pienaar had been concussed in New Zealand. However, I recalled an episode I had witnessed while on tour with the Boks in Argentina in 1993.

Strolling in a mall in the rundown riverside town of Rosario, on the banks of the murky Mar del Plata – the perfect setting, I always thought, for a seedy movie about bandits, quick triggers and drug-running – my fellow rugby writer Louis de Villiers of *Rapport* and I spotted Strauss and James Small having coffee. They called us over, partly to have a chat and partly to rag Louis over the pair of bright purple boots he had just bought and wore out of the shop. And in no time, other members of the team started to arrive … Joel Stransky, Pieter Muller, Heinrich Fuls, the Natalians Mark Andrews, Steve Atherton and John Allan, some of the Transvalers. Soon most of the team was there, cracking jokes and 'birdwatching'. When the time came for them to head back to their hotel for afternoon training, they marched off in a platoon, while Louis and I trailed along. They were a happy group of young men, ecstatic to be back touring, with Strauss clearly their rallying point.

We arrived at the hotel from one direction and, coming from the other, was François Pienaar – by himself. The solitude of leadership is nothing new, perhaps even desirable, but I was left with the impression that Pienaar was something of an outsider and that, if the team was asked to vote on a captain, the majority might have come down on the side of Strauss.

Christie was the most canny of coaches, sensitive to the slightest of nuances, and it may well have been that he wanted to entrench the author-ity of his chosen skipper, a young man not short of confidence and big on ambition who, at the time, worked for the coach's air-conditioning business in Midrand.

Pienaar would prove to be an excellent captain, the right man at the right time. He would form a close bond with President Nelson Mandela – close enough to make Madiba the godfather of his first-born – and would go on to a successful and prominent career outside of rugby.

The naming of the World Cup squad of 26 meant the tournament was upon us. Louis Luyt, who had appointed his son-in-law, Rian Oberholzer, as his tournament director, was, in his own inimitable way, beating into shape the police, hotel groups and airways in order to deliver what he had determined would be the best World Cup ever. The excitement had also begun to take hold among the public, who were suddenly only too aware that not only was the tournament going to be held in South Africa, but the Springboks were actually going to be a part of it.

But that Sunday evening, none of us who had gathered in the con-ference room of the Eastern Boulevard Holiday Inn had any inkling how amazing the journey would be that the Springboks were about to embark upon: the quirks of fate that would guide the team's path, the magical occur-rences that would simply materialise, the epic encounters and individual bravery, the physical presence and spiritual influence of a modern-day saint, and the role rugby would play in reconciliation and nation building. In fact, if one of us ink-stained 'recorders of the trivial' – to use an apt phrase coined by the late rugby scribe Paul Irwin – had sat down to construct such a storyline, he would have been laughed out of the pressroom for being on a flight of fantasy induced by the amber liquid so beloved of sports writers!

SA Rugby had appointed the highly respected Morné du Plessis to manage the team, and he and Edward Griffiths,* the maverick Englishman who had been sports editor of the *Sunday Times* and was then CEO of SA Rugby, were determined that the Springboks would distance themselves from old rugby norms and play a part in the nation's reconciliation.

Griffiths set the tone when he arrived at the World Cup team announcement, dragging along two white boards. He placed them in front of the chairs set down for the official first-team photograph, and promptly revealed the Springboks' motto for the World Cup: 'One team, one nation.' He had not thought to bring along some tape, so the boards could not be fitted together and the players in the front row had to balance them in such a way that the gap between them did not show. Nevertheless, with those four words, the tone was set for the Springboks to reach out to their fellow South Africans, *all* South Africans. The gesture worked, for as the tournament unfolded, there were constant reminders that the team, thanks in no small way to President Mandela's public endorsement, had been taken to the hearts of the majority of South Africans.

But first there was the matter of naming the team – the first Springboks to take part in a World Cup. The squad was read out by Morné du Plessis, 'starting from the back' as per rugby tradition, so that André Joubert became the first player to take his place behind Griffiths' banner. Joubert was followed by Gavin Johnson, then James Small, Japie Mulder and so on, down the positions until No. 8, Rudolf Straeuli, took his place.

There were big grins and the usual horseplay. Balie Swart even took it upon himself to take rugby writer Gavin Rich, who was based in the Western Province, to task over something uncomplimentary he had written about Christie.

'You lay off our coach or you'll get to do with us,' snapped Balie, with his lifelong friend, the huge Kobus Wiese, hovering in close attendance. Soon, however, it would sink in what enormous responsibility, and what a great honour, had been bestowed on the chosen 26.

These were they, 11 backs and 15 forwards:

---

* *Griffiths would later become general manager of SABC's* Topsport *programme, but only after adding the phrase 'to be faxed' to the lexicon when Luyt fired him by this means.*

André Joubert (Natal, fullback); Gavin Johnson (Transvaal, fullback/ utility back); James Small (Natal, right wing); Japie Mulder (Transvaal, centre); Christiaan Scholtz (Transvaal, centre); Brendan Venter (OFS, centre); Chester Williams (WP, left wing); Hennie le Roux (Transvaal, flyhalf); Joel Stransky (WP, flyhalf); Johan Roux (Transvaal, scrumhalf); Joost van der Westhuizen (Northern Transvaal, scrumhalf).

Balie Swart (Transvaal, tighthead prop); Marius Hurter (Northern Transvaal, tighthead prop); James Dalton (Transvaal, hooker); Chris Rossouw (Transvaal, hooker); Pieter 'Os' du Randt (OFS, loosehead prop); Garry Pagel (WP, loosehead prop); Mark Andrews (Natal, lock); Kobus Wiese (Transvaal, lock); Hannes Strydom (Transvaal, lock); Krynauw Otto (Northern Transvaal, lock); Ruben Kruger (Northern Transvaal, flank); François Pienaar (Transvaal, captain, flank); Robby Brink (WP, flank); Adriaan Richter (Northern Transvaal, No. 8); Rudolf Straeuli (Transvaal, No. 8).

As always with Springbok teams, it was a seemingly unmanageable cocktail of Afrikaans- and English-speakers, diverse religions, various schools, competing provinces, opposing views, dissimilar tastes and disparate levels of seniority – all of which made you marvel that, when the occasional moments of disharmony broke out, there were not more serious consequences.

Chester Williams was the only 'player of colour', to use a phrase that I don't much like but which is, sadly, unavoidable in South Africa. Williams would become the face of the squad in the hectic days leading up to the opening game against Australia at Newlands, largely because he was the focus of South African Airways' World Cup advertising campaign. His face, accompanied by the slogan 'The Waiting Is Over', stared out from billboards at airports and alongside highways.

At a 'good luck' banquet for the team at the Sandton Sun, Williams' celebrity was confirmed when Ian Bromley, SAA's marketing manager, bid R150 000 for a painting of Williams in the auction, the proceeds of which went to the Chris Burger Fund for Injured Players (later the Chris Burger/ Petro Jackson Fund).

Unbeknown to all but the inner circle, however, the brave little wing, who always achieved amazing feats on the rugby field despite the seeming absence of calf muscles, was in a desperate fight to stay in the tournament. In the Boks' only warm-up Test, against Samoa at Ellis Park in mid-April, he had tweaked a hamstring, and when the squad gathered for Christie's extreme build-up, the leg was still bothering him. By 15 May, 10 days from the RWC kick-off, Williams could still not stretch to full pace, and Du Plessis and Christie knew that a decision had to be made. They bit the bullet, and Williams withdrew.

Pieter Hendriks was immediately called in and Williams, whose withdrawal was a massive blow for the image of local rugby, flew home. Little did Williams, or Hendriks, know what fate had in store for them.

The naming of South Africa's management team – Morné du Plessis, Kitch Christie and Edward Griffiths – had, somewhat inadvertently, delivered the perfect combination. It was a template which, astonishingly, would never again be used. In Du Plessis, the team had a universally respected former Springbok captain, a man in touch with the demands and sensitivities of the time, who would actually *manage* the team, as opposed to being merely a ceremonial figure. His dignity and sportsmanship would impart norms of behaviour that would stand the team in good stead.

Griffiths delivered a masterstroke when he decided to forego his normal executive duties in order to take on the role of the team's media liaison officer. Highly intelligent and with a wonderful capacity for lateral thinking, Griffiths,* who has written more than 20 books, including biographies on Naas Botha, François Pienaar, Joost van der Westhuizen and Gary Teichmann, understood the media and the need for the team to reach out to all communities.

In the past, Springbok teams had tended to be uncommunicative and grouchy, but during the World Cup the Springboks' press interviews would become the most popular.

Griffiths rolled out the players to the press in numbers (other than Ruben Kruger, who avoided press conferences like the plague, even when he was allowed to speak Afrikaans!). The men managed to charm the media, who were not given that kind of access to the other teams. And during the difficult moments of the campaign, when heated tempers and heightened emotions could have inflamed the situation, Griffiths expertly brought down the shutters.

With Du Plessis and Griffiths in charge of day-to-day affairs, Christie could focus on coaching. Taciturn and none too comfortable with the media, the coach was free to deal with his players and undertake the constant analysis and scheming for which he was famous. Christie was the man who had once had the balls to push his keys across Louis Luyt's desk with

---

* *At the time of writing, Griffiths was back in rugby as CEO of Saracens Rugby Club in London.*

the words, 'If you want to drive the bus, Doc, I'll get off.' Now the man who said he had been hired to do an 'ambulance job' knew exactly what he wanted, and he put together a support group dominated by Transvalers: Frans Verster, doctor; Evan Speechly, physiotherapist; Rudi Joubert, technical director; Ray Mordt, fitness coach; as well as Hennie Bekker, forwards coach, and Gysie Pienaar, backline coach.

Unnoticed by most of us was a coach attached to Transvaal, who spent a lot of time with a camera on his shoulder capturing images Christie wanted to study or show to his players – a young man by the name of Jake White.

Christie was determined to make the Springboks the fittest side in the forthcoming tournament, but it was a difficult time for him. As mentioned, the national squad, dubbed the SA President's XV for the occasion, had been booed when they played Western Province (I made a note at the time that the Newlands crowd reminded me of the rabid bunch at The Gnoll in Neath), Christie had to endure strident criticism over his decision to leave Tiaan Strauss out of the squad, and shortly after the squad had been finalised, the Boks were given a roasting by the King's Park crowd as they hung on to win a warm-up game 27-25 – ironically, exactly the same score by which they had beaten Western Province.

On top of this, Christie's training methods, which involved hard sprints and any number of steps-ups on the concrete benches at the Wanderers rugby club, were being questioned by medical experts, who were quoted as saying he would 'break' the team before they even got to the tournament. Former Springbok wing Ray Mordt was in charge of fitness, and his speciality was to chase the players up and down the steep first hole of the adjacent Wanderers Golf Club. Christie remained unmoved by the criticism. 'I don't know scientific fitness,' he harrumphed, 'but what I do know is rugby fitness, and I know what I'm doing.' As it turned out, he did – as the tournament drew closer, the players were so fit and strong that they would challenge the coach: 'Is that the best you can do, Coach? C'mon, Coach, give us some more!' When Christie or Mordt would call it a day, they'd say, 'No! Let's do one more sprint up the hill; another set of push-ups!'

Morné du Plessis, who with road-running guru Tim Noakes had been a prime mover in the establishment of the Sports Science Institute in Newlands, Cape Town, admitted that Christie's punishing approach worried him. 'The intensity of the training astounds me,' he told me. 'They practise twice a day, and then they still go and do a gym session. These guys are on a different physical plane to what we were.' Much later, as the sun was setting over Ellis Park on the afternoon of 24 June, all this work would pay off handsomely.

Christie had his plans worked out. He plotted a 'high road/low road' scenario ahead of the opening game against Australia – the high road being a win against the world champions to earn an easier quarter-final (probably against Samoa, at altitude, at Ellis Park), followed by a semi-final against France; the low road being losing to the Wallabies and having to go through England and New Zealand to reach the final.

Du Plessis, meanwhile, threw himself wholeheartedly into the logistics of getting the team through the World Cup. He started by asking the players to sign a code of conduct in which they pledged loyalty to each other and dedicated themselves to the task ahead. Du Plessis had impeccable credentials: his father, Felix, had been a Springbok captain, his mother, Pat (née Smethurst), a hockey captain for South Africa, and his uncle, Horace Smethurst, a soccer captain for South Africa. But, above all, Du Plessis possessed the common touch.

Perpetually stooped forward, as if deeply concerned (his team nicknamed him 'Ruggles', because he resembled the giraffe-like mascot of the tournament), his brow wrinkled in concentration, Du Plessis radiated sincerity and honesty. On the playing field, he left a legacy of having captained the Springboks to 13 victories in 15 internationals, and his players looked up to him.

The code of conduct he put before the 1995 Springboks spoke volumes for the man himself:

I, [insert name], hereby undertake and pledge my word of honour in support thereof, to honour and abide by the following code.

That I shall at all times, and on every occasion, conduct myself in a dignified manner and with pride, so as to ensure that all my actions are worthy of the proud traditions of Springbok rugby.

That whilst wearing this jersey, I shall at all times remain gracious in victory and honourable in defeat, yet never shall I surrender whilst enjoying the privilege of wearing the Green and Gold.

That the Springbok team and its interests shall always be placed above my own ambitions, and my contribution will serve only to enhance the proud history of Springbok rugby.

Du Plessis could not have guessed how often his players would be put to the test against their own code, but his prescience was uncanny. In the course of an interview shortly before the tournament started, he told me: 'There is no way you go into the World Cup just being competent in your physical and technical ability. You've got to have something extra – another dimension is going to be needed to win the World Cup. I think that dimension will be on a spiritual level; something much deeper … and, of course, a bit of luck!'

His planning was meticulous and went beyond rugby. Cognisant of the outcry caused by the playing of the old national anthem at Ellis Park, Du Plessis resolved that his team would know the new anthem, 'Nkosi Sikelel' iAfrika', which would be sung in tandem with 'Die Stem', off by heart and sing it with gusto. To this end, he arranged for Anne Munnik, wife of former UCT rugby captain Peter and an expert in Xhosa, to teach the squad the lyrics and how to pronounce the words, clicks and all!

The team threw themselves into the exercise with enthusiasm. Rudolf Straeuli raised peals of laughter when he pointed out that it would be quite difficult to 'click' while wearing a gum guard. It would be a source of great irritation to all the players when the moment was corrupted in Clint Eastwood's 2009 movie, *Invictus*. In it, the Springboks were portrayed as being opposed to the new anthem. Some of the players were shown crumpling up the slips of paper on which the words to the anthem were written and throwing them away, whereas the team was actually quite chuffed to have learnt the words of the song.

Subsequent to 1995, it would become a requirement for new caps to learn the anthem. The legacy of Du Plessis' foresight is that Springbok rugby teams have ever since sung the anthem better than their counterparts from other sports – even if, in most cases, dreadfully off-key.

The Springboks were bonding and were extremely fit, but a few more key moments would bring together all the elements necessary for success in their opening game against the highly favoured Wallabies in Cape Town. First, Nelson Mandela made a surprise visit to the Springboks' training ground at the naval base in the Silvermine Nature Reserve near Tokai. In a spontaneous moment, Hennie le Roux grabbed a Springbok cap from the head of Japie Mulder and presented it to the president. Mandela, who had taken to referring to the team as 'my boys', was touched by the gesture, and perhaps that's where the idea originated for the president to wear the No. 6 jersey at Ellis Park a few weeks later.

Next, for the launch of the World Cup, it had been decided that all the teams would gather for a luncheon at Groot Constantia wine estate. It was a good idea in principle, but in practice it proved a nightmare for SAA, who had to fly 14 teams (South Africa and Australia were already in the Cape) from Johannesburg, Bloemfontein, Durban and Port Elizabeth to Cape Town and then back again. Some of the teams grumbled about the inconvenience, especially when a lashing rainstorm swept the peninsula. Water streamed through gaps in the marquee in which the ceremony was held, requiring much evasive action, and at one stage the Scottish team was drenched. But all in all it was an amazing experience to see the great and good of the game in one place at the same time.

And some markers were laid down. James Small made a point of sitting with his back to the All Blacks and never even looked at Jonah Lomu, never mind making eye contact!

The captains were asked to troop down to Simon van der Stel's beautiful Cape Dutch homestead for an official photograph and, even for me, used to dealing with famous sportsmen, it was an awesome moment to suddenly find myself in the company of François Pienaar, Michael Lynagh, Sean Fitzpatrick, Gavin Hastings, Will Carling and Philippe Saint-André. Judging by the expressions on the faces of the captains of some of the minor countries, the moment was equally overwhelming.

Then, ready, steady ... and just before 'go' on 25 May, an announcement was made by SA Rugby that went down like a lead balloon in certain rugby regions. However, it would play a significant role in helping President Mandela to pacify those in the ANC who were starting to look askance at this impending festival of a sport that many still saw as the preserve of the white right. The brainchild of Edward Griffiths, the announcement read that, henceforth, all national under-17, under-19, under-21 and under-23 teams would have to include a quota of players from disadvantaged and underprivileged backgrounds, i.e. black players. It was a stipulation that would never gain popularity among administrators, coaches and fans but which, at the time, was necessary to drive rugby's transformation.

Behind the scenes, too, much was going on ... clandestine meetings between unions, players, agents, television moguls and sundry shady characters that would be revealed almost as soon as the tournament was over, and that would change rugby forever.

But that was later. Thursday 25 May was upon us. Which road would the Springboks take?

4

Somewhere over the rainbow

Merle McKenna (now McLintock) listened to the crackling voices in her earphones, nibbled at the aerial of her walkie-talkie and looked anxiously at the many bright, expectant faces around her. The tunnel to the dressing rooms at Newlands Stadium in Cape Town was a seething mass of excited young faces, brightly coloured costumes, security personnel, television crewmen and sundry officials. McKenna was waiting for her moment of truth – the countdown to when she could give the signal to set in motion the opening ceremony of the 1995 Rugby World Cup.

McKenna had prepared a pageant that would highlight South Africa's colourful diversity and warm hospitality. Soon she would send 1 400 performers, 'many of them just babies', running onto the field from the main tunnel and the four corners of the stadium in a display she hoped would not only go smoothly but would emphasise the qualities of the 'Rainbow Nation' – then quite a new notion, inspired by the release of Nelson Mandela, the first democratic elections and the country's brightly coloured new flag.

'Ten, nine ... three, two, one – go performers! Go commentators!' And from every corner they came running, little kids in costumes depicting the 16 nations taking part in the tournament. McKenna need not have been concerned. Her show was an immediate success. Her thought, that 'children have a lovely warmth to them', radiated from the field, and in the stands emotions started to well over. In the press enclosure I was standing next to Freddie Hendriks of *Rapport*, a wonderfully gregarious individual whose life would be tragically cut short a few years later while working as a press officer for SA Rugby, and right behind an old pal of mine from Argentina, the rotund and jovial Nicky Gonzalez del Solar, a former Puma hooker.

When McKenna's little gauchos, representing Argentina, made their appearance, Nicky turned to me with tears flowing down his cheeks. In typical fashion, he exclaimed: 'Ah, Dahnee, all my life I never saw!' I was already close to tears, but then Freddie, a coloured man who had not been able to vote in his own country until the year before, turned to me and sobbed: 'I am so proud to be South African!' That was it. Nicky, Freddie and I hugged and wept tears of joy and comradeship; later you would have been hard-pressed to find anyone who did not dab away a tear on that wondrous occasion. Even the weather conspired to make the day perfect.

It was a day, oh what a day it was – one of those bright Cape winter afternoons where you felt you could reach out and touch the mountain. With the eyes of the world on South Africa, Rugby World Cup 1995 got off to a start as emotional as it was spectacular, as memorable as it was significant, and finally, joyously, vibrantly and colourfully African.

The dominant colours were green and gold: South Africa's green and gold, and not the reverse combination of Australia. The weather was perfect, the opening ceremony showed off the rainbow people to best effect, the mood was happy and the crowd chanted 'Nelson! Nelson! Nelson!' with genuine affection when the president appeared on the field to officially declare the tournament open.

The Springbok match-day XV chosen to take on the world champions contained a touch of serendipity, or providence, which, as the tournament progressed, seemed to steer them away from the rocky outcrops of disaster time and again. For it was not the combination Christie had had in mind during the days of hard training that had led up to the opening match. It also provided me with a 'scoop' – an exclusive story your opponents are not privy to and which editors love to gloat over. (Of course your readers don't give a tinker's cuss whether it was an exclusive or not.)

I had arranged an interview with Christie prior to the start of the tournament, and I asked him whether he had decided on his starting team for the opening game. In typical Kitch fashion, he turned my question back on me, replying with one of his own: 'What would *you* do?' Christie loved to make us journos wriggle a little, or expose our lack of knowledge, so I gave it some thought and replied: 'The one thing that worries me is goal-kicking. Hennie le Roux [Christie's preferred choice at flyhalf, as he wanted someone willing to play right on the advantage line to involve the loose forwards in attacks] is accurate from short range, but he doesn't much like kicking for the posts, which could become a problem. And André Joubert can be most erratic from a longer range. I would therefore go with Joel Stransky at flyhalf to give the team a strong kicking game and move Le Roux to inside centre, giving the team another playmaker and an additional kicker.'

I have to admit that I have always been a proponent of the specialist inside centre, or second flyhalf, in the mould of New Zealand's second five-eighths.

Morné du Plessis was sitting in on the interview, as preferred by Christie, as he was wary of being misquoted. The coach pondered my advice for a while, nodded and said, 'Hmm, not bad. At least you know your rugby.' We continued to discuss the opening game, and I tried to get Christie to give an opinion on whether an ageing Wallaby side was still up to the challenge, but he parried every lead, merely repeating his 'high road/low road' scenario.

A Sunday newspaperman needs big, insightful stories, and I felt I had not come away with much from the cagey Christie – until I flipped open the laptop and started to go over the tape. It dawned on me that the coach might, in fact, have given me the team that he intended to pick, so I decided to take a flyer and predict that Stransky and Le Roux were the aces up Christie's sleeve. And, luckily enough, that's how it turned out. It got the World Cup off to a good start for me – much to the chagrin of some of the other journos, who thought that Edward Griffiths, my former sports editor, had leaked me the story.

The opening ceremony provided the perfect kick-off to the tournament, and once again demonstrated the intrepid spirit of South Africans, as McKenna had pulled it off with the smallest of budgets and in very little time; in fact, she was not supposed to have been a part of it. 'I ended up putting together the ceremony purely by chance,' she recalled. 'At the time, my company, Pro Touch Eventing, had the SA Breweries contract for all the below-the-line stuff surrounding the Springboks: clothing, banners, billboards, etc. So that's what I was overseeing for the tournament.

'One day, while I was chatting to Rob Wagner [CEO of WP Rugby Union], he mentioned that they were really battling to put together the opening ceremony. They'd seen a lot of pitches, but nothing that they really liked, and he asked me if I'd come up with some ideas. So I chatted to Rian Oberholzer [tournament director] and put together a presentation of what I felt the ceremony should look like. I'll never forget ... he looked at my presentation, leant back in his chair and said: "I'll support you on this one."

'The theme was "Diversity in Africa", and the budget was really tight. We could not compete on a technological level, so the only thing we could really do was show off the vibrant colours and variety of Africa. So that's what we did – the Rainbow Nation – while also giving a typical South African welcome to the other countries that were here. I wanted to use

1 400 people. We held casting sessions around the country, but we just didn't get very far. And then Old Mutual in Pinelands allowed us to go in … they had a massive staff. For two days we cast, and we ended up using a substantial number of Old Mutual staff and their families.

'The next problems I ran into were when and where to rehearse, the cost of the costumes, the cost of feeding everyone, the cost of the make-up – the cost, the cost, the cost! So it was a case of rehearsing in little pockets. We went to the people and rehearsed parts of it where they were, a school hall here, a field there. We only ran that show in its entirety once – the day before the event. The performers came in from all four corners of the stadium and through the tunnel – we had dance captains who took charge of each position.

'Even the day before, we had to dress them, feed them, make them up – 1 400 people! Not so easy in Newlands with its narrow little roads! We had to colour-code the participants – off the buses with their little bags, on with the show, back to the buses … I was terrified that we might lose someone's child, but it was amazing how everyone pulled together and did their part.

'The only real curve ball occurred the night before, over the anthem we had recorded with the Drakensberg Boys' Choir, as television needed a back-up tape in case there were problems with the sound from the field. I had contacted the powers that be in government to find out which anthem to play, "Nkosi Sikelel' iAfrika" and "Die Stem" back to back, or the new, combined one, and was told to go with the new one.

'Then, on the evening before the event, Edward Griffiths came into the OB van and asked to hear the anthem … and flipped when he heard it. He screeched at me, "Why that one? The team don't know it. There's no way I'm going to allow the team to be thrown by not knowing the words of the anthem!" So we went back into the studio until late into the night and retaped it.

'We had second-by-second schedules from the minute the event started to the minute it finished, and Malcolm Gooding took such pride in and ownership of his task as master of ceremonies, doing a magnificent job with the voiceover. And we got lucky with the weather. Leading up to the opening game there had been so much wind and rain that I remember one of the choreographers looking up and appealing to the skies, "Oh God, please! Enough with the effects now!" But on the day, it was just perfect.'

Some of the other effects were equally powerful. Leon Schuster's humorous 'Hie kommie Bokke' (based on the tune of the Mexican folk song 'La Cucaracha') became an unofficial anthem to South Africa's World Cup, PJ Powers gave an earthy rendition of 'The World in Union', and Jennifer Jones sang the ballad 'Where the World Begins', which was written especially for the tournament.

'The World in Union', a traditional work arranged by Charlie Skarbek, a British composer and lyricist, was first sung at the 1991 tournament and became the theme song of every subsequent Rugby World Cup. With its focus on unity and its beautiful melody, it was remarkably apt for both South Africa and the game itself, capturing as it does the spirit of camaraderie that pervades the rough-and-tumble game of rugby. The melody is taken from the Jupiter Suite in Gustav Holst's seminal work 'The Planets', and was originally adapted by Holst for its use in the Anglican patriotic hymn 'I Vow to Thee My Country'. It was first sung as 'The World in Union' by New Zealand soprano Dame Kiri Te Kanawa, and subsequent versions were by PJ Powers and Ladysmith Black Mambazo in South Africa, Shirley Bassey and Bryn Terfel in Wales, United Colours of Sound in Australia and All Stars in France.

Everyone recognises the tune, but few know the lyrics. They are particularly appropriate:

The World in Union

There's a dream, I feel
So rare, so real
All the world in union
The world as one

Gathering together
One mind, one heart
Every creed, every colour
Once joined, never apart

Searching for the best in me
I will find what I can be
If I win, lose or draw
It's a victory for all
It's the world in union
The world as one

37

As we climb to reach our destiny
A new age has begun
We may face high mountains
Must cross rough seas
We must take our place in history
And live with dignity
Just to be the best I can

That's the goal for every man
If I win, lose or draw
It's a victory for all
It's the world in union
The world as one

As we climb to reach our destiny
A new age has begun
It's the world
The world in union
A new age has begun

SA Rugby could not have wished for a better start to the tournament, and the only thing that could have spoilt so perfect an occasion would have been if the Springboks had lost to the star-studded Wallabies. Adding to the tension was the fact that a number of the Boks had come down with a tummy bug on the morning of the match – something they kept quiet about but that would have an unfortunate recurrence after the final four weeks later. But how the team responded to the exhortations of the highly animated crowd and a nation sitting to attention in front of thousands of television sets on that Thursday afternoon of 25 May 1995!

In the end, that remarkable day not only produced one of the great Springbok victories, but also went down in the annals of history as a most special day in South Africa's embryonic democracy. If ever the country had a reason to feel proud of its association with one team, this was it; an occasion of such good humour, goodwill and endeavour that it could only be surpassed by something truly spectacular at Ellis Park on 24 June ... but few dared think that far ahead.

The Springboks overturned pre-match perceptions and turned the game itself on its head as they strode to victory in spite of minimal possession. They might not have seen too much of the ball, particularly from the line-out, but let no one doubt that the team showed the qualities reflected in the words of 'Shosholoza', a song created by mine and railway workers to lend rhythm and impetus to their manual labour: to work, work and push, push, push as one.

By all logic, the Springboks should not have won the game. Seldom will a team be so comprehensively outplayed in the line-outs and still emerge victorious. That they did is a tribute to their preparation, Christie's strategies, their incredible determination and their collective confidence, and this in players whose ability to rise to the occasion had been in doubt.

Balie Swart and James Dalton could take great satisfaction from the result, as there had been question marks concerning South Africa's scrum. However, once the Boks had gained ascendancy in the first two set pieces, it was Australia who was on the defensive. The normally belligerent Dalton, although struggling to find his line-out jumpers, repaid Christie's faith in him with an utterly disciplined and focused performance. He got through a mountain of work, keeping the pressure on George Gregan and contributing to the defensive effort. He might also have had a deserved try had referee Derek Bevan not ruled that he had lost the ball when driving over the line after a free kick.

In the other crucial area of doubt – midfield defence – Hennie le Roux and Japie Mulder blunted the threat of Jason Little and Daniel Herbert, causing the latter to become so frustrated that he played into South Africa's hands by persistently trying to batter his way through instead of releasing the ball to his support players.

The Newlands crowd made amends for the ribbing they had given François Pienaar and the Springboks a few weeks earlier in their warm-up match against Western Province, and the captain responded by turning in one of his finest games in the green-and-gold jersey. His excellent performance is commemorated in a superb *Sunday Times* picture by Australian photographer Colin Whelan, under the strapline 'How to Wallop a Wallaby'. It shows Pienaar flattening Aussie talisman David Campese, and his ferocious tackling, with the likes of Ruben Kruger, Rudolf Straeuli, Os du Randt and Hannes Strydom in support, that rattled the complacent and overconfident Australians. Although cleaned out in the line-outs, South Africa's loose forwards ensured that almost every ball that was dropped or dislodged in the tackle went the Springboks' way, and it was this possession that enabled the home team to remain competitive throughout the game.

Pieter Hendriks, the man who should not have been there but for

Chester Williams' injury, scored a gem of a try, courtesy of an excellent skip pass from Mulder. The move had started when James Small's anticipation had carried him to a good position on the left after he had been part of the build-up on the right. Making the score even more special was when Hendriks, brandishing his right fist in triumph, wheeled powerfully past a beaten Campese as he headed for the line. It was a graphic moment that illustrated the beginning of the end for Michael Lynagh's ageing defending champions.

André Joubert, regally aloof, exuded confidence and played the tactics perfectly by pinning the Wallabies back with long kicks, while Joel Stransky, with his second 22-point haul in eight Tests, joined the elite club of those who have scored points in all four ways, performing with the authority and variation South Africa had been looking for.

Although Stransky's goal kicks were not from difficult positions, he coped with the pressure better than did his acclaimed and experienced opposite number, Michael Lynagh. Stransky's vital drop goal, which took the Springboks into a 20-13 lead, was the first scored by South Africa since the retirement of Naas Botha, and little did anyone realise what an omen that would turn out to be! After his late elevation to the starting line-up, Stransky had passed his examination with flying colours.

Of all the Springboks, however, the most valuable contribution came from Joost van der Westhuizen. Having honed his passing skills, the tall scrumhalf had matured into a decisive option-taker and a genuine world-class player, destined to become one of his country's greats. Van der West-huizen's explosive pace off the mark and strength in the tackle made the Wallabies uneasy, and they were forced into guarding against his breaks. Also his defensive work, in particular the pressure he put on Gregan and Lynagh, was critical in the gradual breakdown of Australia's confidence.

As mentioned, the Boks struggled in the line-outs, with James Dalton battling to get his timing right, particularly to Mark Andrews, which allowed John Eales to put in a towering performance. However, in the end fortune favoured the bold Boks. The Cape Doctor, or southeaster, which came up in the second half proved an unexpected difficulty for the struggling Wallabies, and accounted for them being unable to get away from their goal line for the greater part of that half; it also caused Lynagh to make uncharacteristic mistakes, such as fluffing a drop-out.

Then, after a well-worked ploy involving Van der Westhuizen and Straeuli, a drop attempt by Stransky hit an Australian hand, which provided the 5-metre scrum platform for the flyhalf's match-clinching try. The Wallabies' thorough preparation might, ironically, have aided in their defeat, leading them to expect a back-row move, involving a back-flip between Straeuli and Pienaar, instead of Van der Westhuizen breaking wide to create the space for Stransky to punch through.

Finally, as former All Black Laurie Knight summed it up, the match was won by the smaller pack with the larger heart, and the Boks had taken the off-ramp leading to the high road … but they would find it to be riddled with potholes, challenges and mishaps.

On some cosmic level, the vagaries of fate were at work. Sitting in the crowd that day was a young man, just a month shy of his 19th birthday, his face festooned in the colours of the new flag, drinking in the occasion; a man destined to play quite a role in future Rugby World Cups. His name was Bob Skinstad.

5
Lights out

There is an old sports writer's saw that the best stories break in the pub ... and it has to be said that they often do – mostly late at night! This was true for me after the wonderful opening game of the 1995 Rugby World Cup, when I ran into a group of rugby officials who were in jovial spirits and feeling flush with the success of the day's events – so flush that they let slip some details of the machinations going on behind the scenes.

At the time I did not realise just how much *was* going on, and on how many levels, but it provided the first indication of a sea change about to happen in the game. It also gave me a front-page story in the *Sunday Times* of 28 May under the headline, 'Newlands euphoria gives boost to "Big 3" pay talks'.

This is the story I stumbled onto: representatives of Rupert Murdoch's News Corporation (Newscorp) had been meeting with southern hemisphere rugby union administrators with a view to forming an alliance that would culminate in rugby union turning fully professional – at least in the bottom half of the globe. Earlier, Murdoch had caused consternation within the ranks of both rugby union and rugby league circles when he offered players substantial sums to play in a tailored-for-TV Super League competition.

In typical fashion, those I contacted denied that any meetings had occurred with Newscorp, but the fact was that South Africa, New Zealand and Australia were well advanced in forming the body that would become known as SANZAR (South Africa, New Zealand and Australia Rugby). As I was able to write at the time: 'The three unions are keen to obtain a new sponsor for an expanded Super 10 interprovincial competition following the decision of SABC's *Topsport* not to renew its contract.' In addition, there was mention of a southern hemisphere Test series – what was to become the Tri Nations.

'It is believed that other pay TV stations, such as Kerry Packer's Channel 9, will enter the bidding to buy a slice of a game which, thanks to Thursday's rainbow celebration, reached unprecedented levels of universal popularity,' I wrote. As it turned out, I had only half the story, as another group, working outside the structures of the IRB and the southern hemisphere Big 3, were at work trying to set up a rebel professional circuit.

At the time I was onto something, but what was going on in boardrooms, pubs and coffee shops from Sydney to Johannesburg, as well as at clandestine meetings in the cities where the World Cup was being held, was nothing short of the title Peter FitzSimons would later give his excellent book about the intrigues playing out behind the scenes: *The Rugby War*. It was indeed a battle for the soul of the game, involving the two Australian media magnates, Murdoch and Packer, disaffected players willing to swap years of tradition for lucrative wages, television stations wanting to 'own the product', avaricious agents and double agents, and administrators who did not really get along but who were forced into a coalition to stave off the threat of the raiders. The extent of the skirmish would not emerge until after the conclusion of the tournament.

In the meantime, there was a World Cup going on … By beating the Wallabies, the Springboks had accomplished Christie's first goal, which was to avoid a potential landmine in having to play England in the quarter-final – provided, of course, that the Boks won their next two pool games, against Romania and Canada. It seemed an easy enough task, but the Eastern Europeans responded to an earlier magnanimous gesture by François Pienaar by putting up an unexpectedly competitive showing in their match at Newlands, and the game against the 'fighting' Canucks in Port Elizabeth would provide untold drama, both on and off the field, which would reverberate for days afterwards.

Having seen the Romanians lugging their meagre rugby belongings around in plastic shopping bags, Pienaar arranged, through the kind offices of former Junior Springbok flyhalf Gavin Cowley (one of the unluckiest men never to gain a full cap), to have them properly kitted out in Adidas gear and provided with tog bags. On the field, however, the Romanians were everything but a rag-tag bunch and put up stern opposition against a rejigged Springbok side – Christie having made the decision to give his entire squad an outing. Pressed about the potential foolhardiness of his actions, Christie was his usual pragmatic self. 'They're also Springboks, you know, and any Springbok side should have the beating of Romania.' In the end it took two pushover tries from captain of the day, Adriaan Richter, to get the Boks home, 21-8, but the coach was vindicated.

However, it was enough to make Christie think again about the outing against the Canadians in Port Elizabeth, and he made some late changes to the side he had intended to play, including the return of Pienaar. His trepidation was well justified, as that was the night the lights literally went out! It is doubtful whether even the imagination of a *Boys' Own* comic book writer at its most fertile would have come up with the events which played out on that fateful night at the Boet Erasmus Stadium.

The Canadians loved the gladiatorial aspects of rugby, but no one really gave them a chance against the Boks – which might, of course, have contributed to the truculence that marred the match. The Canadians had but one thought in mind – not to be bullied – but in the Springbok camp the emphasis was on keeping up fitness, improving accuracy and trying new combinations. My job was to provide feature stories for the *Sunday Times*, and for that week's pieces (as reporters like to refer to their articles), I picked Rod Snow, the Canadian prop who hailed from the icy wastelands of Newfoundland, as I was intrigued by his story, and Springbok flank Ruben Kruger ... largely because I'd identified him as the unobtrusive kingpin in the Springbok pack.

My choice of subjects for the stories proved to be prescient, as they resulted in Kruger acquiring a nickname that even the foreign press adopted, while Snow would end up figuring prominently in the game in a way in which he never intended. When I had informed Edward Griffiths that I wanted to do a feature on the Free Stater, who as a schoolboy had caught my eye with his unshaven neck and immense presence in the Craven Week, he warned: 'I'll see what I can do. Ruben doesn't enjoy doing interviews and I don't think you'll get much out of him.' I think the fact that I could speak Afrikaans helped, because Kruger did agree to a brief chat – and Griffiths was right, I did not get much out of him!

So I had to rely on quotes from Christie, who provided Kruger with a most apt nickname, and Morné du Plessis.

Christie bestowed the moniker on Kruger in the oddest of places – the lawns in front of the old Elizabeth Hotel. Breaking with convention, as was typical of the man, Christie called the team out for an impromptu line-out practice. I trailed after them in the hope of picking up a quote or two from the coach.

'Ruben?' said Christie in that forthright way of his. 'You guys [the press] don't really know what he does or what his value is to the team, but I can tell you he's indispensable. He's my silent assassin.' And there it was: the perfect description of a man who would become one of the great Springboks, and the natural headline for my story. Kruger became a good friend in the teams I reported on: humble, unpretentious, never giving anything but his very best.

Years later I had occasion to do a TV profile on Ruben Kruger and his charming wife and childhood sweetheart, Lize (before their daughters were born), and he was immensely proud to show me the home he had built for her on the Silver Lakes Golf Estate in Pretoria. Kruger was shy and didn't really enjoy being in front of the camera, but the day provided some insight into who he was. Opening a cupboard, he showed me a collection of all the Springbok jerseys he had ever worn; the shorts, the socks ... even the training jerseys and shorts because, as he explained, they were too precious to give away!

I am writing about Ruben now because of the lump I have in my throat, and I feel the need to record his contribution now rather than later. During an immense 1995 season, he was awarded a try by referee Derek Bevan in the 'monsoon' semi-final against France in Durban, which he admitted might just as easily have been denied ('sometimes they give them, sometimes they don't'), but he was adamant that he was robbed of a certain try by Ed Morrison in the final at Ellis Park. 'There's just no way that it wasn't a try,' he said. 'I had the ball tucked into my chest, Os was shoving me from the right and the other forwards were on my left. When I went over the line, I fell on the ball and no one else got near it.' This he said without a tinge of bitterness.

Sadly, after the highlights of 1995, Kruger's career would be dogged by injury and misfortune. He had formed a lethal partnership with fellow Free Stater and protégé André Venter, but suffered a terrible blow when, after scoring a try in the first minute of a Tri Nations Test at Eden Park in Auckland in 1997, he broke a leg while trying to force his way over for another in the 11th minute. It says much for the esteem in which Kruger was held that, when he awoke in hospital early on Sunday morning, the first people to visit him were All Black captain Sean Fitzpatrick and their coach, John Hart.

Kruger fought his way back to be included in the squad for the 1999 World Cup, although he was unable to unseat Rassie Erasmus at flank or persuade Nick Mallett that he was a better option at No. 8 than Bob Skinstad (Gary Teichmann having unforgivably been left at home). Then, the following season, there was the shock discovery of a malignant tumour, which he would fight for 10 years.

What a sad irony that this strong, quiet man, who had served Springbok rugby with such pride, dedication and distinction, would be taken down by the same stealthy killer that claimed the life of the man who gave him his nickname. Ruben died on 28 January 2010, and a few days later most of his former teammates were present to say farewell at a huge memorial service, during which Morné du Plessis and André Venter, himself confined to a wheelchair, delivered eulogies. It was a day on which strong men wiped away tears, and I was reminded of what Du Plessis had said of 'Ben' in Port Elizabeth 15 years previously: 'He had that strongman quality every team needs. You hardly saw him and you very seldom heard him, but all teams need strong, quiet men; he radiated a quality of hardness, which is very important.'

As the World Cup gathered pace towards the knockout stages, Kruger's ascendant star was but one of many in the squad. Whereas the Springboks were not given much of a chance to win the tournament, the touring rugby press were starting to notice that, in the likes of Kruger, Os du Randt, Mark Andrews, Joost van der Westhuizen, André Joubert and a good few others, the Boks possessed some world-class performers. They could easily meld into a team that, in the words of former All Black Murray Mexted, 'could win this damn thing!'

Port Elizabeth is not known as the friendly city for nothing, and the mood was festive and happy on the evening of the Canada match. The great embankment on the far side of the Boet Erasmus field was virtually obscured by braai smoke as local fans, and many from the Eastern Cape interior, settled in for a rare chance to see the Springboks in action. The pitch at this stadium is uniquely laid between two massive sand dunes, with the grandstand backing into one side and concrete terraces on the other, and it lies east–west rather than north–south, as rugby fields normally do to avoid the menace of the setting sun.

As the match was taking place in the evening, the sun was not going to be a problem, but bright lights, or the lack of them, certainly were. The teams stood proudly to attention for the singing of the anthems, and then, just as the strains of 'ons sal lewe, ons sal sterwe, ons vir jou Suid-Afrika!' were fading away, the floodlights went out. Most of us were momentarily blinded and then, in the haze, we could make out the players discussing what to do next; the murmur in the crowd rose to a buzz, and soon the embankment on the far side seemed infested by a wondrous swarm of fireflies as thousands of spectators 'flicked their Bics'. Police helicopters circled overhead with their searchlights on, imparting an eerie, surreal atmosphere.

Soon, however, amusement turned to annoyance as the players trooped off the field and back up the stadium's long tunnel and people began to wonder whether the game would go ahead. At the time we did not realise it, but the situation could have become quite ugly, as without electric power, organisers could not use the PA system to keep the crowd informed. However, some of the lights in the stadium must have been on a different circuit, because there was enough of a glow for me to see as I rushed into the bowels of the ramshackle old stadium to find out what was happening. I bumped into Kitch Christie in the dimly lit corridor outside the Boks' dressing room. 'Welcome to Africa,' he snapped, but James Small, who was not part of the match-day squad, was more upbeat. 'If I can't play, no one can, so I pulled the plug,' he cracked.

Fortunately, at Louis Luyt's behest, the organising committee had invested in a R5-million standby generator in case of just such an emergency. Unfortunately, when it kicked in, a major power cable blew. Rian Oberholzer would later reveal how a roadie with experience in staging pop concerts had donned leather gloves and held the cable together while others worked around him to restore power to the area. But, as it turned out, that was not the only fuse that would blow that night in Port Elizabeth.

There was a loud cheer as the floodlights eventually glowed to life, and finally referee Dave McHugh, who was destined to have quite a history with the Springboks,* blew his whistle for the kick-off 46 minutes after the scheduled time. There was an immediate air of hostility as the Canadians tried to get under the skins of the Boks with off-the-ball niggles, and the South Africans were allowing themselves to become annoyed. The Boks had more nous for the game, though, and with two pushover tries from Adriaan Richter and solid goal-kicking from Joel Stransky, they led 17-0 at half-time. Stransky made it 20-0 seven minutes after the restart, but the game was by now out of control, with any number of cheap shots and tramples going on. As the tension mounted, a succession of players required attention from first-aid officials.

The lid finally came off in the 70th minute. Canada, sparked by their

---

* *In August 2002, Dave McHugh found himself embroiled in another hot-tempered incident while refereeing a Test match in South Africa. In one of the most absurd incidents I ever witnessed, a fan from Potchefstroom, Piet van Zyl, ran onto the field three minutes into the second half of a Test between the Springboks and the All Blacks at the ABSA Stadium in Durban and tackled McHugh with such force that he dislocated the official's shoulder. For his trouble, Van Zyl was worked over by AJ Venter and Richie McCaw, but the incident was most damaging to South Africa's image. McHugh had to be replaced by England's Chris White, the Boks lost a thrilling Test 23-30, and Piet van Zyl was later fined and banned from all rugby stadiums.*

Cape Town–born centre Christian Stewart (whom the South Africans afterwards blamed for inciting the Canadians), were mounting an attack down the right-hand touchline. Springbok centre Christiaan Scholtz made contact with Canadian wing Winston Stanley before he got the ball, causing him to spill it towards the touchline. Then Pieter Hendriks body-checked Stanley and swung an elbow at him as they went after the ball. They tussled, and the next moment Canada's fullback, Scott Stewart, who had been in a red mist for most of the game, came charging in with a forearm hit on Hendriks.

And boom! All hell broke loose. James Dalton came running in right next to the referee – to break up the fight, he would later claim – and got shoved on the chin by Scott Stewart. Players from both sides were joining in the fray, punches were flying, people were falling down and referee McHugh was blowing so hard on his whistle that he was going purple. Finally the fracas settled down. Blood was streaming down Hannes Strydom's face from a cut opened by a punch from Rod Snow (the scar of which is still evident today), the players were glaring at each other and McHugh was deciding how he would sort it out … and what repercussions his decision would have.

The Irishman called over Dalton, Snow and Canadian captain Gareth Rees, a great servant of his country playing in his third World Cup, and sent them off the field. At first it seemed as though Strydom had also been given his marching orders, but he was leaving with physio Evan Speechly to have the blood stemmed and his wound stitched. McHugh had decided that Dalton, 'the third man in', had been the instigator, although the South Africans all thought Scott Stewart and Winston Stanley were the culprits, while Snow and Rees were dismissed for retaliating.

After that, the sting went out of the game. The Boks sealed the win (20-0) they needed to top the table in Pool A and qualify for a quarter-final against Samoa at Ellis Park. This was not a time for match reports, so to get the story behind the story, we Sunday writers all rushed back down to the dressing rooms, hoping for a response or two ahead of the more structured press conference. François Pienaar was understandably livid. 'I was surprised when James [Dalton] was sent off,' he said. 'I didn't think he was involved. He's distraught, but I'm sure he'll get off. He was the peacemaker. We'll have to look at the tape, but we never started the off-the-ball stuff. If a guy starts throwing punches at your guys, you have to rely on the ref or you have to look after your teammates.'

Canada's manager, Ray Skett, summed it up perfectly: 'The game started in the dark and finished pretty black,' he said, and Kitch was Kitch: 'Now we know what they mean when they say the Royal Canadian Mounties always get their man!' Later there was an instance of Griffiths and Du Plessis' astute management at work. While the media waited in the press-room and the clock ticked past midnight, they arranged for the coach to pull up at a side entrance and whisk the team away so that nothing might be quoted in anger that would be regretted later.

But that would not end the fallout. Despite a spirited defence mounted on his behalf, Dalton was suspended for 30 days, and was thus out of the tournament, while Rees and Snow did not bother to contest their dismissals, as for them the tournament was over anyway. In addition, both Hendriks and Scott Stewart were cited by officials for having been the instigators of the brawl and, on the basis of the then relatively new concept of television footage, suspended, which bundled the Springbok out of the tournament.

For South Africa, however, there was a happy, if curious, twist in the tale: Hendriks' departure opened the door for the return of Chester Williams, thanks to an odd regulation that allowed a suspended player to be replaced in the squad – and how fortuitous that would prove to be.

Dalton broke down in tears during a radio interview as he tried to come to terms with the fact that his dream had turned into a nightmare. However, these personal setbacks were put into perspective when news broke of the appalling neck injury suffered by Max Brito of the Ivory Coast in his team's final pool match, against Tonga, which would leave him paralysed for life.

For the Springboks, however, the fairy tale was still unfolding – just three more games to win the World Cup. But fate had much more in store for Pienaar and his men.

As the team settled into the Sunnyside Park Hotel in Parktown for their quarter-final match against Samoa, even the local black press expressed touching and poignant indications of the extent to which all South Africans were being swept along by the World Cup. Aggrey Klaaste, legendary and respected editor of *The Sowetan*, South Africa's biggest black newspaper, admitted that he was surprised by the flood of interest in the tournament, which caused him and his staff to modify their approach to the 'foreign game of rugby'.

'When the World Cup was about to take place,' Klaaste said, 'we honestly felt it had nothing to do with us. But to our amazement, the interest among our readers was just so high. I even picked it up in my own home when I heard the women of the household arguing over the rugby. I suppose that is the nature of a World Cup tournament. The people get swept along. We started to run stories on the tournament, and the response from our readers was such that we realised it was necessary for us to demonstrate a commitment to the cause of the Springboks.'

The Sowetan then came up with the definitive headline of the tournament: 'Viva Amabokoboko!' Klaaste explained that the new nickname, which resonated throughout the land, had been inspired by the name Pirates fans affectionately called their soccer team. Although known as the Buccaneers, their fans also called them the 'Amabuccabucca'. A subeditor had come to Klaaste with the suggestion of using 'Amabokoboko', and the editor was delighted. 'I thought it was wonderful,' he recalled. 'It was in the spirit of the whole thing, and after that it just caught on.'

6

Sink or swim

The deserted streets of Johannesburg added to André Joubert's depression as he sat in the car with a big brown envelope in his lap. He was being driven back to Ellis Park from the Rosebank Clinic, and the envelope contained X-rays of his damaged left hand. The excited voices emanating from the radio tormented him even more, for the broadcast was coming from the rugby stadium where he was going.

Just an hour earlier, Joubert had been at the stadium – not as part of the crowd, but on the field, playing for the Springboks against Samoa in a match that aptly illustrated the concept of sport as a substitute for war. It was the quarter-final of the Rugby World Cup, and the South Sea tribesmen tore into the Springboks as if they were a hostile force invading their islands.

Joubert, memorably nicknamed 'the Rolls-Royce of fullbacks' by England coach Jack Rowell in 1994, had suffered a sharp blow to his hand 'about eight or 10 minutes' into the game when he was caught by the swinging arm and fist of Samoa's combative fullback Mike Umaga (older brother of future All Black captain Tana).

'The Doc [Frans Verster] saw something was loose [in my left hand], but we decided to strap it and carry on,' Joubert recalled. 'Later, however, when I took another knock on it, our physio, Evan Speechly, said it had been decided to take me off.

'My hand was swollen and bruised, and I realised it was serious. It was decided to take me for an X-ray immediately, and we left Ellis Park. I was hoping for the best, but a picture doesn't lie and it showed an image of a broken metacarpal [a bone in the palm] in my left hand. There goes my World Cup, was all I could think. To say I was depressed would not be strong enough; even the fact that the Boks were winning well and that Chester [Williams] was scoring four tries meant nothing. I felt like crying when Kitch asked, "What's the story?" and I had to say, "It's broken."

'However, that night at the function, Mark Ferguson [the match doctor] said, "Come and see me, let's see what we can do." We had been given some time off on the Sunday, so I had gone home to Durban [where the semi-final against France would be played], but I flew back to Joburg to see Mark. He suggested that they put a pin in to join the break and that we do it immediately. After the surgery the hand was strapped and I returned to the team. Kitch wanted to know how sore it was, and when I replied that it wasn't too bad, he got me to play a game of table tennis [Joubert is left-handed] against Joost and I was surprised that I coped quite well. The hand was not too bad after all.

'I still didn't think I had any chance of playing, though, and that's when they came up with the idea of the decompression chamber [hyperbaric chamber] to try to accelerate the healing process. Mark Andrews had hurt his shoulder against the Samoans, so he was my travelling companion for the week while we underwent the treatment at the CSIR in Pretoria. Basically it meant that we sat in this steel cylinder for two and a half hours a day while they lowered the pressure and pumped in oxygen, which helps to make the swelling go away. It would have been quite an ordeal had I not had that walking encyclopaedia, Mark, along to keep me entertained – he talked and I listened!

'When we flew down to Durban I was starting to feel as if I might make it. Then we were contacted by an Irish doctor who had been following the World Cup, and he told us about a protective glove they use in hurling [a Gaelic game played with a ball and stick]. He promised to send us a glove, but it didn't arrive until the Saturday morning of the semi-final. And, appropriately, when we unwrapped it, it was green – which I suppose was not too odd, coming from Ireland!

'By that stage the decision had been made that I would play, and the doctors had also made a little plastic cover to go over the break. So that's how we did it; the cover, the strapping and then the glove. For extra stability I asked the docs to strap my point finger to my middle finger, but there was no chance to try it out. The first time I caught a ball with the protective stuff and glove on was in the game … so you can imagine when all that rain came down, I was shitting myself!'

Joubert was not the only casualty from the quarter-final. The Springboks won convincingly (42-14), but were mercilessly and often illegally hacked down by what I described in my match report as the Samoan 'axe men'. The casualty list included Andrews, who had a damaged shoulder as a result of being shoulder-charged when he was nowhere near the ball. Joost van der Westhuizen was laid out by a swinging arm from Mike Umaga that struck him across the face as he chased after his own grubber, while Ruben Kruger and Kobus Wiese also had to be taken off.

The Samoans, often the beneficiaries of support reserved for the Cinderellas of the game, made no friends on this afternoon and afterwards added insult to injury when their captain, Pat Lam, speaking privately to a Kiwi writer from Auckland rather than at the official post-match 'presser', claimed his team had been subjected to racist taunts by the Springboks.

Mike Umaga was cited for dangerous play by the World Cup disciplinary officials and banned for 90 days – subsequently reduced to 60. Even though the attitude of the Samoans and the efforts by the New Zealand journalist to foment the racial opprobrium to which the South Africans were so vulnerable left a sour taste, the supernatural force that seemed to be guiding François Pienaar's team had again been at work.

Chester Williams was not meant to have been part of the game because of the hamstring injury that had so cruelly knocked him out before the start of the tournament. However, Pieter Hendriks' suspension and a loophole in the tournament rules (plugged for subsequent tournaments) allowed him to make a comeback, and he celebrated by scoring a record four tries.*

The Springboks were through to the semi-final, at Durban's King's Park, where they would take on France, who had beaten Ireland in their quarter-final. Kitch Christie, forced to go easy on his injured troops and unable to stage a proper practice session because of the absence of Joubert and Andrews, wondered aloud what fate still had in store for his side. Little did he know that he should not have tempted the powerful forces of nature as the Boks headed for yet another episode from the realms of fantasy.

Soaking rain began to fall on the Kingdom of the Zulus on the afternoon before the semi-final, and on the morning of the game – Saturday 17 June – it was still teeming down. The esplanade was completely obscured when I looked out from my room in a high-rise beachfront hotel. Still, I thought, Kitch Christie's shock decision to play his primary line-out lock Mark Andrews at No. 8, a position he had not played since school, might pay off in what was going to be a war of attrition among the forwards. Noticing how the French used their tall forwards to peel off the back of the line-out, Christie had decided that he needed the grunt of Kobus Wiese and Hannes Strydom at lock, and the tall presence of Andrews at the back of the formation to stop *Les Tricolores* from throwing there.

The ploy worked for Christie, and he would repeat it in the final – but

---

* *Stefan Terblanche would score five tries against Italy in 1999, and Tonderai Chavhanga six against Uruguay in 2005.*

for a different reason. This time, it was to exploit the All Blacks' lack of height at the back of the line-out.

Andrews, though, nearly fudged it before he even got the chance to run onto the pitch, but fortunately his roommate Joel Stransky's quick thinking saved the day. Stransky recalled taking a phone call one afternoon.

'I roomed with Mark the whole way. We were in our room, lying on our beds relaxing, when the phone rang. It was Kitch. He said, "Is Mark there?" I said, "Ja, just hold on, Coach." I gave the phone to Mark, they went chat, chat, then Mark said, "No, Coach, I don't think I could." I said, "Well, what did he say?" "He asked if I could play flank." "And you said no?" Mark said, "Ja." And I said, "Are you fucking mad!" He said, "What do you mean?" I said, "Mark, it's the semi-final of the World Cup. You have to play *anywhere* the coach wants you to." Then the phone rang again. This time, Coach said, "Can you play No. 8?" "Yeah, Coach, of course I can!" said Mark.'

The monsoon presented quite a problem for us intrepid laptop-wielding reporters as we set off for King's Park. I had gone out to buy a plastic raincoat, only to find that the outdoor shop had sold out of the nifty little fold-into-a-packet type of covers, as well as all their rain suits for golfers. So I bought a dark-green jacket, but its towelling lining was indicative of the garment's water-resistant qualities. As I left the pressroom that had been set up in the old Kingsmead soccer stadium and pulled on the jacket, the rain drops went straight through the outer covering. At least with the lining I could turn the thing inside out and use it to dry myself later on, when I had to resort to emergency measures in order for my match report to reach the *Sunday Times* on deadline.

From the room-service trolley I had helped myself to a black garbage bag in which to wrap my laptop, but all my precautions proved to be useless once we reached the press seats in the stadium. The writers had been given prime seats right on the halfway line, and well forward – in fact, so far forward that there was no cover from the roof. The whole area was awash. The desk was sopping wet, and because there were no drainage holes in the seats, you actually ended up sitting in a little pool of water.

There was a room set aside for the media inside the stadium, but so many had retreated there that there were no telephone plugs or power points available – and my old Olivetti needed, at all times, to be connected to both if I was to file my story.

My brief for the afternoon was a simple one: 'We're giving over the back page to the semi-final – fill it!' Difficult but doable if you have a match to report on, but it soon became apparent that there might not *be* a match. Referee Derek Bevan was concerned for the safety of the players in the pools of water – as one of the assistants remarked, 'Someone might drown' – and whether it was even possible to play rugby in these conditions. No problem, we'll come back tomorrow, but *big* problem filling the back page. I stashed my laptop indoors and went down to the field to assess the 'state of play'. I soon discovered that 'coming back tomorrow' represented a massive problem for the Springboks.

Natal Rugby Union officials were feverishly trying to find a way to ensure that the field was playable – even sending on some of the Zulu staff to try to sweep away the biggest pools and sending an SOS to the adjacent Durban Country Club, one of South Africa's top golf courses, to try to borrow some pumps to suck the water off the field. The crowd was in remarkably good spirits, as Durban's rain was, at least, warm, and oblivious to the drama playing out on the field.

In the meantime, I had picked up a story that the Springboks' jerseys had presented some problems. Joost van der Westhuizen, Joel Stransky and André Joubert, among others, normally played in short sleeves, but because of the wet conditions, they wanted to play in long sleeves – especially Joubert, who felt that the sleeves would help him catch the high balls that the French were sure to launch at him.

However, if they decided to wear the jerseys of the reserves, the jersey numbers would be wrong, and spare jerseys had no numbers at all. When Morné du Plessis informed officials of the situation, he was told that under no circumstances would this be allowed. The Bok camp then tried to convince match director John Jeavons-Fellows, a member of the IRB, that the original jerseys had been taken away in the Springboks' bus. Even Louis Luyt got involved, but Jeavons-Fellows put his foot down and said that if the Boks did not run out in the correct numbers, they would be in danger of forfeiting the match.

Forfeiting the match? No way! Yes, certainly. But when I saw Louis Luyt angrily exchanging words with French RWC director Marcel Martin, I soon became aware of a far more serious problem. The reason for their altercation was shocking. If the game was abandoned before it could start, or at any point once it had started, and the teams were level with South Africa not having scored more tries than the French, then, according to the rules of the tournament, the Springboks would lose the match.

The rules clearly stated that in the event of such circumstances, the team with the least number of players red-carded in the tournament would be deemed the winners. South Africa, of course, had James Dalton sent off in Port Elizabeth, while the French had no send-offs. It would have been a dreadful conclusion to South Africa's tournament, and later Luyt would reveal that he was convinced Martin was doing his level best to have the game called off.

The rules made no provision for a postponement, and it also transpired that the Springboks had already checked out of their hotel and were due to fly back to Johannesburg after the game that night. If an emergency postponement was decided upon, they would have had nowhere to stay.

Bevan, however, was a man schooled in the great rugby tradition of the Welsh valleys and he was determined that there would be no contrived ending. There was a spot in the World Cup final up for grabs and he wanted the teams to slug it out toe to toe. While waiting to see what would transpire, I experienced a surrealistic moment that has lived with me ever since. Some of the Boks had emerged from the dressing room to look at the pitch and get some fresh air, and Joel Stransky, in running shoes and a tracksuit top, came over to me and casually asked, 'Do you think we're going to get on?'

I told him what I knew, but I was astonished at how calm he was. Here he stood on the brink of a World Cup semi-final that would be played in the worst conditions imaginable – or would not take place at all – and the Springbok flyhalf was as relaxed as if we were discussing where we might meet for a beer afterwards!

'Weren't we?' quipped Joel when I interviewed him for this book and mentioned the incident. But he then went on to give some insight into the kind of temperament required to succeed in a cauldron of pressure that few ever experience.

'I've always had this view that in life we should try not to worry about things that are out of our control,' Stransky explained. 'I didn't always get it right – for some games you get more nervous than for others. For me, whether the kick-off was at 3 p.m., 5 p.m. or 8 p.m. was not much of an issue – for me, the mornings were always the worst. Time just seemed to drag. But once we got to the ground, I was normally quite calm. And I think that when we got to the ground that day, we were probably nervous. It was the Cup semi-final, and I think that's when natural instinct takes over. For me, that means to calm down and not stress, because there is nothing you can do about it.

'If you did sit there and stress and worry before a game, you just used up all your energy from nerves. You worried about things that were completely out of your hands. I was fortunate that I could switch off. I think that's why I was a good goal-kicker. If you chat to a psychologist, he will tell you that you cannot concentrate for 80 minutes. Cricketers cannot concentrate for a whole session or for three sessions in a row – you have to have the ability to switch off and switch on again, and I think the guys who can do that are the ones who can deal with the pressure. I am fortunate that it is something I was blessed with. We were very aware that if we did not get on the pitch, we were out. However, I had great faith in Doc Luyt. He would never have allowed that to happen – he would *never*! We would have played in a swimming pool if need be!'

Soon there was a lull in the deluge, and then word came that an attempt would be made to start the game in half an hour. It was decision time for me. I clearly couldn't risk getting my laptop or cell phone (one of those old brick-like jobs) wet, and the landlines had been knocked out. How to get my copy through? The only solution was for me to hightail it back to the pressroom at Kingsmead Stadium, where there were hopefully TV screens, electrical power and working telephones. For the first edition, I hastily dictated some copy about the threat of forfeiture hanging over the Boks, the goings-on among officials, the weather and other conditions, and the literal pool of water the semi-final would be played in.

'Thanks,' said the chief sports sub, Gavin Schmidt. 'We'll fill the page with pictures and you can go big on the match report.' And then it was on: an hour and a half after the scheduled start, Derek Bevan blew the opening whistle of one of the most remarkable Test matches ever. From the outset, the players slipped, slid and sent up sprays of water as they tried to gain control of the ball. Some later described the game as a farce, and I suppose it was, but it stands out in my mind as one of the most nail-biting matches ever.

The Boks started off well, forcing a pushover try by Ruben Kruger to lead 10-0 after 24 minutes. But by half-time it was 10-6. Then 13-6, then 13-9, then 16-9, then 16-12, then 19-12, then 19-15 as Stransky and Thierry Lacroix (who would later in his career guide Natal to a Currie Cup victory in the same stadium) gave an exceptional display of goal-kicking while often having to move their kicking tees to spots where they did not float and where their studs could get some grip in the water-logged turf.

And so the Springboks were leading 19-15 with four minutes to play. The French were running rampant and the Boks were making mistakes. Stransky's kick-off didn't go 10 metres, James Small knocked on and Lacroix sent a high kick onto Joubert. The fullback, seemingly oblivious of his broken hand, had taken everything thrown at him, sometimes with the help of Small, but this time he dropped the ball. Big Abdel Benazzi came steaming in, picked up the ball and hurled himself at the line. A try would have made it 19-20, and regardless of the conversion, there would simply not have been time for the Boks to get back in front with just over a minute left to play. It seemed impossible that Benazzi would be stopped – but he was, short by just centimetres.

Small threw himself head-on into the bigger and heavier Frenchman, they connected, right shoulder to right shoulder, and the big loose forward's outstretched hand, straining to deposit the ball over the line, came down just short. To this day, Benazzi and his teammates contend that it was a try, but while making the updated *Springbok Saga* series for SuperSport, I was able to study the footage in super slo-mo, time and again, and I have no doubt that Benazzi did not score. Amazingly, the line was visible; amazingly, Bevan saw it too and did not award the score.

Ironically, Bevan then made a mistake, because the ball had spurted forward off Benazzi's hand. It should have been a scrum to the Boks, but Bevan awarded the put-in to the French. Less than a minute to go. Scrum collapses. French get another scrum awarded to them, some of their backs come rushing in to add weight, but down it goes again. A third reset, and this time the ball emerges and is flicked to Lacroix, who is hit hard by Stransky and Hennie le Roux.

This time the scrum goes to the Boks, and they know they have to get the ball, kick it out, and they're through to the final. It's a do-or-die situation, and Kobus Wiese utters immortal words as he grabs tighthead prop Balie Swart, who had been down injured with a torn rib cartilage, to go down for the hit. 'You can go up, and you can go down, but you're not coming back!' The hit is good, Chris Rossouw scoops the ball back, Johan 'Johnny' Roux passes it to Stransky, and he sends it spiralling away into the stands before immediately jumping for joy with the rest of the Springboks. The vanquished French just crumple into the mud, many of them in tears.

Sport truly is the theatre of life.

The Boks are in the final. Unexpectedly, perhaps luckily, but gloriously ... in the *final*. When it was all over, my match report for the *Sunday Times* filed, I sat shivering (in Durban!) and caught the eye of former Wallaby lock Peter FitzSimons, who was covering the tournament for the *Sydney Morning Herald*. We shook our heads simultaneously, incredulous at what we had just witnessed.

I rather liked the last line of my match report: *'Vive le François!'*

7

The man in the No. 6 jersey

Laurie Kay, airline pilot and aerobatic flyer, might have been on a Saturday afternoon flip with his mates, just the four of them skimming through the sky above Johannesburg. But today was different. Today was 24 June 1995, and this was not just any aircraft – this was a Boeing 747 Jumbo, and Kay and his mates were headed for the airspace above Ellis Park Stadium.

Their mission was a secret, designed to stun and leave a lasting impression. And that it would. Kay directed the Jumbo over the stadium and swooped as low as possible. As he and his big flying machine suddenly loomed over the roof of the South Stand and the thunder of the jet engines drowned out all other sound, a lasting and glorious memory was created in the minds of all who were present.

This was the *pièce de résistance* of Merle McKenna's closing ceremony – a moment so huge that it would never be forgotten, no matter whether the Springboks won or lost. And she had pulled it off. The crowd was in complete awe and abuzz with excitement. And yet the contrast between the mood of the men in the cockpit and the people in the stadium could not have been greater. Although the pilots were keyed up, they were mostly quiet, their attention having been focused on arriving above Ellis Park at exactly the right time, as they had promised.

Kay remembers the day as though it were yesterday. 'I only got involved when they said, "Let's put a 747 over the stadium." That's the Boeing 747, the one with the bulge. It's a huge piece of metal. The day that we flew over the stadium, it was very light – about 230 tons. We were just four people on board and we had a light load of fuel. The aircraft's weight could go up to about 365 tons.

'I'd been involved in aerobatics and stunt flying my whole life, and display aeroplanes at air shows, so it was not as if it was something new to me. It was just wonderful to be given the opportunity to have a 747 at my disposal, as opposed to what, in comparison, was a model aeroplane. There was no way we could fly over the city to practise, plus you have to remember that it was a commercial plane – utilised daily – so all our preparation was done in the simulator. In any case, we wanted to keep it a surprise – we didn't want the nation to know about it, so we couldn't practise the flight in a 747 prior to the actual event.

'It took quite a lot of planning. We had meetings with Ellis Park, Johannesburg City Council, Merle McKenna, SABC producer Ken Kirsten, civil aviation, the air-traffic controllers, military air-traffic controllers – there were such a lot of loose ends to tie up. And the insurers, of course.

'One thing we were worried about was light aircraft, which are permitted to fly up to 8 000 feet. We thus had an air-traffic controller in place on the roof of the stadium so that when we left the relative calm and quiet of controlled air space and we came down to uncontrolled air space, we would be in touch with civilian and military control. Remember, there was also [going to be] a fly-past by some vintage planes, and there were helicopters around.

'We issued what is called a Notam [short for Notice to Airmen], declaring Ellis Park a prohibited area for any light aircraft to fly over. You didn't want four big farmers from the Kalahari suddenly deciding after a couple of *dops* to fly over the stadium to lend the Bokke some support. They would have looked like gang-raped owls if they had suddenly seen a 747 looming into view! So we advised every single pilot by means of the Notam to stay clear of Ellis Park.

'We knew about the helicopter and the other aircraft and were in radio contact with them. We had to obtain special clearances on air navigation regulations. There are specific heights below which you're not allowed to fly over built-up areas and public gatherings, but, fortunately, in consultation with Civil Aviation Authorities, those regulations were waived, and they didn't stipulate a height. So that was my passport to stay out of jail!

'You have to realise that the Jumbo is a really big airy. It's a BIG aeroplane. You know, it's 200 feet long and 200 feet wide (which means its wingspan, 61 metres, would barely fit into the width of the field, which is 70 metres). That's 4 000 square feet. I think if one did the calculation, you'd find it covers an acre of ground.

'Ellis Park was simple. It wasn't difficult flying, but it was aggressive flying. People still ask, "Hell, wasn't it dangerous?" But I don't know if you ever flew into the old Hong Kong airport? With that Hong Kong approach, you were actually flying directly towards a mountain. You couldn't line up with the runway from a long way out because there was a horseshoe of mountains around the old Kai Tak Airport. So when you broke out of the cloud, you had a mountain in front of you with a big chequerboard on it, and then you had to visually turn and line up – in bad weather, strong wind, cross winds, turbulence, driving rain. June in South Africa we had wall-to-wall blue skies. When we practised in the simulator, we factored in all the possibilities and we stacked the odds against us ... so on the day of the flight it was actually quite straightforward.

'Beforehand, I went onto the field at Ellis Park with a Global Positioning System (GPS) to get the exact position; I also went up onto the roof of the stadium, and onto the Berea Hills just to the north. I wanted to know what the people in the stadium were going to see and feel; what I would see from the cockpit was not so important. So, by spending a lot of time at Ellis Park, on the roof, in the stands, then up on the hill, I got a good idea of what was required.

'During planning, Ken Kirsten said, "I want you over the stadium at 2:32.45." My next question to him was, "How much leeway do we have?"

'"This is international TV; we're going out internationally, so it must be 2:32.45," he replied. I thought, bloody hell, this isn't *Airwolf*! Then he said, "Can you be over the stadium for a second pass within 90 seconds?" That's when Merle McKenna looked at me and I remember her raising her eyebrows as if to say, "Well?" I said sure, even though I had never thought of putting a 747 into that kind of turn.

'The aeroplane would come in from the south. I obtained a GPS position, then I took an ordinary little compass and measured the bearing between the goalposts. I then took a pretty high-definition map, which actually showed Ellis Park, but I just needed to double-check it as well to program it into the aircraft's computers. Then I just drew a line southwards, which I knew was lined up with the goalposts, and I looked for a prominent feature on the ground, which happened to be a sports club, the Southern Suburbs Sports Club, which was also shown on the map. Then, whenever I did a trip to London or wherever, I looked for it. When I spotted it, I knew that with that line from the sports club, I would pass right over the centre spot.

'I measured the distance – I think it was 3.96 nautical miles – so I could calculate on the old "speed-equals-distance" that when I left that point on the ground, it would take one minute and 26 seconds before 2:32 and 45, the time they wanted us there, if I was pointing in the right direction to fly there in perfect conditions. If we had a head wind, I'd have to fly a little faster; tail wind, a little slower. The only difficult thing about it was making sure that we were pointing at Ellis Park at the right time.

'There was also a fleet of historic SAA planes – their time was 2:32. We allowed 45 seconds for them to get out of the way, because you know, once we were on the run-in, if these guys were late, we would have had a problem.

'There were just four of us: my dear friend, Senior Training Captain Selwyn Thomas; the co-pilot, Senior First Officer Wim Fourie; and Senior Flight Engineer Don Coppard. Selwyn was the clever guy, and he worked out when we had to turn – the first time from the south to the north to bring us in over the Touchdown restaurant at Ellis Park. I had noticed a crane working at the Johannesburg Stadium. Sometimes the operator parked the jib horizontally and sometimes vertically, which I had to keep in mind. Also, flying so low with the gear up, there were all kinds of signals shouting at us in the cockpit. We got airborne at about 2 p.m., and the whole thing lasted just over 40 minutes.

'From flying air shows, I knew that there were two things that got the crowd going: the visual part of it, and to feel the sound – the thumping. On the first pass, just before we got to the stadium, we rotated quite markedly and poured on maximum thrust so that we were pointing the tailpipes into the stadium, and we released big sound. They told me later that the stadium shook.

'I put her down again at Jan Smuts, and it felt as though there was no one there to meet us. We taxied into an area that was pretty tight, parked this great big airy, shut it down, and out came a guy with a wobbly set of stairs. And there was Linda, a crew driver, shouting '*Kom! Kom!*' I don't think we even signed any documents. I got in my old 450 Merc and raced home to watch the game, missing only the first 10 minutes.'

The idea of flying a 747 over Ellis Park on the day of the final had grown from a desire to do something really memorable. 'Newlands had been good,' Merle McKenna recalls, 'but the problem was how to follow it. That's why I have huge respect for Louis Luyt. He summoned me to his office and said to me, "How are you going to make the closing ceremony better than the opening one? That was RWC and it was Newlands, but this is SARFU and Ellis Park. So what are we going to do?"

'I said that the only way we could top it was to take to the air. SAA had been keen to get involved, and the obvious idea of a flyover just got bigger and bigger until someone said, "No one's ever done it with a Jumbo before." I told Doc Luyt that I needed a bit more money and his permission to do it. He said, "You've got it," and let me get on with it. That's why I say he

63

was such a good delegator and why I have such respect for him. I spotted him watching from the Touchdown restaurant on occasion, but he never interfered.

'For me, the moment that stands out was when I said to Laurie, "And you, Captain Kay, will come in at 2:32 and 45 seconds ..." His eyebrows shot up and he said, "Sweetheart, you don't understand. Do you have any idea how many tons of machinery we're talking about?" I don't know where I got the cheek from, but I said, "Unfortunately, *you* don't understand. If you don't come in then, don't come in at all." But Laurie pulled it off perfectly. Afterwards he would joke that he had been more nervous of me than of flying the plane.'

All over the city and the rest of the land people were getting ready for the final, putting beers on ice, setting the braai fires or donning Springbok jerseys and heading for the stadium. Ellis Park was then quite new and state-of-the-art, in spite of being situated in a quite insalubrious part of town. At the *Sunday Times*, photographers John Hogg and John Hrusa, along with Raymond Preston, who was then with the *Financial Mail*, had arranged for motorcycles and runners so that the film they exposed could be rushed back to the *Times* offices, which were then in the futuristic, glass-encased building at 11 Diagonal Street, next to the Stock Exchange. I had arranged to be dropped off and then met again after the match was over, as parking then, as now, was a hassle at Ellis Park.

I was just about to set off when the duty news editor came into the sports department and asked if I still had the office cell phone I had been issued with for the duration of the tournament. 'Why?' I asked.

'Because I might need it for a reporter to cover a big story that might be breaking,' she said. I could not help but say, 'I don't think there's going to be any bigger story than the one I'm about to cover,' as I handed over the phone (fortunately by then I had my own), hoisted up the heavy old Olivetti and headed off to be part of the biggest day in South African sports history.

Ellis Park was buzzing with excitement. From high up I watched the team buses arrive, feeling a connection with, a wave of empathy for James Small, and then headed to the press seats – just in time to be bowled over as the Jumbo suddenly roared over the East Stand like a spaceship in a sci-fi movie. Under its wings, the message 'Good Luck Bokke' was clearly visible. I had missed the first pass from the south. As I made my way to my seat, I was amazed at how well the crowd was singing the workers' song, 'Shosholoza', which had grown so popular during the tournament. Jenny Crwys-Williams of Radio 702 had drummed up support for the singing of 'Shosholoza' on her show, and before the game, she and fellow announcer Dan Moyane had been on the field teaching the people the words and getting them to sing along. It worked so well, I often think SA Rugby should get them back for every Test match.

The atmosphere was electric and it was as if someone had turned up the voltage even higher when President Nelson Mandela appeared on the field. 'He's wearing a Springbok jersey!' I yelled to my colleague, Clinton van der Berg. 'He's wearing a Springbok jersey!'

'Nelson! Nelson! Nelson!' reverberated around the stadium. Down on the ground, All Black captain Sean Fitzpatrick looked the Springboks over and realised that his team was in deep trouble. President Mandela wearing François Pienaar's No. 6 jersey as a motivational tool was special, but as an act of reconciliation, it was unsurpassed. By embracing a sporting symbol many in the country detested, Mandela succeeded in uniting a fractured nation like never before. It brought the crowd together and galvanised the Springboks. As one of the Fleet Street corps wrote: 'The Madiba Magic is something you can feel and touch.'

'What Madiba did was an absolute masterstroke,' Morné du Plessis recalled in an interview I conducted in 2006 for a book on the Springbok badge. 'It was not a calculated or premeditated gesture – purely his feeling at the time. To see him coming into our dressing room, radiating brightness, enthusiasm and humility into a very sombre atmosphere, will remain with me forever. A Test-match dressing room is a very serious place and the tension can be unbearable. Each player is in his own space, caught up in his own thoughts, perhaps trying not to think, and it being the World Cup final, it was worse than normal ... And then Madiba arrives with that glow that seems to surround him.

'He's happy, he's smiling and, what's more, he's wearing a Springbok jersey. No one could ever describe the scene, or the effect it had on us, properly. The look on the guys' faces, the mood that came over them, is just something I'll never forget. It's imprinted on all of us ... And then the atmosphere on the field. Madiba's arrival in our jersey had galvanised the crowd and they just could not stop chanting his name. It was as if I was dreaming. It must have had an effect on the All Blacks.'

Sadly it was all too fleeting, but the moment of unity engendered on that bright Highveld winter's afternoon will always be special to those who felt it. It was neatly summed up by Archbishop Desmond Tutu in an interview with *The Star* a month later. 'I did not expect this, but I am proud to wear a Springbok jersey when, a few years ago, even a few months ago, it was an anathema. I try to say what I believe is true and this thing, which was a very divisive and ugly symbol, could in fact have been magically used by God to weld us together. No one of us could ever in their wildest dreams have been able to predict that rugby … could have this magical effect.'*

The All Blacks were the overwhelming favourites. They had registered a unique Grand Slam on their way to the final, beating Wales, Ireland, Scotland and England, but it was the manner of their demolition of the latter in the Newlands semi-final (played on the Sunday after the Springboks had ousted France) that sent tremors of trepidation coursing through South African veins and gave a whole new meaning to the term 'swart gevaar' (a phrase popularised by apartheid governments, meaning 'black danger').

England had knocked the reigning champions, the Wallabies, out of the tournament thanks to a last-gasp drop goal by Rob Andrew in their quarter-final, but they had no answer for the juggernaut that hit them in the semi-final. The result, a win for the All Blacks, was never in doubt. Whereas the Wallabies had got their tactics hopelessly wrong by trying to match the big England forwards, the All Blacks concentrated on playing fast and wide with the clear intention of getting the ball to Jonah Lomu.

The match was a triumph for Lomu. He scored four tries by running around, through and straight over the hapless English tacklers – the first consigning South African–born Mike Catt to an unfortunate place in the annals of rugby history as the hapless victim of one of the Tongan Torpedo's powerful surges.

'He crashed through tackles like an earth mover,' wrote Bill McLaren. Their No. 8, Zinzan Brooke, added insult to injury as he cheekily dropped a goal after collecting a failed touch kick, taking the All Blacks to an

---

* Sadly it seems that the No. 6 jersey Madiba wore has not been preserved for posterity. Some years later I was working on a SARU publication called The Badge and contacted the Nelson Mandela Foundation to try to find out where it was. Verne Harris, head of Memory Programmes of the Nelson Mandela Archive, did not know in whose possession the jersey was, saying that as far as he knew it had been given to the Eastern Province branch of the ANC to be used as a fund-raiser. As far as I know it has never surfaced.

impressive 45-29 victory. England had regained some pride with a few tries of their own after being 3-35 in arrears at one stage.

'They made an unbelievable start,' said England captain Will Carling. 'I have never endured anything like it. Lomu is a freak, an incredible athlete. The sooner he goes away, the better.' Lomu had made an incredible impact on the World Cup, and he would make an even bigger impact on the very fabric of rugby union. Somewhere in the world, Australian media mogul Rupert Murdoch was watching. After the game, he picked up the phone and called Sam Chisholm, his man in charge of television. 'Get me that man,' he is rumoured to have said.

But that was another story, brewing in the background, which would ultimately lead to the creation of SANZAR. Next up was the World Cup final between the two greatest rivals in the game – the Springboks and the All Blacks. It was to be their 39th meeting. South Africa had 20 wins, New Zealand 16, and two games were drawn ...

8

'Not for 60 000, for 43 million'

Massive Attack was still on James Small's mind as the Springboks, the anthems having been sung, lined up to face the All Blacks' Haka. But he was not thinking so much about the big wheel as he was about the giant who stood facing him and whom he would soon be physically confronting.

'My God, he's a big ****!' Small thought to himself as, for the first time, he took a good look at Jonah Lomu. The All Blacks went into their finger-twitching, arm-slapping ritual. 'Ka mate! ka mate! ka ora! ka ora!' they yelled, and the Springboks, arms linked and determined not to be cowed or show any fear, advanced on the New Zealanders as they eye-balled each other.

Small locked his eyes on Lomu, but then Kobus Wiese stepped in front of him, demonstrating to Small that he would not be on his own when the time came to stop Lomu. According to Wiese, it was a sudden impulse. 'I looked him straight in the eye,' Wiese said later, 'and he blinked and looked away. I knew then that we had them.' According to popular legend, Ruben Kruger was, for once, heard to break his silence when he caught his direct opponent Mike Brewer in a steely glare and snarled: 'I've got your number, mate.'

In keeping with the incredible storylines that had played themselves out in the course of the tournament, there was also a tale to tell about 'one-eyed' English referee Ed Morrison – no affront intended, as Morrison genuinely had the use of only one eye, which made his feat of being appointed to handle a World Cup final all the more remarkable.

Morrison was the man who had red-carded James Small in a match between South Africa and Australia at Ballymore, Brisbane, in 1993, making him the first Springbok in history to be sent off in a Test. The punishment was for swearing, or verbal abuse of the referee, as they call it in the disciplinary tribunal. Small had not been impressed by Morrison's appointment.

'How can you have a ref who has only one eye, for goodness' sake? Surely his depth and linear perception must be skewed? Never mind *one* eye – to ref a World Cup final, the bloody ref should have eyes in the back of his head!' Small made this comment after the RWC final, in relation to an incident that had happened during the game. Small had passed the ball to Joel Stransky, but Morrison called him back for a forward pass. It put an abrupt end to a promising blindside breakout that might have resulted in a try. But this came later ...

Morrison blew the opening whistle and the two teams were into it – the very first touch of the ball perhaps an omen of things to come. Andrew Mehrtens tried to catch the Springboks unawares by stabbing the ball along the ground, but failed to get it to travel 10 metres. The result was an early penalty to the Boks, putting the All Blacks under immediate pressure. But Sean Fitzpatrick was not considered to be the best captain in the tournament for nothing, and he soon had his team focused and playing more fluid rugby.

Unlike the opening game, this, to me at least, was not a joyous occasion. It was too nerve-wracking to be enjoyed. There was too much at stake, and the stats I was keeping – line-outs, ball retention – were showing that the All Blacks were the better side. It was close all the way, with Joel Stransky and Andrew Mehrtens matching penalties and drop goals. As the match wore on, my colleague Clinton van der Berg would say to me, 'I think we're going to do this,' or 'The Boks are getting on top,' and I would reply, 'I don't think so. We're getting cleaned out in almost every phase.' This was especially apparent in the line-out count, where the lanky Ian Jones was playing the game of his life.

Passages from my match report in the *Sunday Times* reveal a bit of my pessimism, but also the key sequences that eventually gave the Springboks the edge.

With the All Blacks playing with more rhythm it seemed for long periods that the black panthers would break through – either in creating space for the dreadnought on the left, Jonah Lomu, or by exploiting the extra attention the Springboks were paying to New Zealand's lethal weapon.

But on the day the Springboks revealed the determination and plain old-fashioned guts to hole the big cruiser below the water line whenever he threatened. François Pienaar and Mark Andrews brought off a big hit on the youngster early on, Joost van der Westhuizen pinned his legs, James Small compressed his space and a thumping tackle by Japie Mulder had the effect of galvanising a Springbok team who seemed to be fading midway through the second half. With the Boks positioning James Small wider, in the tramlines, Lomu was often forced inside or unable to get into his stride and the moment the crowd had feared, when Lomu was finally given a run on the outside, was snuffed out by Mulder.

Mulder put Lomu down harder than he'd ever been dumped before, but Van der Westhuizen, who would also contribute another key play near the end of the game, made arguably the most important tackle of the game, in the 12th minute. The All Blacks brought Lomu steaming through from the blind side and he crashed clean through in front of South Africa's posts. There was only one Springbok left in his way, a No. 9 on his back, and Van der Westhuizen stood his ground, dipped down, grabbed the churning legs in an iron grip and broke Lomu's momentum. Mark Andrews got back in time to help knock the giant down.

If Lomu had scored then, or made enough ground to unload to the ever-present Josh Kronfeld for a try at the posts, the game might have been lost. To me, it has always been the moment the pendulum swung in the Boks' favour, as the Boks drew heart from Van der Westhuizen's brave example and started to settle down.

In spite of the All Blacks' greater fluency, the fact that the Springboks came closer to scoring a try gave them a mental edge. Ruben Kruger, Os du Randt and Hannes Strydom were convinced the flanker had been driven over the line after a scrum on the All Blacks' line, but referee Morrison said he was unsighted.

'There was a mass of bodies and it was impossible to see whether or not the ball had been grounded,' he told a RWC publication. 'In fact, it was an easy decision to make, because if you can't see it, you can't give it.'

Kruger, however, was adamant that he had scored, as I mentioned in an earlier chapter. 'There was absolutely no doubt in my mind that it was a try. I picked up the ball and there were Springboks on either side of me as I went over the line and fell on the ball. No All Black got in the way. It was a try,' he said afterwards, but he typically took a philosophical view. 'As it turned out, it might have been a blessing. If we had scored then, we might have relaxed and stopped putting the All Blacks under pressure.'

Stransky's first drop of the game, in the 31st minute (many forget he kicked two), made the score 9-6 to the Springboks. That was the situation at half-time, and in the 54th minute, Mehrtens kicked a drop to make the scores level again. It was cut and thrust, and every time the All Blacks got the ball to Lomu, the green ants swarmed all over him; although the Boks did get the benefit of a forward-pass ruling that had the pockets of Kiwis in the ground howling indignantly.

Mehrtens fired off another drop, which missed, and it became apparent that, this being the World Cup of twists and turns, extra time – 10 minutes each way – might be required to separate the two teams. The Springbok management and François Pienaar were all too aware that a draw was out of the question. According to the rules, if the teams could not be separated in score or tries at the end of extra time, then the number of red cards would come into play. Yet again, James Dalton's dismissal in Port Elizabeth was potentially the sword of Damocles.

The All Blacks held territorial ascendancy and, in the 77th minute, 55 000 hearts (not counting the 5 000 Kiwis) stopped beating when Mehrtens was put in an ideal dropping position 32 metres from the posts. It seemed he could not miss, but Van der Westhuizen strained every sinew in his body to rush out and dive at the slick little flyhalf's kicking foot ... causing Mehrtens to have to readjust his angle, the ball slewing off to the right.

So extra time it was to be – for the first time in the Rugby World Cup. The All Blacks gained a psychological boost when they were given a penalty near the centre spot within seconds of extra time starting. Mehrtens, with a superb kick, raised the flags to put New Zealand 12-9 up. The Boks, however, were starting to look the stronger outfit. An up-and-under by Stransky and a spirited chase saw the Boks force a maul just before the changeover, and it was Sean Fitzpatrick who was penalised for diving over the top. Stransky's nerve held, the kick from 35 metres went over, and it was 12-all with the last 10 minutes left to play. With no tries and the score deadlocked, the Boks knew they had to score.

And they did. This was my description of the dream passage of play, which appeared in the *Sunday Times* under the headline, 'Super, Super Stransky'.

Then came the sequence which made the Springboks the world champions. Rudolf Straeuli, having just replaced Mark Andrews, won a 22 m drop-out after André Joubert had put the ball deep. The Bok pack forced a scrum, a wheel, reset and then Joost van der

Westhuizen sent the ball spinning to Stransky. Catch, drop, foot swinging through and the crowd behind the posts rising in unison providing the signal for Ellis Park to erupt in joyous celebration.

The rest is a blur. Six minutes [it was actually longer] in which one could hardly bear to look. SA's musketeer spirit of all for one and one for all held for all of the 104 minutes it took to decide a winner, and the epic journey which started against the same traditional and respected opponents at Ellis Park in August 1992 ended with the Springboks back on top of the world.

Most who were watching the game remember the match as ending right after Stransky's classic drop kick – they have no recollection that the game lasted another eight and a half minutes and that the flyhalf, in fact, missed a penalty that would have stretched the lead.

Stransky recalls that he had never hit a ball as sweetly as the winning drop goal. 'François called a blindside move – the one where Joost taps the No. 8's backside [Rudolf Straeuli was by then on the field, replacing Mark Andrews], which triggers the move in which he breaks away from the formation without the ball. And with Joost's speed, he could be six, seven metres away in a flash, getting away from the blindside flanker, before the ball even reaches him.

'Then he would have had André Joubert on his outside, Rudolf on his inside – there were times when we [practised] it with me on the inside [in fact, Stransky scored a try off Joost's back-flip in the opening game at Newlands]. It was really the foundation of a lot of our back-row moves. We made the call, it was the right call, but I think the All Blacks had obviously studied us, because when Joost put the ball in, Bachop [New Zealand scrumhalf] never looked at me once as he was coming round, which meant he was going to chase Joost around the corner.

'So as he came round I called Joost, got his attention, and pulled my hand across my throat, signalling, cancel! cancel! Mehrtens was standing wide and there was a massive, gaping hole for me to step into and make a kick.

'Kitch had spoken about the drop in the week building up to the final, and [the opportunity] suddenly opened up for me. So I shouted, "cancel!" Joost got the message, shouted to Rudolf to let him have the ball, sent the ball spinning to me, Bachop tried to dive and block the pass instead of coming at me to block or narrow my angle, and I had all the time in the world to step and swing my foot as Mehrtens was coming at me from the side, off my left shoulder, rather than head-on. I don't think I have ever struck a ball as purely as I hit that one.

'In the week before [the final], we were practising on a really hard field at the Goudstad Teachers' Training College. The forwards were doing line-outs and I had gone along to do some place-kicking. Because I was striking the ball really well, I packed it in after about half an hour. However, Kitch came over and said to me, "Why don't you kick more drop kicks?" My initial reaction was, it's not as easy as it looks – first you've got to catch the ball, you've got to drop it right, it's got to bounce right and, on top of that, you've got the likes of Zinzan Brooke and Mike Brewer charging at you.

'But Kitch was adamant – he planted a seed – so Johan Roux passed and I dropped, and on that hard surface I was just awful … the ball was bouncing too high and too quickly. However, there was an upside: because of that hard surface, my timing got really good. You had to be perfect, like nipping a chip off a bare surface. I started to hit them a bit better, and when we got down to Ellis Park on the Friday for our captain's run, I was hitting my practice shots just brilliantly. When I struck that one in the game, it was just right. I looked up, and it was spinning perfectly. I could see where it was going, right on line, and just knew it couldn't miss – unless a hurricane came up and blew it off course.'

Videos and photographs showed that the adrenalin-charged Stransky had struck the ball so well that he could have attempted the drop from much further back and still have succeeded. The party started right there and then, the biggest celebration South Africa had ever known. People of all races were dancing and hugging in the streets, jumping into the harbour at the V&A Waterfront in Cape Town, doing mad and silly things. Never before had one team done so much to unite one nation.

After the game, François Pienaar said that they had had the support not only of the 60 000 supporters in the stadium, but of 43 million South Africans – a masterpiece of public relations.

It was a time of pure, unadulterated joy …

But I had a job to do and a paper to bring out. Alongside a picture by John Hrusa of a smiling Pienaar holding aloft the Webb Ellis Cup, the *Sunday Times* front-page headline trumpeted: 'Our "guts and glory" boys … and the rainbow nation rejoices'.

My front-page piece written for the late edition said, 'The secret of success … was in the tackle'.

New Zealand had the ruck, Australia had the winning way – and South Africa had the tackle. The definitive quality of South Africa's surge to world champion status is the resolute, muscular defence of the Springboks. In the build-up to yesterday's final the All Blacks had amassed an awesome and praiseworthy record for scoring tries. Less conspicuously the Springboks had shown that there was plenty of merit in stopping them. The All Blacks had their juggernaut Jonah Lomu, and his shadows, Josh Kronfeld, Frank Bunce, Walter Little and Glen Osborne, who could mesmerise and prise open or, in the case of the large Lomu, simply batter down defences. The Springboks promised that they would stop them. And they did. François Pienaar and Mark Andrews knocked the big man down after James Small had slowed him in the way no-one else had been prepared to – he simply got in front of him and hung on for dear life.

Joost van der Westhuizen dipped down and put a pair of pincers around Lomu's legs, little Chester Williams snapped like a terrier at his ankles, André Joubert would not let go of Lomu's jersey and Japie Mulder, when Lomu finally found some space on the outside, torpedoed him and put him into touch. The Springboks blunted the threat of Lomu, soaked up whatever else the All Blacks threw at them, and simply refused to allow their line to be crossed. Dogged, unremitting defence. That is what finally made South Africa champions of the world.

Not just in yesterday's stressful 104 minutes – throughout the tournament. When François Pienaar finally received the William Webb Ellis Trophy [I got the name wrong!] from a similarly attired President Nelson Mandela it was in the knowledge that his team had not conceded a try in either the semi-final or the final.

As Van der Westhuizen said: 'The difference between us and the other sides was that they stood off Lomu while we queued up to tackle him.' The big All Black would end his career without having scored a try against the Springboks.

The *Sunday Times* of 25 June 1995 also ran stories about the SABC and M-Net being upset by what they termed Louis Luyt's 'devious deal' to sell television rights to Rupert Murdoch's Newscorp, which had been announced on the Friday before the final. Another feature story informed South African readers on the doings of said Rupert Murdoch and, tucked onto the end of the front-page lead, was what newspapermen call a 'blob'. It read: 'South African Rugby Football Union president Dr Louis Luyt angered the international rugby world with a gloating speech during the official closing ceremony at Gallagher Estate last night. Soon after Luyt's speech, the All Blacks left the dinner in disgust. The All Black captain, Sean Fitzpatrick, snapped at a television reporter: "I hope you got that down, mate. It's a disgrace." Soon after the All Blacks walked out, international referees, as well as other visiting sides represented at the banquet, also left.'

These discordant notes at the end of a glorious day laid down the script for the next few years between South Africa winning the World Cup, defending it in Wales in 1999, and the RWC tournament in Australia in 2003.

9

A walkout and
a girl called Suzie

Colin Meads had a face like thunder as he strode towards the exit of the
Gallagher Estate conference centre. The legendary All Black's heavy eye-
brows were pulled into a jagged scowl and his body language spoke of fury.
'Hello, Colin,' said the reporter, 'is there a problem?'

'That *bastard*,' snapped the man whose gritty voice put an inflection
on the word like no other. 'That bastard insulted us. We're out of here!'
And he stormed past, the rest of the All Blacks following in their black
blazers.

'Who?' the reporter called after Meads.

'Louis Luyt!' he shot back as the phalanx of All Blacks, with coach
Laurie Mains and captain Sean Fitzpatrick following hard on the heels of
their manager, strode out. And following right behind them came the
French and then the English, soon followed by the group of referees.

I was that reporter. I had got to the banqueting hall in Midrand,
midway between Johannesburg and Pretoria, where the closing ceremony
of the 1995 Rugby World Cup was held, quite late after completing my
match report, my front-page 'think piece' and a small story on Kitch
Christie's announcement that he intended to quit as Springbok coach.
I had had to fight my way through heavy traffic because of the celebrating
fans making their way out of the city to try to catch sight of their
heroes.

I rushed into the hall to find the party breaking up. Many of the teams
were following the All Blacks, who, my fellow reporters told me, had been
incensed by Luyt's allegedly gloating speech. I looked at my watch, realised that there might still be time to get the story into the *Sunday Times*,
and phoned the news desk – only to be told by the news editor that 'the
paper has already been put to bed'.

'I think this is quite important!' I yelled. 'The All Blacks have just
walked out of the Rugby World Cup's closing banquet because they were
insulted by Louis Luyt.'

'I don't think we can hold the paper back for that,' came the reply.

'Just call Ken Owen [editor of the *Sunday Times*]!' I shouted. And when Owen came on the line, I told him what I had just seen.

'Give it to me; we haven't got much time,' he said, and took down the 'blob', which appeared in the front-page lead. 'South African Rugby Football Union president Dr Louis Luyt angered the international rugby world with a gloating speech during the official closing ceremony at Gallagher Estate last night. Soon after Luyt's speech, the All Blacks left the dinner in disgust. The All Black captain, Sean Fitzpatrick, snapped at a television reporter: "I hope you got that down, mate. It's a disgrace." Soon after the All Blacks walked out, international referees, as well as other visiting sides represented at the banquet, also left.'

That was the only reference to the walk-out that made the Sunday papers, but Luyt's alleged triumphalism was seized upon by both the South African and the foreign media in their Monday reports. Luyt's combative, dictatorial style and his 'you're either with me or against me' approach to all things, especially the press, tended to rub people up the wrong way. But it troubled me that I had not actually heard his speech.

Further outrage was expressed because he had presented Welsh referee Derek Bevan with a gold watch, for unstated reasons but immediately misinterpreted as some kind of sinister reward for his role in the semi-final against France (afterwards French reporters would refer to Bevan, in slang, as *Monsieur Goolwash*).

I wondered whether the All Blacks and the other teams weren't perhaps guilty of sour grapes, and whether Luyt's lack of charm had not perhaps been misconstrued as gloating. This was especially pertinent after the tournament, when All Black coach Laurie Mains alleged that his team had been poisoned ahead of the final by a mysterious woman called 'Suzie'.

That night, Luyt was tired and angry – angry because the Springboks were late, angry because he had been against having the closing banquet out of the city and was proven right by the difficulty people had in getting to Midrand, and seriously pissed off because, in the course of his speech, Sir Ewart Bell, the Irishman who was chairman of RWC, had said SARFU had 'helped' the IRB to stage the tournament. The big doctor had felt that the worthies of the RWC, whom he scathingly referred to as the 'gin-and-tonic and scotch-and-soda brigade', had not done very much themselves.

And he was tired because he was fighting on many fronts: putting together the deal that would result in the formation of SANZAR, the

Super 12 and the Tri Nations, and because he was aware of the activities of an Australian called Ross Turnbull, who was determined to pirate rugby union and set up a rival organisation, called the World Rugby Corporation (WRC). Luyt had been to London and back, the SANZAR deal had been announced to angry outcries and criticism from the SABC and M-Net, and he was probably feeling a little betrayed by François Pienaar and the Springbok team for whom he had gone out on a limb to ensure that they got everything they wanted for the World Cup.

Later it would transpire that the Springboks had been late because Edward Griffiths had cornered them at their Sandton Hotel to tell them not to do anything silly and sign contracts they might regret. Griffiths knew that the WRC was hunting for players and offering big money, but he wanted the guys to know that the SANZAR agreement would enable SARFU to offer the players a deal that would ensure that they would be well paid and able to continue playing Test rugby.

Speaking to them at the hotel after the game was the only chance he would get, knowing that they would scatter to the four winds once the celebration party got under way. He also knew how badly Turnbull and his cohorts wanted the signatures of the world champions. In fact, without the newly crowned World Cup winners, the WRC would not fly. When the players finally emerged to catch the bus to Midrand, they were besieged by jubilant fans and were so late for proceedings at Gallagher Estate that they were accused of being rude.

So what exactly did Luyt say that got the All Blacks in such high dudgeon? Other than pick the memories of people who had been present, I didn't think we would ever know. Then, while I was busy researching this book, I learnt of the existence of a videotape of the speech and managed to track down a copy. This is what happened.

Luyt was called up to the podium by Sir Ewart Bell and presented with a Rugby World Cup plaque. Sir Ewart said, 'Louis, it was your ambition to have the final of the Rugby World Cup at Ellis Park, and also it was your ambition to have South Africa win the Cup. You must be a proud man this evening.'

Frenchman Bernard Lapasset, then in his first term as chairman of the IRB, was also on stage. Luyt fulfilled the usual protocols, and then said:

Before I speak, I'd like one man to come up here – Rian Oberholzer [then married to Luyt's daughter Corlia], come up here, please.

Ladies and gentlemen, of course to us South Africans this is a great day, of course this is what we've been waiting for for so many years. We boasted in 1987 that the real World Cup was not won by New Zealand unless we were there, then in 1991 we boasted again, we weren't there ... In 1995 we proved it, that if we were there we would have won. [Luyt looks down smiling, to applause and laughter.]

I want to say one thing: so much was said about Rugby World Cup, but if there ever was one man who made this possible, one man who worked around the clock, one man who did everything for South Africa – he was never at home – then it's this man Rian Oberholzer. [Turning to Rian and beckoning him forward, to much applause.]

I'd like to thank the government of South Africa for their support; I want to thank you all for your support. To [muffled], Richie Guy, Colin [Meads], all of you, I want to say, thank you. It was wonderful to play against the All Blacks, because I believe that today we saw the two best [rugby] nations on this planet, to coin a phrase that I read on Tuesday in London.

I read in a newspaper [that] a lady called Miss Bellamy [name not clear] – I didn't know a lady wrote about rugby, but she did – and she said that if there's a better team on this planet, I would like to see it, and she also said that if there are other planets with teams, they would lose to the All Blacks. So we're from Mars [lifting his right hand and smiling]. From Mars, we thank you, we are there.

The All Blacks are the greatest rugby nation, with us, not next to us, on earth. Because next time they'll beat us, most probably, and then we'll beat them again. It was the perfect script, the perfect script written by whoever, to have South Africa play New Zealand, the Springboks against the All Blacks. And I want to say thank you to those magnificent Springboks, you have done our country proud, you have brought this magnificent trophy home, where it belongs [meant as a crack?].

I heard my coach for today, Kitch Christie, told his players that he was not available henceforth. I want to tell him, you haven't spoken to me yet, pal! You will be available, okay? And so will Morné du Plessis, you will be available, right! We built a perfect Team South Africa, perfect management. To the management, Morné, Kitch and your team, how much better can you get? How much better can we get [loud applause]?

It might have been better had Luyt stopped there, but he had other things on his mind. The audio becomes unclear, some words are muffled, but his irritation, possibly because of the clandestine wheeling and dealing that had been going on with the WRC, was clear when he addressed his captain.

> François, I want to talk to you, I want to talk to you, at the very quickest too. I heard that [name inaudible, possibly Murdoch's] name was mentioned here [perhaps a reference to Bell's speech], it's [indistinguishable]. We must never lose the rugby culture. Sir Ewart, today we showed you we will never lose it. Rugby union is part of our culture, it will always remain part of our culture, and this is the way we show [indistinguishable] that we are there, rugby union.
>
> I thank you for your support, and I thank you for coming here. I thank you for supporting this country. We went through very difficult experiences, tumultuous experiences. There was a time that the Rugby World Cup was going to be removed from South Africa. We fought for it, we kept it here, and we showed the world that we could host it here – host it here in a way that will be very difficult, by … Wales to emulate. Thank you very much [shouts and applause].

At this point it seems as if Luyt is about to step off the podium, but a puzzled expression flits across his face, as if he were having second thoughts about something. So he turns, holding up his hand, and goes back to the microphone.

> In South Africa we have funny ways, very funny ways. I sat down with a number of colleagues and we decided, who do we pick, who do we pick as a man we respect? And we decided, a man who didn't have the whistle today but had it for the first game, we decided that Derek Bevan was the man we would like to pick to hand something to. So I would like Mr Bevan to come up please.' [Bevan comes up in a RWC blazer, shakes the doctor's hand, is handed a small parcel and departs the podium.]

Luyt then continues:

> The most wonderful referee in the world, we believe [holding up both hands]. We may be wrong, but to us, he was. It's that man,

80

thank you, Derek. And to Wales, who'll present the 1999 World Cup, we say thank you for giving us people like Derek Bevan. I know you can't beat us on the 2nd of September [South Africa's next Test-match assignment], you've got to play the world champions and they're going to defend their title, and England of course is going to have Twickenham ready for us.

Singling out a referee who had controlled two of South Africa's key games in such a way was clearly a mistake. At this point, what could be described as derisory noises from the room are audible. But Luyt, and whoever else might have been advising him, clearly felt that it was necessary to make some gesture of gratitude to Bevan for having ensured that the semi-final against France was played.

Remember, Luyt implicitly believed that Marcel Martin was trying to influence Bevan to call it off, so that James Dalton's red card in Port Elizabeth would result in France advancing to the final. However, in his autobiography, Luyt claimed that he been asked by Johan Prinsloo, the CEO of the Transvaal Rugby Union, to make a presentation to Bevan on behalf of the referees, 'as he had been voted the best referee at the tournament', and remarked: 'In hindsight, this was perhaps the dumbest thing I have ever done.'

And there was a sting in the tail of Luyt's address, which lasted for slightly more than eight minutes, which again indicated his suspicion that the players were up to something. 'Will Carling, you'll have to start renegotiations on your contract, like François must start with his … Thank you very, very much [what sounds like derisive shouts, perhaps cheers, heard from the room]. Thank you from South Africa, all of you. Remember that we can and will host big tournaments. Thank you very much.'

Did Louis Luyt insult the All Blacks? Was Mike Brewer right in walking up to Luyt's table to verbally insult him, as documented in Luyt's book? Were the All Blacks justified in staging a walkout?

You be the judge.

But all of this was forgotten a couple of days later, when the Springboks piled into an open-top bus to go on a victory parade through the streets of Johannesburg. James Small recalls one youngster running alongside the bus from the moment it departed until it completed its eight-kilometre route at the Civic Theatre. The players took turns to hold up the pot of gold they had found at the end of their rainbow, and once again South

Africans of all races laughed and cried, cheered and whistled, hugged and danced and felt very good about being South African.

Unfortunately, the euphoria did not last long. The Mad Dog – Ross Turnbull was given this nickname when he was a player – was roaming around with the lure of big money and looking for players to bite. The players, it seemed, were being seduced by talk of all this filthy lucre. Rugby officials adopted the stance that they were fighting for the future of their game. And then, to crown it all, the All Blacks' bitterness was ramped up a notch when Laurie Mains made the startling claim that his team had been deliberately poisoned two days before the final, and that it had severely affected their performance.

Mains mentioned a mysterious waitress called Suzie, who was never traced and has never come forward, and claimed that she might have spiked the team's tea and coffee, which were served in large urns at their hotel, the Sandton Crowne Plaza. This hotel is a big establishment on one of Joburg's busiest intersections and has often been home to the Springboks.

To this day, New Zealanders will claim that their team had been nobbled whenever they discuss the momentous events of the 1995 Rugby World Cup. The Kiwi press talked emotively of 'the sight of All Blacks being sick by the side of the pitch' (it still pops up on Google), but Evan Speechly, the Springboks' physio on the day, says he has no recollection of any of the All Blacks throwing up on the side of the field, 'and if anyone had been, I would have seen it and probably helped to attend to him. I know that some of them – as well as some of their security personnel – had been sick, but I have no recollection of anyone being sick during the game.'

The food-poisoning furore surfaced again with the release of the auto-biography of the man who had been in charge of the All Blacks' security during the World Cup. Rory Steyn had been Nelson Mandela's chief security officer, and his memoir, *One Step Behind Mandela*, published in 2001 and ghostwritten by e-tv's feisty Debora Patta, was seized upon in New Zealand as proof that some nefarious deed had been visited upon their team. Or, as this excerpt from Wikipedia puts it: 'He claims that the All Blacks had "definitely been poisoned" before the 1995 Rugby World Cup final, becoming the first high-profile South African to acknowledge any wrongdoing.'

In his book, Steyn relates that on the Thursday before the final, most of the All Blacks visited a cinema complex. Steyn accompanied prop Richard Loe (one of the reserves for the match). Loe vomited immediately after the movie, while Jeff Wilson had severe stomach cramps. Steyn said he knew then that he had a serious problem on his hands.

'We raced back to the hotel and when I got up to the doctor's room it looked like a battle zone – like a scene from a war movie,' Steyn said. 'Players were lying all over the place and the doctor and physio were walking around injecting them.'

Steyn then made a strikingly contradictory claim. 'I was a police officer, I worked with facts. What my eyes told me that night was that the team had deliberately been poisoned.' What facts, you have to ask? He also made another startling claim unsupported by fact. Mains allegedly employed a private investigator in an attempt to get to the bottom of the mystery, who reported back that a Far Eastern betting syndicate had paid a waitress called Suzie at the All Blacks' hotel to put something in their water.

'South African rugby fans remained sceptical of this theory and preferred to put it down to sour Kiwi grapes,' Steyn says. 'To my fellow South Africans, I want to say this: Stop all those cheap jokes about Suzie, the food poisoning and whingeing Kiwis. It happened. There is no doubt that the All Blacks were poisoned two days before the final. The All Black team never whinged about it. If anybody whinged it was their media and, boy, can they whinge. In fact, the New Zealand team management took a decision not to use the poisoning as an excuse, not to even mention it.'

A pact they might have broken, as the press did come to know about it and Mains did suffer the fate of having his name forever coupled to Suzie on Google. The private investigator has never come forward or been exposed and no betting syndicate ever uncovered.

A person with a different take on the poisoning allegations is Tony Rubin, who was general manager of the Sandton Crowne Plaza (now the Southern Sun Grayston) during the World Cup. Tony is now the managing director of the Maropeng a'Afrika complex in the Cradle of Humankind World Heritage Site near Krugersdorp, and this is what he told me.

'On the Thursday before the World Cup final, some of [the All Blacks] came downstairs and they were about to go out. And I said to Rory Steyn, who was their security liaison man, "Rory, what are you doing? I'm responsible for the team's welfare and they can't go out." He said, "Don't worry, they're going out with me and I'll make sure that they're okay." The South African liaison man with them said, "Don't worry, we're taking them to a friend of mine's place and everything will be okay." So off they went. Not all the team – about five or six of them.

'The following morning [the Friday before the final], I got to work at about 6 a.m. and the All Blacks' doctor [Dr Michael Bowen] was waiting outside my office. I asked what was wrong, and he answered, "We have a problem – the team's got food poisoning."

'I said, "Are you sure?" You can't make a statement like that, because food poisoning can only be confirmed by doing proper tests. He replied that he was sure. I said we'll have to check why or how, but in the meantime I asked him to get stool samples so that we could have tests done to see what had caused the food poisoning. He said, "That's already organised. Laurie Mains has a friend at Morningside Hospital [quite nearby] who's in the pathology department and we're sorting that out." I asked him to make sure that I received a copy of the results, which he undertook to do. [Rubin never received a copy of the results.]

'Jonah Lomu then came down to breakfast – as always wearing those earphones of his. Jonah was a loner who kept very much to himself. Engrossed in his music, he was in a different world. I asked him how he was, and I'll never forget his reply: "I'm fine, but some of the boys have got little girls' tummies." He made a big joke of it. He ... hadn't gone out with them.

'But it got worse. Everyone stopped speaking to me and they became very withdrawn. Zinzan Brooke, one of the really nice guys who often came by for a chat, started to avoid me; Andrew Mehrtens, who had always been quite friendly and easygoing, gave me the cold shoulder – I was suddenly persona non grata.

'Yes, five of them were very, very ill – but not all of them. The day after the final, I took Sean Fitzpatrick and Colin Meads to the Royal Johannesburg Golf Club, and in my car on the way, Sean said to me, "Tony, we were beaten by a better team on the day."

'The team checked out on the Monday, and after they left, house-keeping went in to clean the rooms and we found used bottles of peri-peri sauce from a takeaway fish outlet. I sent them away for lab analysis and what came back indicated that if someone had consumed that sauce, there was a strong likelihood that they would have contracted a 24-hour bug. They would be man down. And that is what had caused the problem.

'The guys were on such a strict diet. The doctor used to check on the menu all the time. In fact, their food was extremely bland. And the night before the meal they did, in fact, have chicken burgers – and there's no way a chicken burger could do what happened to them. All of the staff working with the team had to eat what the team ate. They were not allowed to go to the staff canteen for meals, so once the team had eaten, we would eat exactly what they did.

'None of my staff got ill. Mains claimed [the poison] had been in the tea or coffee, but the tea or coffee came out of the urns in the kitchen. If that had been the case, a great many more people would have been under the weather. It was something that Laurie Mains dreamt up. Laurie was one of the people on the bus who went out for dinner that night. I don't know if the group split up, but he should have taken responsibility.'

Rubin remains upset by the slight on his reputation and the manner in which his employers, Southern Sun, decided to handle the issue. 'Their PR department said to me, "Look, for better or worse, we're not speaking to the press." I objected and said that there was a true story to tell. I was upset that it was my name and my reputation that were being dragged through the mud. In fact, I thought it was a most serious accusation against us. I said, "There's a story here, so let's tell the story."

'I felt I was let down and that we should have defended ourselves against a scurrilous and unjustified accusation that also cast our country and the World Cup organisation in a bad light.'

As with Louis Luyt's speech, you be the judge. 'Suzie' has never been found, nor has she come forward to either sell or tell her story. But how sad that an unsubstantiated accusation was allowed to sully an occasion that Sean Fitzpatrick described as 'the most memorable World Cup of all for what it meant to a country and a nation'. And he said this in 2010, while promoting the seventh World Cup, to be staged in New Zealand in 2011.

In a surprising development, Laurie Mains would become coach of the Ellis Park–based Cats in the Super 12 competition, taking them to two consecutive semi-finals, in 2000 and 2001, and also become a key figure in the palace revolt that led to Luyt being forced out of a union that he had turned into one of the richest in the world.

10

Money, the root of all evil

'There are 550 million reasons for doing this,' said Louis Luyt as he faced a media scrum in the teak- and yellowwood-panelled reception room at Ellis Park Stadium. It was 23 June, the day before the 1995 Rugby World Cup final. Luyt was flanked by the chairmen of the other two major southern hemisphere rugby unions: Leo Williams of Australia on his right, and Richie Guy of New Zealand on his left.

The press conference had been called at short notice, and the three administrators were about to declare the start of the professional era in rugby. For Luyt, the chief spokesman, had just announced a US$550-million deal over 10 years with Rupert Murdoch's Newscorp, granting the organisation television rights to all rugby under the jurisdiction of the three unions.

With the scribbling of a few signatures, 100 years of rugby's tradition as an amateur game (which by then was a complete farce in any case) was over-turned and the SANZAR alliance born. It would result in the inception of the annual Tri Nations competition and the expansion of the existing Super 10 competition to the Super 12, creating arguably the hardest tour-nament the game has ever seen. The move caught the traditional northern hemisphere partners of the southern hemisphere triumvirate by surprise. They huffed and they puffed and declared their outrage, but the dam wall had burst and, by August 1996, the IRB officially renounced amateurism and condoned pay for play.

As I've briefly mentioned, the Ellis Park press conference was the result of feverish negotiations during the previous month to head off what officials in Australia and New Zealand believed was a 'hostile raid' on rugby union in their region. In April, Rupert Murdoch had launched Super League, a full-scale assault on Kerry Packer's Australian Rugby League (ARL).

Murdoch was dissatisfied that Packer's Optus pay television channel held all rights to rugby league, and he wanted a slice of the action for his Foxtel network. So he did a Packer on Packer by doing in rugby league what Packer had done in cricket with his World Series Cricket. Murdoch's agents decided to set up a rival professional rugby league series, and they went around offering big salaries to ARL players – but, most alarmingly

Frik du Preez and Albie Bates (on the ground) tackle Chris Laidlaw in Wessel Oosthuizen's iconic photograph taken during the All Black tour of South Africa in 1970

Dr Danie Craven with his dog, Bliksem. Doc Craven was instrumental in the creation of the Rugby World Cup tournament

Left: New Zealand captain David Kirk holds the Webb Ellis Cup aloft at the culmination of the first Rugby World Cup in 1987. The All Blacks have not won the Cup since, but will 2011 be their year?

Wallaby captain Nick Farr-Jones and David Campese with the Cup in 1991. Australia beat England in the final at Twickenham

Below: PJ Powers and members of Ladysmith Black Mambazo rehearsing for the 1995 Rugby World Cup opening ceremony

all photos @ Grant Leversha

Top right and right: Performers at the 1995 Rugby World Cup opening ceremony

Merle McKenna (now McLintock), who organised both the opening and closing ceremonies of the 1995 World Cup, SARFU tournament manager Rian Oberholzer and RWC tournament manager Craig Jamieson on the field at Ellis Park before the start of the final. Their superb organisational skills ensured a magnificent and memorable tournament

Me with the late Ray Gravell, the man who gave me my nickname, at St Helens, Swansea, in 1994

The wettest World Cup game ever. Morné du Plessis (centre) and Kitch Christie (right) survey the field in Durban ahead of the Springboks' clash against France in the semi-final of the 1995 Rugby World Cup. André Joubert can be seen behind Du Plessis

The wet conditions at King's Park Stadium on 17 June 1995 are amply illustrated in this action shot of André Joubert kicking the ball; note the green hurling glove on his left hand

The Lomu Factor – Joost van der Westhuizen's crucial tackle on Jonah Lomu in the final on 24 June 1995

Lomu and James Small compete for
the ball while André Joubert looks on

Ruben Kruger prepares to stop
Jonah Lomu, while Japie Mulder
hangs on tightly

@ Gallo Images

The moment critique ...
Joel Stransky drops the ball
onto his foot as Andrew
Mehrtens desperately tries to
block the kick. Stransky later
said: 'I don't think I have ever
struck a ball as purely
as I hit that one '

@ Gallo Images

Stransky, Mehrtens and Josh Kronfeld
follow the trajectory of the ball ...

@ Gallo Images

... and it's over! Stransky and
André Joubert celebrate

Left: The men in the No. 6 jersey. President Nelson Mandela congratulates François Pienaar, after presenting him with the Webb Ellis Cup

Above: It's ours — Pienaar lifts the Cup

Pilot Laurie Kay sets the Jumbo 747 on its tail and blasts the crowd before the final of the 1995 World Cup at Ellis Park

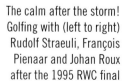

The calm after the storm! Golfing with (left to right) Rudolf Straeuli, François Pienaar and Johan Roux after the 1995 RWC final

Above: Bob Skinstad, Joost van der Westhuizen and André Venter listen to instructions from Nick Mallett at a training session during the 1999 Rugby World Cup in Glasgow, Scotland

Right: Jannie de Beer kicking one of his five successful drop kicks against England in the 1999 quarter-final at the Stade de France in Paris

Worried men. Nick Mallett, Alan Solomons and Brendan Venter watch the Springboks go down to Australia in the 1999 semi-final at Twickenham

Right: Corné Krige, me and Nick Mallett at the Ernie Els Invitational at Fancourt, December 2001

Above: Uneasy lies the head ... Harry Viljoen (second from left) talks to (left to right) Percy Montgomery, Jake White and André Vos during a training session in Cardiff, Wales, in November 2000

Right: And then came Straeuli ... The Springbok coach and his captain, Corné Krige, face the press in Dunedin, New Zealand, in August 2003

Mike Greenaway, Clinton van der Berg and me doing what the Irish do at The Club, Dalkey, November 2004

With Rod Kafer (left) and Phil Kearns (centre), commentating from the Telstra Stadium in Sydney, July 2007

to administrators of the 15-man code in Australia and New Zealand, also to union players.

Murdoch's attack on rugby league, however, turned out to be a catalyst for the changes that would transform rugby union. Australian and New Zealand officials realised that they had to defend their game by offering the television mogul an attractive product ... but unbeknown to them, other wheels had been set in motion.

Packer had brought Geoff Levy, a South African–born lawyer living and working in Sydney, into the fray to assist in efforts to head off Murdoch's Super League. And Levy then had a brainwave: rugby union might, in fact, provide a much better option for Packer. Levy realised – correctly – that while rugby league was, in fact, a very small game concentrated mainly in Australia and parts of northern England, rugby union was a universal sport on the verge of staging its third World Cup.

Levy possessed a fertile mind, and he came up with the concept of an international professional rugby circuit involving the best players in rugby union, and this embryo would metamorphose into the World Rugby Corporation (WRC), which could be offered to Packer.

Levy mooted his plan in influential circles. Sensing resistance because of the difficulty of circumventing rugby union's entrenched committee system – from club level to the IRB – he soon realised that he would need a partner to help develop and sell the concept. And he knew just the right man – former Wallaby prop, former chairman of the New South Wales Rugby Union and former Australian representative to the IRB, Ross Vincent Turnbull.

Turnbull, at the time, was out of favour with the establishment because of a scheme he had brokered to establish the Waratahs' headquarters at the out-of-the-way Concorde Stadium (where a semi-final between Australia and France was staged in the first RWC in 1987). He jumped at the chance of joining forces with fellow legal man Levy. A pugnacious character who was the embodiment of the bluff Australian, Turnbull threw himself into the WRC with gusto, refining Levy's plan and using his connections to get players to sign on with what rugby administrators derisively referred to as 'a circus' ... when they finally got to hear about it.

It was a time of much intrigue, clandestine arrangements and secret meetings. Super League fizzled out eventually, but Australian and New Zealand officials knew they had to bring South Africa into the frame to have any chance of success, while simultaneously Levy and Turnbull were effectively planning how to hijack rugby union and deliver it into the hands of Packer. Finally, the rugby officials from the antipodes were forced to eat humble pie and ask Luyt to bring his business acumen to bear to fine-tune their offering, take charge of the SANZAR bid and face up to Murdoch's heavy hitters.

Turnbull played on the players' mistrust of officialdom. He found a receptive audience when he told them of the money they might earn in the WRC, for in spite of the massive amount (originally announced as $550 million and later edged up to a tidy $555 million) Luyt had announced at Ellis Park, players were not confident that they would get a liberal share of the loot. During the press conference at Ellis Park, Luyt revealed a great deal about the prevailing attitude with this answer to one of my questions:

'Right now, 30 of the world's leading players are getting up in Sandton, preparing for tomorrow's final,' I said. 'Have you told them of this [development] or slipped a press release under their doors?'

'I don't need to talk to the players,' was Luyt's curt reply.

Little did he know that he would soon have to, for hardly had the World Cup hangover eased when news of Turnbull's activities began to emerge. I first got an inkling of what was going on in the British papers while I was covering the British Open (won by John Daly at St Andrews), but Luyt was distracted by a furious row that had broken out between him, the SABC and M-Net over the Murdoch contract. The broadcasters complained about the fact that the rights – worth R2 billion at the time – had been 'secretly sold to a broadcaster who did not have a footprint in Africa'.

There were dire rumours that rugby would not be seen on local television and that Murdoch would establish a pay-to-view network in South Africa, but in the end it proved to be all bluster from Russell MacMillan (M-Net) and Robin Kempthorne (SABC). The broadcasting rights were settled as Luyt and Griffiths had said they would be: M-Net agreed to a subcontract with Newscorp, which, in time, would be the launch pad for the highly successful specialist sports broadcaster SuperSport, which sprouted from M-Net.

Ironically, MacMillan and M-Net would play a key role in the collapse of the WRC, but not before a furious round of threats and counter-threats, heated meetings, angry video conferences, legal incursions and court appearances. It gradually emerged that Turnbull had managed to get the buy-in of the Wallabies, the All Blacks and the Springboks, and that players from especially England and Ireland were ready to sign with him.

Luyt's instinct was to send them to hell and offer contracts to a new group, but Griffiths worked hard to convince the World Cup–winning Boks that there was no substance to Turnbull's offer, that his scheme could not work and that they would be better off staying with the establishment.

It transpired that Harry Viljoen, a former Transvaal player and Junior Springbok who had coached Transvaal, Natal and Western Province and who would end up coaching the Springboks, had been instrumental in introducing Turnbull to the South African players. François Pienaar was deeply involved in this scheme, and most of his teammates were ready to jump ship with him.

Later it emerged that all but two – Chester Williams and Brendan Venter – had signed Turnbull's pieces of paper.* Fortunately these players were saved from a tricky situation when the skipper did not hand over the contracts but kept them in his possession while the bargaining with SA Rugby continued. And it was not only the Springboks – obviously representing the diamonds in the necklace – who were involved in the wheeling and dealing. Other players, rallying around Tiaan Strauss, were also keeping a sharp eye on proceedings, partly to share in the booty and partly because they feared being excluded.

These were momentous times. The Springboks were being fêted for having won the World Cup while, unbeknown to all but a few, Ross Turnbull's World Rugby Championship scheme was bubbling under the surface. And within eight days of winning the Webb Ellis Cup, the 13 Transvaal Springboks in the RWC squad were involved in a stand-off with Luyt over money. The players were unhappy over issues such as the ratio between retainers and match fees (even though the game at that point was not professional!), and medical aid cover.

They wanted a better deal, and a fiery meeting at their Wanderers training ground went on for so long that no training, under new coach Ray Mordt, who had replaced an ailing Christie, was possible. Missing a training session was interpreted as a players' strike, and Luyt was incensed. Never one to back off from a scrap, he went on the offensive and cancelled

---

* *Williams, at the behest of his lawyer Frikkie Erasmus, had refused to put pen to paper on the grounds that he could do more lucrative deals as an individual (erroneously, as it turned out).*

the employment contracts of players such as Hennie le Roux and Johan Roux, and demanded that their sponsored cars be returned.

I inadvertently became involved in the squabble when I received a call from Lisa Bon, the former Natal Rugby Union liaison officer, who was then attached to the sports marketing company Masters International, which took care of sponsorship issues for a number of the players. Bon asked me whether I could attend a meeting with some of the players at the Sunnyside Park Hotel, and when I arrived there, I was shown to a conference room. Not knowing what to expect, I was surprised to find 11 of Transvaal's World Cup Springboks seated around the boardroom table: François Pienaar, Hennie le Roux, Rudolf Straeuli, Johan Roux, Gavin Johnson, Chris Rossouw, James Dalton, Hannes Strydom, Christiaan Scholtz, Japie Mulder and Pieter Hendriks. Kobus Wiese and Balie Swart were absent.

Also in the room was Gary Janks, a Johannesburg lawyer who, I gathered, had previously advised some of the players and was now present to counsel them and advise them on their rights. Lisa asked me for advice on how the players should frame the press release they intended making and how to handle any public pronouncements. It was a tricky situation for me as a reporter, as it was my job to report both sides of a story, but I was friendly with a number of the players and sympathised with the stance they were taking. My advice was that they had to stand together at all costs, speak with one voice and not belabour the money aspects too much, as I was surprised to hear what salaries they were already earning! I added that what transpired between us in the room would remain confidential, but that when I left I would revert to being a newspaperman and would report on the story as it unfolded.

Straeuli, a lawyer by profession, played a leading role in the discussions. I spent some time with him and Janks drafting the press release, and then I left. Later I attended the press conference at the Sunnyside Park Hotel and was impressed by the credible statement Janks had crafted, delivered most ably by Pienaar, who was supported by Straeuli and Le Roux.

The upshot of the stand-off was that Transvaal played their first Currie Cup game of the season, against Eastern Province, with a virtual second team and suffered a predictable defeat. However, by standing strong, the players had not only won a better dispensation from their province, but were able to negotiate far more forcefully than might have been the case when they signed up with SARFU.

The players had been bombarded with advice and threats from all quarters – SA Rugby, Murdoch's men, Turnbull and Viljoen, as well as the Wallabies, led by Phil Kearns, and the All Blacks, led by Sean Fitzpatrick, who seemed ready and determined to sign with Turnbull.

My own view was that the players would be making a grave mistake if they decided to sign the so-called Packer deal as promoted by Turnbull. It reminded me of the famous line in *Jerry Maguire*: 'Show me the money!' I had serious reservations about whether Packer was 100% committed, and I was not alone in my doubts.

My misgivings were confirmed when Viljoen invited me to meet with Turnbull, ostensibly to convince me of the verity of the WRC, at his palatial home in Cleveland Road in the plush suburb of Sandhurst in Johannesburg. Viljoen had told me, 'I would never be involved [in the Packer deal] if I didn't believe this was good for the game and the unions.'

When I arrived, I noted in passing that Viljoen had a garden similar to the one adorning the Cascades Hotel at Sun City. During the meeting, Turnbull, thickset, brash and with silver sideburns, made the mistake of telling me that I would be the 'first journalist anywhere in the world' to see the document he was about to show me.

Big mistake. In my briefcase was a cutting from the British newspaper the *Guardian*, containing exactly the same information he was 'revealing' to 'only' me. No one likes to be lied to, so I was less receptive than Turnbull and Viljoen might have wished, and what I saw convinced me that the WRC was unworkable.

The document enumerated on crowds numbering 40 000 in Houston and Tokyo, and even bigger numbers at established venues. I wondered ... such figures for composite teams made up of various nationalities *not* playing in their national colours? The traditionalist in me could not see it working. Turnbull was also quite evasive on whether Kerry Packer was actually committed to bankrolling the whole show.

Viljoen, sitting at a desk on which lay a *Rugby News* magazine with a picture of François Pienaar holding up the Webb Ellis Cup, let Turnbull do most of the talking. Little did I know then that our paths would cross again when he became the Springbok coach and that it would lead to one of the most absurd episodes in my career as a rugby writer. But more on this later ...

There had been plenty of 'wheeling, dealing and mealing', to borrow the title of one of the chapters in Peter FitzSimons' book *The Rugby War*. Great pressure had been brought to bear on the players, business magnate

Johann Rupert's name was mentioned as a possible backer, and the whole saga became a case of 'who is fooling whom?'

The World Cup was won in June, and in early August, trying to get to the bottom of it all, I got my break. Russell MacMillan, then in charge of M-Net's sport, called to confirm that as far as financial matters were concerned, the WRC were skating on thin ice. MacMillan had had a meeting with Jamie Packer, Kerry's son, in which he had been asked whether M-Net would stand surety for the salaries of the Springboks should they sign and hand over their WRC contracts. 'They don't have the money,' said MacMillan. That was the gist of my story, and from that point on, the WRC started to crumble.

Edward Griffiths was able to put concrete offers on the table, and then François Pienaar backed out of an international conference call with Sean Fitzpatrick, Phil Kearns and various WRC representatives. His actions deeply annoyed his fellow international captains, as well as James Small and Hennie le Roux, who squirmed with embarrassment when they were unable to provide the same assurances as the All Blacks and the Wallabies. And although the feisty Turnbull would continue to try to convince the courts of the validity of certain documents he did not have (Pienaar, the 'agent' Turnbull had appointed to conclude contracts with his fellow players, still had them in his possession), the WRC was a lost cause without the world champions. On 11 August, the proceedings were struck from the court roll and Turnbull was ordered to pay SARFU's legal costs.

The Springboks, with the exception of Chester Williams, signed with SA Rugby; the New Zealanders, where some prominent young players had already broken ranks, put their names on the dotted line; and the Australians, feeling that they had been betrayed by the Springboks, reluctantly followed suit when it became clear that there was no other viable option to pursue.

Rugby's establishment had won the war. Griffiths waxed lyrical: 'The threat to rugby in this country has been thwarted. We have faced the rape of rugby in this country and withstood it.'

I had another story to write. It appeared under the headline 'Pienaar's career on the line' in some editions and 'The Springboks are not yours to sell' in others. The article went as follows:

> Springbok captain François Pienaar's career was last night in jeopardy following revelations that he had agreed to accept US$300 000 to act as an agent for the Kerry Packer–backed World Rugby Corporation.

Pienaar could face accusations that he wilfully set out to denude South African rugby of its stars and may face disciplinary action. Just 42 days after South Africa's victory in the World Cup, Pienaar's reputation lies in tatters. Allegations made by the WRC are the latest episode in a sordid tale of deceit which has seen South Africa's leading players locked in bitter pay-for-play negotiations. Pienaar's possible involvement as a key player is a damning indictment.

Pienaar had been promised the fee by the WRC, and Sam Chisholm of Newscorp promised to match the amount if he signed with SA Rugby. And, when the dust settled, he did claim it.

Luyt took delight in allowing *Beeld* newspaper to photograph and publish the cashed cheque for R1 million (converted from dollars) that he had paid to the Springbok captain. Pienaar's teammates were furious, as they had not been aware of the fact that he had actually been paid to act as their agent. It is sad but true that there is not much love lost between the skipper and certain members of the team who had stood at the end of the rainbow on that marvellous day, 24 June 1995, at Ellis Park. In 2005, a reunion was held to commemorate the winning of the World Cup, and when I asked one of the Springboks whether he had enjoyed the party, he sneered, 'You mean the François Pienaar show!'

Far from the World Cup triumph leaving a golden glow in which the Springboks could bask, the ensuing years would be fraught with so much controversy, squabbles and sheer ugliness that it made some of the highlights they managed to achieve simply miraculous.

The euphoria, however, did manage to rub off on other sports. At the 1996 Atlanta Olympics, Penny Heyns won two gold medals in swimming, Josiah Thugwane claimed gold in the marathon and Hezekiel Sepeng silver in the 800 metres. And Bafana Bafana won the Africa Cup of Nations that same year. But the good ship *Springbok* would run into stormy waters, souring their World Cup defence in 1999 and reaching a nadir in Australia in 2003.

Not only did the signing of the Newscorp contract put television in charge of the game – meaning 'product' before people – but it sounded the death knell of long tours and consigned SA Rugby to a system of unequal and unsustainable payment that is still not resolved. It created a new order in which rugby would effectively be managed in four-year cycles, the years separating the World Cups, and would leave a seemingly unsolvable situation in which the top players simply played too much rugby.

Within a year of winning the World Cup, five of the key players in the Springboks' success were no longer involved. Kitch Christie, who, rather unsurprisingly, had been persuaded by Luyt to remain on as coach, was forced to stand down due to ill health; Morné du Plessis, who detested the internecine squabbles and did not approve of the ways of Christie's successor, André Markgraaff, resigned the role of manager; Edward Griffiths, who was too much his own man for Luyt, was summarily dismissed; François Pienaar, who was crassly dropped by Markgraaff, was paying the price for his role in the WRC hullabaloo; and Joel Stransky, the man who put over The Drop, was dropped in turn.

Pienaar's axing unleashed an angry public outcry, reflected in a column I wrote for the British *Rugby World* magazine. 'South African rugby's propensity to shoot itself in the foot hit a bizarre low point when Springbok captain François Pienaar was incomprehensibly left out of the team to tour Argentina, France and Wales. Coach André Markgraaff's decision to axe the charismatic World Cup hero triggered an unprecedented wave of public resentment and indignation. A call-in poll run by the *Sunday Times* attracted 55 000 callers in a matter of nine hours – 95.5% of them demanding Pienaar's reinstatement and the dismissal of Markgraaff.'

Luyt, too, was blamed for Pienaar's dismissal in faxes that clogged the newspaper's machines. One of these was particularly amusing. A teacher from a predominantly Jewish primary school in Johannesburg had helped her class to compile a petition, but she had clearly not read all the remarks, particularly the one from David, aged nine, which said: 'Louis, you prick!'

In a historical context, South Africa's 1996 rugby season set the tone for the quadrennial leading up to the World Cup in 1999 in Wales. It will be remembered for Sean Fitzpatrick and as good a bunch of All Blacks as ever donned the famous black jersey with its silver fern as they triumphantly marched towards the tournament. In this time, Fitzpatrick, already his country's longest-serving All Black, would surpass Willie John McBride to become the most-capped rugby forward of all time, moving his tally up to 83 during an awesome August.

This record was something special, but it paled in comparison to the other achievements of the feisty old pirate of rugby's high seas. Fitzpatrick became arguably the greatest of the men in black. If he didn't have the edge on Colin Meads, then he was at least the equal of the great 'Pinetree'.

The peppery hooker led an impressive New Zealand team that topped the table to win the inaugural Tri Nations series, while also becoming the first All Blacks to win a series in South Africa – thus healing a Kiwi psyche first wounded in 1937, when Phillip Nel's team (dubbed 'the greatest touring team ever to leave the shores of New Zealand') won the series in New Zealand, and exacerbated in 1949, when Fred Allan's side took a 0-4 series drubbing in South Africa.

The 1996 All Blacks met South Africa's world champions in a record five Tests in a single year, beating the Springboks four successive times, to not only clinch the Tri Nations, but take an insurmountable 2-0 lead in the three-match series. A 32-22 win on the field of dreams at Ellis Park restored some pride to the Boks, but all in all it proved to be a winter of discontent, with off-field ructions dominating the news. South Africa's transition to professionalism was traumatic, while from the outset it became clear that the structure of the Super 12 and the Tri Nations put South African teams at a clear disadvantage due to the travel demands.

Interestingly, Markgraaff was then already talking about building the core of the team to defend the Webb Ellis Cup. Gary Teichmann had by then succeeded Pienaar as captain. The blond World Cup–winning skipper's career had come to a poignant end when he was carried off the field suffering from concussion in the Test against the All Blacks at Newlands. It seemed as if injuries and disillusionment dogged the team. While researching the *Springbok Saga** series for SuperSport many years later, I was constantly amazed at the amount of drama woven into the fabric of Springbok rugby.

In 1997, the British & Irish Lions returned to tour after an absence of 17 years, and by then the Springboks were being coached by Carel du Plessis, the Prince of Wings. Du Plessis was a wonderful player but a man with virtually no coaching experience. He was appointed as coach after André Markgraaff was caught on tape uttering racial slurs against certain politicians and officials. The tape was subsequently leaked to the media by one of his disgruntled Griquas players, André Bester, and Markgraaff was forced to resign.

In Du Plessis' preparation of the Springboks for the arrival of Martin

---

* *Springbok Saga is a television documentary series that brought the original Saga series by Pierre Marais, based on Chris Greyvenstein's seminal work of the same title, up to date from 1995 to 2007 (13 episodes spanning one World Cup victory to the next).*

Johnson's Lions, he tended to ignore the importance of a sound goal-kicker. The result was that Teichmann's heavily favoured men dropped the first two internationals and lost the series. Du Plessis was eventually removed as coach, but, ironically, only after the Springboks, in his eighth and last Test in control, scored a record 61-22 win over the Wallabies at Loftus Versfeld.

His successor in 1997 was Nick Mallett, who had been brought into the coaching set-up by Markgraaff, and he would become South Africa's seventh coach since readmission in 1992.

The hard-nosed and bullish Mallett was passed what rugby reporters were already referring to as the 'poisoned chalice'. His era began with a 62-31 win over Italy in Bologna, which set the Boks on a record-equalling run of 17 successive wins that would not be halted until December 1998.

One great victory followed another, in particular a *trés magnifique* 52-10 win over France at Parc des Princes in Paris. It heralded a glorious 1998 as the Springboks once again rose to the top of the rugby pile, winning the Tri Nations for the first time, equalling but failing to beat the record of 17 successive Test wins (set by New Zealand) by going down to England at Twickenham in the last game of the year.

Along the way, the Boks beat the All Blacks 13-3 at Athletic Park in Wellington in the 50th Test between rugby's greatest rivals. It was a victory that would gather lustre as the years passed, as it would take another nine years before the Boks won again in New Zealand. In the return game in Durban, the Springboks trailed 5-23 with 20 minutes to go, but then unleashed some of the best rugby they have ever produced to score tries through Joost van der Westhuizen, Bob Skinstad and James Dalton, to snatch a wonderful 24-23 victory.

It set up a winner-take-all match against Australia at Ellis Park the following week. The Boks duly negotiated this game 29-14, with Skinstad scoring one of rugby's all-time classic tries to clinch the match.

With the Millennium Stadium in Cardiff under construction for the 1999 RWC, the Boks' end-of-year Test against Wales was played at England's home of football, the Wembley Stadium in London. It was Mark Andrews' 50th Test, but the Boks made surprisingly heavy weather of defeating a Welsh side fired up by Scott Gibbs and the Quinnell brothers. The Boks were awarded a controversial penalty try, and the Welsh were further upset by the appearance of a streaker – he later turned out to be a South African – who broke their momentum and snapped their concentration. A try by André Venter sealed the win for the Boks (28-20).

However, it was in the next Test, against Scotland at Murrayfield, that Mallett made his first false move by picking Skinstad to start and dropping ironman André Venter. Time would show that Mallett had disturbed his all-conquering team's chemistry, and even though the Boks got a good win, 35-10, the cracks were beginning to show. Ireland were seen off 27-13 at Lansdowne Road for win No. 17, but the Boks were starting to look jaded as they headed for Twickenham and the Test record.

Mallett wanted to stay loyal to the team that had carried him so far, but he probably erred in playing soldiers who were battling injuries rather than those who were fit. England was a different kettle of fish to the side beaten earlier in the year, and after a dead-simple try by Pieter Rossouw early on in the game, the Boks were strangled by a fresher side that contained the core of the team who would go on to win the 2003 World Cup. They went down 7-13, consigning all us South Africans to a nightmare train ride back from Twickenham when the English fans adapted a popular pop song with which to taunt us: 'Where's your record gone? Where's your record gone? Far, far away!'

Little did we know that we could expect worse days and worse defeats at Twickenham in the not-too-distant future.

Yet the achievements of the team had been nothing short of phenomenal, given the off-field ructions playing out in the background. As Andy Colquhoun phrased it during his excellent editorship of the *SA Rugby Annual*: 'If events on the field were dramatic they were kept pace by events in the amateur committee rooms of South African rugby.'

Louis Luyt's reputation for being a litigious man was validated when SARFU launched two actions against the ANC government. The first was to obtain a copy of a dossier alleging mismanagement and racism, compiled by dissident Transvaal vice-president Brian van Rooyen (a man who was no match for Luyt in face-to-face combat, but who would play a key role in the 'Big Lion's' departure from rugby; he would also, rather bizarrely, end up as president of SARFU).

The second was far more serious. It sought to set aside an inquiry into the affairs of rugby, prompted by Van Rooyen's dossier. Judge William de Villiers was forced to request President Nelson Mandela's presence in the witness box to defend his decision to institute the inquiry, a move that was interpreted as crassly disrespectful of the iconic Madiba. As one commentator put it, 'Challenging Mandela in court is like accusing Mother Teresa of child abuse.'

Luyt was correct on the points of law and he won his court battle, but he lost the war. His opponents and critics banded against him (the National Sports Council threatened a return of rugby boycotts) and he was forced out of office, to be replaced by Silas Nkanunu, the first black president of SARFU.

Luyt's achievements were many: he had run the most successful World Cup ever, in the process creating a blueprint for how it should be done, and he had brought his business brain and tough negotiating skills to bear in brokering a transition to professionalism that was much more lucrative than the players might have anticipated. Yet for him there were no fond farewells. The following year he took up the political cudgels, founding the Federal Alliance to contest the 1999 general election.

Still, despite all the off-the-field drama and controversy, the national team had done well. There was reason to be optimistic about the Springboks having a darn good chance of successfully defending the Webb Ellis Cup in 'Cymru 1999'.

11

No way to treat a captain

Gary Teichmann was lying face down on his physiotherapist's table, receiving treatment for a knee injury, when his cell phone rang. 'Hello, Gary speaking,' he said.

'Hello, Gary. Look, it's Nick here, can you talk?' a familiar, gruff voice said.

'No problem,' Gary said.

'Look, Gary, I've made up my mind. You're out,' the voice announced.

'Out of what?' Gary asked, even though he knew.

'Out of the World Cup,' said the voice. 'I've got to move on, and I've decided you're not going.'

And that was pretty much it. The caller was Springbok coach Nick Mallett, and he had just informed Gary Teichmann, his captain, that he would not be going to the 1999 World Cup, to be held in the UK in a few weeks' time. Not, 'I'm sorry'; not an explanation – just a phone call to jettison a player who had already been captain when Mallett took over in 1997 and who would be by his side for a run of 16 straight victories (17 if you count the 61-22 victory over the Wallabies when Carel du Plessis was still in charge) during a period when racially orientated and other political realities impacted negatively on the team.

To say that Teichmann was shattered would be an understatement. He had been fighting to recover from a knee injury and was winning the battle. Even though his relationship with Mallett had soured, he felt that he would be given a fair chance to prove his fitness. Teichmann had missed out on the 1995 World Cup, and now he would be denied the crowning moment of a stellar career. Mallett's insensitive phone call turned out to be the defining act of the quadrennial between 1995 and 1999.

A lot had happened in that time. Rugby had turned professional, the Super 12 and Tri Nations had added great intensity to the sport and provided an overwhelming workload for the players, André Markgraaff had replaced Kitch Christie, who had then been replaced by Carel du Plessis, who in turn had made way for Mallett, and there had been many successes (including winning the Tri Nations for the first time in 1998). But Mallett's decision to leave out Gary Teichmann and take Bob Skinstad to RWC 1999 instead caused shock waves ahead of the tournament. They would reverberate for years to come and be considered the reason why the Springboks failed to win a tournament many felt had been theirs to lose.

Teichmann, who today runs a successful earth-moving business in KwaZulu-Natal, is still puzzled about why Mallett had dropped him. He admits that even though the passing years have dulled his anger, the hurt still runs deep. 'I expected [not to be selected in] 1995,' he said when I interviewed him for this book, 'even though I had been part of all the preparation and knew there was always a chance I might get in. I thought Tiaan [Strauss] would make it. It certainly wasn't like 1999, when I really struggled to come to terms with the unfairness of [not being selected]. Nick and I had had quite a good rapport. We spoke a lot, analysed the opposition, discussed selections – not that I had a say in selection – but we spoke about it; bounced things off each other. However, our relationship had deteriorated, for whatever reason, and all that had died. So obviously I knew something was going on, because he was avoiding discussing things with me – particularly on the Tri Nations trip to New Zealand and Australia [in 1999].

'I got injured in Dunedin [the Test against the All Blacks in which Mallett picked rookie halfbacks Gaffie du Toit and Dave von Hoesslin and openly criticised their play afterwards]. We lost heavily [0-28]. In essence, I don't think I had a bad game; the score looked worse than it was. Then I got injured and was put out of the Australian game, where we got hammered [6-32].

'I knew something wasn't right, but I didn't think it would impact on World Cup considerations, as we still had some other games to get through in the Currie Cup. From that perspective, I didn't see it all ending then. I had a knee injury, but it was nothing drastic. We'd played a lot of rugby, if you take the number of games, the 17 Tests and then straight into the Super 12. It was more [of] a strain, but I did have a sense of unease.'

When the popular Natalian was axed, it sparked a massive public outcry, which was exacerbated when the charismatic Bob Skinstad (who had gone to the same school as Teichmann – Hilton College – but had found his rugby fortune at Stellenbosch and with Western Province) was selected in spite of carrying an injury. Few young players, before or since, have made as big an impact as Skinstad when he first arrived on the scene, and as far as sporting *causes célèbres* go, the reason for his injury was as big as they come, cloaked in mystery and gossip as it was.

Teichmann says he was aware that there was a strong push for Skinstad, which mainly emanated from Mallett's assistant, Alan Solomons. 'Ja, we were aware [that that was going on]. Remember, [Mallett] had moved André Venter around in spite of the fact that we had a nice trio going in the form of Rassie Erasmus, André and me. We had spoken about what Bob was doing, which was to make a nice impact when he came on; it was working well for us. I had, in fact, asked Nick: "Is the press pressurising you into starting with him [Bob]?" And he never answered me. He would just brush off [my question].

'Bobby was a special player, you know, in that he could change [the run of play], but I think he was doing that job as an impact player very well. It didn't necessarily mean that you had to slot him in [in the starting line-up], because the crucial work that André and Rassie were doing upfront was the reason why he could come in and have an effect later on [in the game].

'Nick also felt that on our last trip to the UK [at the end of 1998], the games were much closer [than the previous year, when there had been some big scores] and that the teams were catching up on us. He didn't ever consider that the players were bushed. Look at those 17 Tests; it was just bang, bang, bang. There wasn't a lot of substituting, so the guys were all playing in all of the games. Even in the game against England [in which the Boks failed to set a new record of 18 consecutive wins], it wasn't as if we were totally outplayed. We didn't do certain things well that we normally did well, but we only lost 7-13. Looking back, perhaps Nick took [the loss] harder than we did. [England] were hyped up to [stop us from breaking] the record – they lifted their game, and we made a couple of mistakes. Perhaps Nick was looking for someone to blame.

'Alan Solomons? It's all bloody guesswork, but Nick always insisted that *he* made the decisions. So even if Solomons was biting his ear, Nick had the final word. There had been indications that Nick was edging towards Bobby, but it was just so illogical. The guy was injured and hadn't been playing top-level rugby. I think every sportsman knows that sooner or later you're going to get dropped. You don't play sport without knowing that your day will come. It happens to everyone.

'But when you do get dropped, you expect that it is for someone playing at [your] level. That was the big problem I had – [being] jettisoned for someone who hadn't been playing and who was, in fact, less fit than me. What can you say? I wasn't going to try and change Nick's mind. I can't even recall what I said. I couldn't believe it. We still had to go through the Currie Cup. Why did he have to make the decision then and there? At best, let me think in my own mind that I can make it, and who knows what might have happened. To just be discarded like that was the hardest to put up with – after all, I wasn't some fringe player.

'I would have loved to have been part of the World Cup. I think it's the pinnacle [of a rugby player's career]. There were times I didn't think I'd get one cap, and then to win the first Tri Nations and go on that run of 17 wins. But at the end of the day you can't get it out of your head that the World Cup is something unique and you missed it. The pain goes away, but a part of you always aches to have been part of it. But in saying that, I am also grateful for what I had. You know we had a fantastic team, we had a good run – if you think where we had come from – losing to the All Blacks, losing to the British Lions – we had been through the pain. But, ja, I think the World Cup is the ultimate.

'That was the thing. Nick felt that he had to change [things] because of that last tour and us not thrashing everybody. If you look what we did to Scotland and Wales previously, we thumped them, and we beat Ireland because Bobby had two good breaks. But it also wasn't convincing, because in previous years we annihilated them. So Nick felt that he wanted to change the way he wanted to play, which I don't believe was right. I think there was a lot of tiredness in the team and it wasn't necessarily about the way we played. He felt that Bobby would make the difference without, perhaps, looking at the reality of why he was able to make an impact late in games.

'Rugby is pretty simple – you stick to what works for you. You can make subtle changes, but at the end of the day it's about the players – how committed they are, how they combine as a team, how much they play for each other, and how they read and respond to the match situation on the day.'

Teichmann concluded: 'Watching that World Cup … [the Springboks] never really got going. I don't know why. I wasn't in the team to experience it, but certainly as a team they never seemed to hit their straps. They seemed unsettled. I think Nick was pretty lost without Henry [Honiball]. He had built his whole game plan around Henry, and as soon as you took that factor out, he was lost. But he had already made the decision on Bobby, so it was hard for him to go back. He made the decision on a notion and not what he was seeing in front of him. It's not Bobby's fault; in the end it might have harmed him more than it did me.'

Mallett might well have believed that Teichmann's desire and form were waning. Fuelled by Solomons, who had had a long association with Skinstad, an undeniably dynamic young loose forward, Mallett might also have believed that the player could work his magic from the opening minute rather than as a substitute in the last quarter. In Skinstad, with his vision and sublime passing skills, Mallett could perhaps see the key creator for the Springboks (as he had been for the Stormers and WP). He even considered – quite seriously – whether Skinstad might not be converted into an inside centre, the key playmaker in the Springboks' hit-up style, especially in the absence of Henry Honiball. But in the end he was blind to the fact that Skinstad was not properly fit.

Skinstad had been in the form of his life in the Super 12. I have an image of him bounding out of the tunnel with a big grin on his face, revelling in his youth and radiating his joy and good fortune at living in this time and being in this place to play rugby – while getting paid for it. He was handsome, outrageously talented, erudite and extremely marketable, as attested by the sponsorships he attracted from Adidas, Ford and Guinness.

But then came the fateful night of 18 April 1999. Earlier in the day, the Stormers had got their season back on track with a 28-19 victory over the Canterbury Crusaders, the reigning champions, who would go on to successfully defend their title that year. After the game, the Stormers hosted a get-together for the Kiwis at a pub in Claremont called The Green Man (of which Joel Stransky was a shareholder). At some point during the evening, Skinstad became incensed and left in a huff. It was raining. Skinstad drove too fast and lost control of the high-powered vehicle supplied to him by Ford. The car skidded into a wall; Skinstad hit his left knee on the dashboard and suffered one of the most celebrated injuries in the history of South African rugby.

Rumours abounded about what had happened at the club. The most lurid gossip alleged that Skinstad had got into a scuffle with Crusaders scrumhalf Justin Marshall and had been kicked on the knee. Those who were there, though, say there was no fight. Skinstad himself repeatedly denied the allegations, to the point where he eventually declined to talk about it. It was amazing how the story stuck in the public mind, though.

Marshall might have been the cause of Skinstad's irritation, but there was no brawl. A prominent sports surgeon confirmed to me that the injury – a partial tear to the posterior cruciate ligament – was consistent with receiving a hard bang to the knee.

Skinstad made the mistake of flying to Johannesburg instead of immediately seeking medical help, but the upshot was that he was out of the Super 12. Speculation immediately started about whether he would be fit for the impending World Cup.

Acres of newspaper column inches were expended on The Knee as the Currie Cup season unfolded and Cymru 1999 drew nearer. Referring to my notebook for the period, I came across notes of side-by-side interviews with Skinstad and Teichmann about their injuries. Skinstad talked of the plaster coming off, about doing lots of upper-body work in the gym and keeping busy by doing promotional work for his sponsors. Teichmann said he was training pretty hard, that there was no instability in his injured knee, that he was feeling quite refreshed, and that he was two to three weeks away from playing again.

At that point it seemed that Skinstad had little chance of being ready for the RWC. Then, in late July, I inadvertently became involved in the unfolding drama surrounding the two No. 8s. I had travelled to Bloemfontein to cover a Free State versus Western Province match in which Skinstad was slated to make a brief appearance off the bench. Soon after checking into the City Lodge, I received a call from John Dobson, then editor of *SA Rugby* magazine and later to make a name for himself as the coach who grabbed the opportunity of the Varsity Cup to lead a revival at UCT.

'You're not going to believe this,' Dobson said. 'Nick is going to drop Gary Teichmann and take Bob Skinstad to the World Cup.' I was dumbfounded. It transpired that Dobson had had dinner with Mallett the night before, when he had revealed his thoughts on the upcoming World Cup.

Mallett and I had a good working relationship during his tenure as coach. In that time, I had written a column for *SA Rugby* magazine in which I suggested that rugby officials and coaches should consult with the press before making big announcements, as they always left holes in their stories. In response, Mallett told me to get hold of him if I felt I had advice to give or that something in the team was going off-track.

'Don't wait until things have gone wrong and then write about it,' was the gist of his words. 'Call me and tell me about it.'

So I called, but Mallett's cell phone went unanswered. I tried a number of times and eventually decided to leave a message. I apologised for interfering (the truth is that it would have been a very good story for the *Sunday Times*) but explained that I had heard of his intention to drop Teichmann. In essence, I implored him not to make a hasty decision, as the deadline for naming the World Cup squad was still a couple of weeks away. I suggested that he give both players a chance to prove their fitness and make his decision at the very last minute. I was so convinced that he would be making a mistake that I said axing 'Teich' would destroy the chemistry of his team.

Mallett never did call back, but years later, when he was no longer coach, we both attended one of those inane breakfasts at which sporting figures are the main attraction. I was surprised when, in his talk, he referred to my call and admitted that dropping Teichmann had been his biggest mistake.

Events in South African rugby have a way of justifying the over-the-top 'Rugby Bomb Bursts' headline, and this was such an occasion. Mallett, a grab-the-bull-by-the-horns kind of guy, felt that if he was going to drop Teichmann, he had to get the job done. Not one for sentimentality, he then made the call to Teichmann to tell him that he had decided to do without him. His reason? Teichmann was no longer assured of his place in the starting line-up. He then promptly called a press conference and announced that Joost van der Westhuizen was the new captain, while absurdly claiming that he felt the team needed an Afrikaans-speaking leader.

Momentous events had taken place in South African rugby. The Springboks lost a series to the All Blacks in 1996 and to the British & Irish Lions in 1997, they suffered record defeats against New Zealand and Australia, Kitch Christie died in April 1998, his successor, André Markgraaff, suffered his 'Rugbygate', and Carel du Plessis was quickly ousted and replaced by Mallett – the fifth coach in four years.

Louis Luyt had been forced to stand down after the damaging scrap with government and was succeeded by Silas Nkanunu, even though CEO Rian Oberholzer was effectively running South African rugby. However, Nkanunu's appointment met with the approval of ANC politicians and their acolytes, who continued to snipe at the Springbok badge and rugby's lack of transformation.

But Mallett had imparted new ideas and had a firm hand on the tiller. In 1998, he had taken the team on an exceptional run of victories. It included a rare win over the All Blacks in New Zealand and South Africa's first Tri Nations trophy. But the arrival of the next World Cup year, 1999, brought about a sudden and dramatic change in the mood and fortunes of the Springboks.

The change to professionalism had introduced a new dynamic, the worship of Mammon. The promise of a handsome stipend persuaded SARFU to accept an invitation for the world champions to play a Test against Wales in Cardiff in June to mark the official opening of the Millennium Stadium, built on the site of the old Cardiff Arms Park (the name everyone called it by, even though its real name was the National Stadium), which would serve as the focal point of Cymru 1999. This Test would prove to be the beginning of the end for Nick Mallett. The build-up became mired in South Africa's race-obsessed politics, the match itself was a disaster, and there's no doubt that it signalled the moment the 1999 World Cup campaign started going sour.

During a practice session in a cold and wet Cardiff, Gavin Rich and I approached Nick Mallett for comment on the state of the team and his feelings on dispatches from home claiming the need for greater representation of black and coloured players in the Springbok team. Mallett answered quite reasonably that he could not spend too much time worrying about politics, as his mandate was to prepare a winning Springbok team. Gavin filed his story to the *Cape Times*, and the next day all hell broke loose. Mallett's comments had been manipulated into a headline along the lines of: 'Mallett tells ANC politicians to lay off'. It was not quite what he'd said, but the flak Mallett got could not have been worse had he been caught selling state secrets.

Rian Oberholzer, who had become skilled at steering rugby around the many obstacles it faced almost daily, had flown into Cardiff, ostensibly to support the team. But the agenda had changed. Oberholzer was clearly under pressure to pull Mallett into line and read the team the riot act. The press sniffed that something was up, so we hung around outside the team room in the Marriott Hotel, waiting to buttonhole Oberholzer after he addressed the players. When the meeting came to an end, it was immediately apparent that something serious had transpired.

'Fuck this!' snarled Rob van der Valk, Mallett's team manager, as he pushed passed me to the lift. 'Fuck them! If this is what's happening to Springbok rugby, I want no part of it.'

The players, too, looked angry and grim-faced as they filed out of the meeting room. It transpired later that they had booed Oberholzer after he had berated them. Apparently the CEO had told the players rather bluntly that there were imperatives to team selection in the South Africa of 1999 that had little do with rugby form, and that if they wanted to continue to play international rugby and wear the Springbok colours, they had better get used to it.

At the time I was quite shocked at the naivety of the players who seemed to think that they could remain sublimely isolated from the problems of a country that for years had gone under the yoke of a repressive racist system. Some restitution was surely required, and even though the quota system was inadequate and unfair, especially on the players it favoured, to rail against it was as stupid as the old 'keep politics out of sport' catch-phrase in the days of apartheid.

Rob van der Valk chronicled the events of that day in his revealing book *Nick & I*, which did not cause as much of a stir as one might have expected. As it turned out, the Springboks took the field against Wales with an all-white team – the last time that would ever happen.

The Springboks also lost – their first-ever defeat to the Welsh. In my match report, I described it as an 'ambush'. The Millennium Stadium was far from finished, so the small crowd had to sit in a horseshoe behind one of the posts and to the sides. And it turned out that the Welsh rugby union had inveigled SARU to be part of a series of 'rolling' official openings. The Springboks were clearly distracted, they were playing without regular half-backs Joost van der Westhuizen and Henry Honiball (Braam van Straaten, Gaffie du Toit, Werner Swanepoel and Dave von Hoesslin all getting a turn) and were pretty much blown off the park by referee Ed Morrison as they went down 19-29.

It was a big moment for the Welsh. An old man behind me in the press box stood up and said, 'Now I can die.' But the match represented Mallett's second defeat, and Teichmann, for one, believes that the coach took it harder than the players. On top of this, SA Rugby had agreed to a crazy schedule, which entailed the players packing for Wales, returning to South Africa for a day and a half, and then flying to Dunedin on the South Island of New Zealand to commence the defence of their Tri Nations title.

It was not that apparent at the time, but history has since shown that the unity of the Springbok team was severely shaken by events in Cardiff. Mallett was both angered and disillusioned by the unacceptable parameters he was to abide by. The unremitting schedule caused a number of injuries to key personnel, and the upshot was that a slipshod Springbok team was hammered 0-28 (still the biggest defeat against the All Blacks) at the aptly named House of Pain.

And, as it turned out, it was Gary Teichmann's last Test for his country. He had captained the Springboks a record 32 times, earned a record 42 caps as eighthman and set a record of 39 consecutive Test matches. But he picked up an injury and had no part in the next two of the run of four successive losses (the Boks lost 6-32 to Australia in Brisbane – Rassie Erasmus's sole appearance as captain before, portentously, being replaced by Joost van der Westhuizen – and 18-34 to the All Blacks in Pretoria). The Boks managed to halt the slide with a nerve-wracking 10-9 win over the Wallabies at Newlands, but Mallett and gone from Saint Nicholas to the devil incarnate and, far from the highs of 1998, South Africa's prospects of defending their world title now seemed distinctly gloomy.

The introduction to this chapter paints a somewhat uncomplimentary picture of Mallett as an arrogant, insensitive and heartless individual – an impression it is incumbent on me to correct. Nick Mallett, with his cerebral approach to the game, was an extremely good coach of the Springboks – arguably the best of those who have attempted a job that has been likened to leaping out of a plane without a parachute into a crocodile-infested river.

He was in charge for 38 Tests, winning 27 of them for a success rate of 71.05%. It says much about the nature of the job that even someone as strong-minded as Mallett could be debilitated by the pressures.

But it is a fact that Mallett, who was feeling the pinch of constant interference from SA Rugby's administration on issues he felt had little to do with him and impacted on his ability to coach a winning team, handled Gary Teichmann's sacking extremely badly. To his credit, he subsequently often took it on the chin and admitted as much – and in public forums.

He should have properly assessed who of Teichmann or Skinstad was the fittest, he should have thought more deeply about how profoundly 'Teich' was entrenched as the team's captain and the respect he commanded, he should not have allowed himself to be influenced quite as much by Alan Solomons, and, after all that, if he still felt that the Sharks skipper was not the man for the job, he should have flown to Durban to speak personally to someone who had given great service to Springbok rugby. That would have been the right and decent thing to do, and Mallett's tenure will always be blotted by his error of judgement.

As a player and a coach, Mallett was super-confident and forthright, and he possessed an unflinching belief in his own ability and methods. He could be unsympathetic and harsh, use strong language and flaunt his 'Englishness', but that does not suggest he was a bad coach. On the contrary, he was a very good coach, as I've said. His first Test in charge of the team was in November 1997, and it would be 13 months before he tasted defeat when, in December 1998, his exhausted and, in some cases, chronically injured charges failed to beat England at Twickenham.

From the outset, as Gavin Rich recorded in the *SA Rugby Annual*, Mallett stressed that the players would be his first priority, a principle he first introduced into the Bok squad when he was serving (along with Carel du Plessis) as André Markgraaff's assistant during the 1996 tour to Argentina. Noticing that some of the players (especially the big forwards) were booked into economy class on the flight across the South Atlantic, Mallett convinced his fellow management members to give up their seats.

In 1997 in Paris, when he was the head coach, he was dissatisfied with the state and location of the hotel that had been booked for the Boks, so he promptly checked whether the towering and much more expensive Concorde Lafayette could accommodate his team and had the booking changed. That was Mallett – standing up for his players while at the same time signalling his loathing of fat-cat officials who took free rides on the backs of the players.

Having studied at Oxford and been a successful player and coach in France, Mallett was a citizen of the world, and perhaps the ideal personality to be in charge during rugby's transition from an amateur to a professional sport. Some of the players might not have liked it, but he certainly taught them their rights. In the end, however, his dislike of bumbling and, later, pernicious officialdom and the reciprocal feelings this would engender led to him being removed on spurious grounds when he was charged with bringing the game into disrepute. Mallett was widely quoted as having said that Test match tickets were too expensive – some claimed that it was the only thing he ever said that everyone agreed with!

And therein lies a tale. Mallett did not actually say, in so many words, that the tickets were too expensive. At a press conference ahead of a Test match in Durban, a reporter approached him as he was leaving the room and posed the following question: 'Nick, do you think the tickets for the Test are too expensive?'

'Uh, yes, I suppose so,' he replied. The next day, the headline read: 'Springbok coach slams the price of test tickets'.

That was all SA Rugby needed. They wanted a more pliable coach, and Mallett saw which way the wind was blowing. He had had enough of the head-banging, of being called a racist – even an atheist in some quarters – and of having to hire lawyers to fight his conditions of employment. He decided to negotiate an exit package. By the time he left, he had beaten the All Blacks more times than he had lost to them, he'd won the 1998 Tri Nations and been party to a number of record victories, including that run of 16 consecutive wins. And he came close to retaining the World Cup, eventually forfeiting the Holy Grail to a drop goal by Stephen Larkham ... and, it has to be said, the absence of Gary Teichmann.

Mallett's departure coincided with my leaving the *Sunday Times*. I had started to do work for SuperSport in June 1998, making inserts with television producer Peter Trehaeven, and by 1999 I had been placed on retainer. In August 2000, lured by the promise of extending my career into television, I decided to join SuperSport full time, and what an eye-opener that turned out to be.

It would lead to the most bizarre encounter I would ever have with a Springbok coach and cause me great torment about journalistic integrity and morality.

12

Monsieur le Drop

While relaxing in the foyer of the Petersham Hotel in Richmond, London, I suddenly noticed a familiar face peering around a doorway. The person first scanned the area, then quickly crossed the hallway to what appeared to be a stored-luggage room. Next, another face appeared, again familiar, and the same skulking behaviour ensued. 'Those guys look like Nick Beal and Martin Corry [England fullback and No. 8 respectively],' I thought to myself. It was only when a third face appeared, that of England hooker Phil Greening, that I realised they *were* England players. Greening had a shiner I'd noticed the day before on the Eurostar from Paris to London.

I was at the Petersham Hotel, a regular stopover for rugby teams playing at nearby Twickenham, to interview Springbok flyhalf Jannie de Beer before the team's management shut down any further 'media opportunities' for the rest of the week in preparation for their RWC semi-final against Australia.

And the reason (there were five, actually) I needed to see De Beer was to write a feature on the Man of the Moment; the man who, the day before, had slotted a world-record five drop goals and scored a record 34 points to steer the Springboks to an amazing 44-21 victory over England in their quarter-final at the Stade de France in Paris.

But what on earth were the England players doing in the Springboks' hotel? As players and porters rushed furtively to the car park, I finally cottoned on to what was going on. The England team had been so confident that they would advance to the semi-finals that they had not checked out of the hotel in time – now they were being forced to clear out in a hurry because the Springboks had arrived.

The fact that the Springboks had made it to this hotel that overlooked the Thames, and that they were two matches away from retaining the Webb Ellis Cup, was taking time to sink in. It had, after all, up till then been a bizarre tournament, marked by a complete lack of atmosphere and a series of mismatches, as well as plenty of challenges for the Springboks at their initial base in Edinburgh, Scotland.

If you had arrived at Edinburgh Airport and taken a taxi into town or emerged from the main train station and taken a stroll down Princes Street and back up Rose Street, the street of pubs, in search of a pint, you would not have known that the World Cup was on. 'Auld Reekie', with its castle upon the crag, was as charming as ever, but there was hardly any sign that the biggest rugby tournament in the world was being staged there or that the defending champions were in town.

As Andy Colquhoun so aptly summed it up in the *SA Rugby Annual*, 'It seemed [as if] we were witnessing the last amateur World Cup rather than the first professional one.' The organisation of the tournament was amateurish, the rugby not of a high standard, the marketing slapdash, the format (including a complicated system of play-offs to decide quarter-finalists) unworkable and the decision to stage it in different countries impractical.

The mood was set by the opening ceremony at the magnificent Millennium Stadium in the heart of Cardiff, Wales, which, while featuring wonderful performers such as Shirley Bassey, Bryn Terfel, Michael Ball ('Love Changes Everything') and a very young Charlotte Church, was overpoweringly nationalistic. It was all about Wales and very little about 'the world in union'. Louis Luyt was no longer involved in rugby by then, but the bumbling by the 'gin-and-tonic brigade' he so resented provided him with some validation. While South Africa's presentation of RWC 1995 had been superb, RWC 1999 was in many ways a lesson in how *not* to run a tournament.

When Nick Mallett had axed Teichmann ahead of the start of the tournament, it placed the team under severe scrutiny at a time when the players could have done without the spotlight. To exacerbate matters, everyone now had very high expectations of Skinstad (who would fail to deliver). Conspiracy theories about his accident and why he had been included in the squad continued to do the rounds. The most far-fetched tale was that Guinness, one of his sponsors, had bribed SA Rugby to ensure his presence at the World Cup.

This was categorically denied by Rian Oberholzer and Skinstad himself, but still the story stuck – just like the creamy head atop Ireland's famous brew. My employers asked me to corroborate the story, and I finally managed to get a plausible answer when I spoke to Guinness's sales director in the pressroom at Twickenham. He pointed out that it would have been almost impossible to have pulled off a plot to ensure Skinstad's selection.

'Think about it. It cost us £12.5 million to sponsor the World Cup. Then we would have had to find the money to [bribe] SA Rugby and keep them quiet, plus we would have had to get Nick Mallett and his assistants to buy into the plan. It simply could not have been done. We didn't have the money, and you could never have kept such a thing quiet.'

Psychologically, the Springbok team was not in a good place going into the tournament, and injuries and setbacks only added to their woes. Os du Randt and Joost van der Westhuizen had arrived in Britain nursing knee injuries. Joost's would continue to deteriorate, and he would end up having to play in the third-place play-off against the All Blacks with a torn ligament. But the biggest setback was Henry Honiball, who suffered a hamstring injury in training before the first match, against Scotland in Edinburgh.

The tall Natalian had nursed an ankle injury in the weeks leading up to the tournament, but he was expected to be at the epicentre of virtually all the Springboks' attacking ploys. Also, his scything tackling, reflected in his nickname 'Lem', or 'Blade', had made him a player genuinely feared by teams such as the Wallabies and the All Blacks.

Now, his hamstring injury proved to be a major setback. Mallett had hoped to build a pattern around the axis of No. 8 (Skinstad), No. 9 (Van der Westhuizen), No. 10 (Honiball) and No. 12 (Brendan Venter), but he was forced to change to Jannie de Beer, a pivot who preferred to take less contact than Honiball. Yet still one felt the Boks could pull through. After all, De Beer and Venter were lifelong teammates from Free State, while the flame-haired flyhalf also boasted excellent goal-kicking skills.

Injuries are a fact of rugby, and being able to absorb them and adapt accordingly is part and parcel of the six games it took to win the trophy (there are now seven games in the RWC if a team makes it to the final). Honiball had been deeply upset by the way Mallett had handled the Teichmann issue, and he cut a melancholy figure during the tournament. When he was finally declared fit to play, it was right after De Beer's command performance in Paris.

In their opening game, against Scotland, the Springboks did not play well, despite the fact that the crowd contained so many green-shirted South Africans that it felt like a home fixture. They did, however, manage to put together a second-half burst, including a centre's try to Ollie le Roux, to win comfortably enough, 46-29.

But there were warning signs when the 'B' team, consisting of those players who had not played in the opening match, made extremely heavy weather of beating Spain, the weakest side at the RWC, 47-3. As this was an unprepossessing midweek fixture that would have no bearing on my

Sunday reportage, I decided to travel to St Andrews, thanks to the kind offices of Iain Banner and Nina Fiddian-Green, who worked for Johann Rupert's organising arm, to watch Ernie Els, Retief Goosen and David Frost attempt to win the Alfred Dunhill Cup for the third year in a row. And, as it turned out, this opportunity to visit the spiritual home of golf provided me with a captivating 'six degrees of separation' experience.

I was freelancing for SuperSport on this tour, and I had a cameraman accompany me for a story I was doing for the channel on the Spanish rugby team. While chatting to Spain's rugby coach, Alfonso Feijoo, who was to become a prominent mentor in Spanish rugby, I mentioned that I would be going to St Andrews, and that one of the teams competing was from Spain. 'Who in team?' he asked. 'No Seve,' I replied. 'Miguel Ángel Jiménez, Sergio García and José María Olazábal.'

At the mention of the last name, Feijoo's face lit up. It transpired that as a physical education instructor in San Sebastián, he had been one of Olazábal's teachers. As he was keen to take some of the players up to St Andrews to support their Spanish compatriots, I arranged for some tickets to be left at the gate for the Spanish rugby men. I ended up watching the Springboks versus Spain match on TV in a pub in the 'auld grey toon' while the Spanish golfers dethroned the South Africans in the Alfred Dunhill Cup. In the rugby they were obviously less imposing, losing 3-47, but they nevertheless gave a good account of themselves.

It was as if the complete lack of atmosphere or awareness of the World Cup in Scotland had affected the Springboks. Despite the fact that they were the defending champions, they found themselves banished to the backwaters. It was rather like staging the World Cup in South Africa and basing the defending champions in East London.

Worse was to follow. For their next match, against another of the minnows, Uruguay, the Springboks were dispatched to Scotland's soccer capital, Glasgow, to play in its football headquarters, Hampden Park.* If there were 2 000 people in a stadium that can hold 52 000 it was a lot, and

---

* The Springboks have actually played at a number of major football stadiums. The year before, Mark Andrews had celebrated his 50th cap against Wales at Wembley Stadium in London, while the Millennium Stadium was being built, while others are the Parc des Princes in Paris (Paris Saint-Germain), Leeds United's Elland Road, Stadio Renato dall'Ara in Bologna, River Plate in Buenos Aires, Leicester City's Walkers Stadium, Stadio Luigi Ferraris in Genoa and Stade Félix Bollaert in Lens. Great citadels like the Stade de France and Marseille's Stade Vélodrome are multipurpose venues.

the South Africans' game reflected the desultory atmosphere. The Teros (so named after the bird represented on Uruguay's badge) had but one aim in mind as they faced up to the biggest game in their rugby history: to keep the score as low as possible. In order to achieve this, they were willing to risk body and limb by hurling themselves onto the ball and obstructing its passage at any price. One had a sense of foreboding as the Springboks, containing a good number of their first-choice squad, battled to make headway against both a negative team and a referee – Australia's Peter Marshall – who seemed to have taken it upon himself to keep the weaker team competitive.

The Boks' frustration levels were running high because of their inability to suppress the valiant Uruguayans. One felt that they needed the half-time break to settle down and reassess their approach. However, just two minutes away from this breather, fate struck them a cruel blow. It was over in a flash, but the moment was captured on videotape to stand as evidence.

During a ruck, Brendan Venter tried to hack free the ball just as flanker Martin Panizza hurled himself onto it. In the same instant, Joost van der Westhuizen got his hands on the ball and ripped it free – making it look as if Venter was stamping. At first it seemed as if Venter had connected with Bob Skinstad's leg, but there was New Zealand touch judge Steve Walsh holding out his flag, talking to Marshall ... and him reaching for the cards in his pocket and producing a red one! It was a scene from a nightmare. With the quarter-final next, the Boks had lost another of their key play-makers. Video replays showed that Venter's boot had made glancing contact with Panizza's scrum cap.

In their appeal against Venter's suspension, the South Africans could point to the staggering inconsistency of the tournament's disciplinary procedures. There had been no other cautions in the match against Uruguay until Venter was pulled up, which indicated that he should have received a yellow card rather than a red, while in the same game Uruguay lock Mario Lame had blatantly kicked Naka Drotské in the back and got off scot free. Fiji's Marika Vunibaka had not even been cited for a headbutt, while France's Fabian Pelous, who had been cited for turning and stamping on an opponent on the side of a maul, was given only a 14-day suspension for an offence more serious than Venter's.

Venter later told the press that he had been going for the hand on the ball. 'There was no malice intended – I didn't go for his head; the way he went down caused it to get in the way.' Having witnessed the treatment

South African players had received from disciplinary tribunals since re-admission in 1992, I had little doubt that Venter was in deep trouble, but I was nevertheless surprised at the severity of his 'sentence'. Even though the disciplinary committee conceded that Venter's action had not been 'wilful' but rather 'reckless', they slapped him with a 21-day suspension – thus putting him out of action until the day before the World Cup final.

As they say in Glasgow, the Boks were shite, but it was revealing that Uruguay celebrated as if they had won the game! Their coach, Daniel Herrera, rubbed it in.

'We proved that we're not guests who shouldn't be here,' he said at a post-match press conference. 'The Springboks suffered a little shame at their performance against amateurs.'

The next stop was the quarter-final against England, in Paris, and on my arrival at the Hotel St Jacques (now the Marriott Rive Gauche) – in those days the media were still allowed to stay in the same hotels as the team – I was astonished to discover manager Arthob Petersen in residence. Petersen, of whom the press often joked that he had breakfast, lunch and supper for South Africa, had decided he would be of no use at Venter's hearing back in Wales. I would have thought that a well-reasoned appeal from someone who for so long had been a victim of social injustices might well have swayed the 'court'.

The Springboks' objections, however, fell on deaf ears, and they were forced to face up to the fact that they would have to get through their Paris quarter-final against England without Honiball and Venter. Another problem for Mallett was that, in both low-key games against Spain and Uruguay, the 'dirt-trackers' had failed to put significant pressure on those in the 'first' team, making it more obvious for him to persevere with Skinstad, who was manfully trying to mask the continued effects of his injury.

Mallett maintained that his nominated game-breaker was fit, but by chance I saw proof that this was not the case. Wearing goggles and an elastic cap, I was swimming in the indoor pool of the Hilton Hotel in Glasgow, and spotted Skinstad and Percy Montgomery emerging from the solarium. They passed right by me, unnoticed because of my 'disguise'. Skinstad was hobbling along gingerly, his knee noticeably swollen. Soon afterwards, at the daily press conference, the media were assured that he was fine. It says much for his grit that he pushed himself through the quarter- and semi-final matches before crying off the third-place play-off against New Zealand in Cardiff.

The Springboks had left for the World Cup on 23 September to set up their base in Edinburgh. Nearly four weeks later, on 17 October, they arrived in Paris to prepare for their quarter-final match. At Nick Mallett's first press conference at their hotel on the Boulevard St Jacques (ironically the same hotel that would be the Boks' initial base in 2007), the isolation that had been the Springboks' lot in Scotland was neatly summed up by a reporter when he said: 'Welcome to the World Cup.'

The banqueting hall on the second floor had been set aside for press conferences, and it was filled to overflowing with representatives of the London press. After England's solid quarter-final play-off victory over Fiji and a 100-pointer against Italy, one could detect an air of confidence among the Fleet Street mob. Their money was obviously on Martin Johnson and his men, and not Joost van der Westhuizen's Springboks, to advance past the Stade de France to the semi-finals.

And for most of an intense first half in the futuristic stadium, which had hosted the FIFA World Cup football final the previous year, it seemed as though they might be right. The Boks, heavily penalised by Scots referee Jim Fleming, struggled to get into stride.

I had learnt from AC Parker, the legendary rugby writer and sports editor of *The Argus* – and one of my mentors – that press-box decorum requires one to be neutral and composed. However, Fleming's questionable rulings and mounting penalty count against the Boks – two scrum penalties had been awarded when the ball had already reached the inside centre – made me forget my own code and I shouted out: 'The man is a fucking cheat!', causing Sue Mott, award-winning feature writer of the *Daily Telegraph*, to turn in her seat and tick me off: 'Strong language, sir!'

Suitably chastened I pulled my neck in, but moments later I was somewhat vindicated when the French reporter sitting next to Mott jumped up, screaming, 'Eet ees scandalous! Eet ees scandalous!' after Fleming had once again penalised the Boks. Fleming's touch judges were New Zealanders Paddy O'Brien and Paul Honiss, and André Venter later related how O'Brien, waiting behind the posts alongside the Boks as Paul Grayson lined up a penalty attempt, remarked: 'This so-and-so's not going to allow you boys to win, mate. You had better get the ball up in their half.' As it turned out, O'Brien's advice was most prescient!

Joost van der Westhuizen's predatory instincts and Pieter Rossouw and Percy Montgomery's attacking skills kept the Boks in front, though, eventually allowing the skipper to score a marginal try in the left-hand corner. In later years, with the help of a TMO (television match official), that try might not have been awarded. Van der Westhuizen had squirmed away from any number of defenders and his dive for the try had taken him diagonally along the goal line, rather than squarely across it. However, he felt he had managed to touch the ball down in-goal before Richard Hill bundled him into the corner flag. Replays were not that clear, but the fact that Honiss ran around to the posts and Fleming gave the try indicated that the officials were satisfied that the ball had been grounded – and, to be honest, gives the lie to my condemnation of the match official.

The Boks led 16-12 at the break, but none of us had any inkling of the drama that would unfold in the second 40-minute period. It started with a penalty to England, which Paul Grayson goaled to make it 15-16, but the stage had been set for the diffident Jannie de Beer to have greatness thrust upon his shoulders. Whether by design, as the Springbok camp claimed, or by accident, De Beer started to drop off second-phase ball and switch passes, rather than falling back into the pocket behind the forwards. His first drop kick went over in the 47th minute and the fifth, and last, in the 84th minute of extended time. Before this, no one in the entire history of the game had kicked more than three drop kicks in a Test match, and now De Beer had dropped five. He also kicked five penalties and two conversions (of Van der Westhuizen's try and a late show-stopper by Rossouw) to set a Springbok record of 34 points in a Test as the Boks surged to a 44-21 victory.

Afterwards the deeply religious flyhalf came up with one of the quotes of the tournament: 'The Lord gave me the talent and the forwards gave me the ball.' And so to London, where De Beer would again find himself in the glare of a harsh spotlight. Some were of the opinion that Mallett should pull an ace out of the pack by playing Honiball against Australia, but after such a performance, how could he drop De Beer?

And so I met with De Beer at the Petersham Hotel in London. He was humble, albeit nonplussed by all the attention he was receiving, and determined to pass some of the kudos to his teammates. 'Personally, I don't want to take credit,' he told me as we settled down for a long talk. 'The other guys stuck to the game plan and provided the opportunities. It was just one of those days ... every one I tried went over.

'You know, the drop kick is something you have to have in your back pocket to use if the game situation calls for it. England's defence was hard to break down. They hold their defensive line very well, they don't get out of alignment, but they tend to wait for you to come at them and then smother you. The fact that they didn't charge up on defence made it easier for me. Australia will be completely different. They will put a man on you ... George Gregan, for instance.'

De Beer was also at pains to set the record straight about his spirituality, as some of the tabloids had tried to depict him as some sort of evangelist freak who believed God was on the side of the Springboks. 'My religious beliefs have been totally overstated. I am not a *dominee*, but my faith is very important to me.

'We were poor as kids, but I came out of a God-fearing house and had good values instilled in me. I don't want to force [my religion] on others.'

De Beer had an obvious rugby hero: 'From the time I can remember, Naas [Botha] was the man – that's who I modelled myself on.' And, looking ahead to the semi-final against Australia, he added a portentous remark about his direct opponent, Stephen Larkham. 'You've got to look out for him. He's an exciting player.'

The Wallabies dominated the opening minutes of the semi-final match, but the Springboks held the ascendancy in the periods on either side of half-time. In an epic war of attrition, both teams had their chances but could not cross the other's line – the Springboks having been forced into ultra-defensive mode as early as the fourth minute when an attempted expansive attack by them had gone wrong.

Skinstad, for once, had made an intrusion into the line, and he threw one of those flat passes of his to Robbie Fleck. The centre popped the ball up for Montgomery, coming up at speed, but the fullback, who would have been in the clear, was unable to hold on to the ball. Instead it was kicked through by the Wallabies and De Beer had to fall back to his own line to clear. The approach was right, as the Wallabies in all probability did not expect South Africa to attack out wide, but the mistake, and the moment of panic that resulted, saw the Boks crawl back into their shells.

With the benefit of hindsight, that failed attack was crucial to the eventual outcome of the game. Had the Springboks scored then, the match might have taken an entirely different course, as the Wallabies would have been forced to adapt their structures. Instead the shutters came down as the Springboks tried to do to the Australians what they had done to the English, by attempting to set De Beer up for field-goal attempts.

There were times when the situation cried out for the ball to be moved, but it seemed as if the team as a whole had decided that it was simply too dangerous. They tackled and they fought, but it appeared as if the Australians had done enough when they led 18-12 with time running out. De Beer, however, landed a penalty to narrow the gap. Then, in the 83rd minute, the public-address system boomed into life, announcing that there were two minutes left to play. The two minutes came and went, and still referee Derek Bevan did not blow the final whistle.*

Then, in the 88th minute, Bevan awarded the Springboks a penalty, and De Beer stepped up to place the ball 10 metres from the right-hand touchline and 36 metres from the posts, a stiff, cold breeze and splattering rain blowing into his face. Miss and the game was over; succeed and force it into extra time, 10 minutes each way, and the winner would go through to the final in Cardiff. Only Van der Westhuizen had been beyond this point before; Mark Andrews and Os du Randt, the other survivors from 1995, had already been substituted.

It was as difficult a kick under as much pressure as you can imagine, but De Beer kept his head down and split the uprights to take the match into additional time. First blood in extra time went to the Boks when De Beer kicked a penalty to give them the lead, 21-18, for the first time in the match, but then Matt Burke landed his seventh penalty to level the scores again. Into the last period of 10 minutes, and one felt that it was the Wallabies who were tiring. But fate had a surprise in store for South Africa, the country that had won the 1995 World Cup with a Joel Stransky drop goal.

In the third minute (of the last 10), Wallaby flyhalf Stephen Larkham received the ball in an unpromising situation over to the right and near the Springboks' 10-metre line. Instead of setting off on one of his eel-like runs, he chose to drop; an ungainly-looking action resulting in a surprisingly clean strike that sent the ball on a wobbly flight between the uprights. From where I was sitting high up in the stands you could see the shock on the faces of the Springboks. With panic mounting, Van der Westhuizen picked the ball up behind a scrum and was penalised. Many thought that the ball had been out, but nevertheless Burke coolly kicked his eighth penalty to give the Wallabies a 27-21 victory and propel them into their second final in Britain.

Up till then, in four World Cup tournaments, on just two occasions

---

* *These days, with the introduction of official timekeepers and referees indicating when the clock has been stopped, timekeeping is much more accurate, eliminating the discrepancies that often occurred because referees were expected to add time on for injuries and stoppages.*

had extra time been needed to separate two teams. The resolve of the Springboks was evident, given that they had been involved in both. South Africa had won the 1995 World Cup in extra time and now, in only their second appearance in the tournament, they went down to the Wallabies after additional time had been played in the semi-final at Twickenham.

Interestingly, this match would turn out to be the last of Jannie de Beer's 13 Tests. He had signed a contract with London Scottish, a move motivated mainly by the fact that he could never be assured of starting a game for the Boks with Honiball in the picture. He had also frequently battled injury, and no doubt he wanted some financial security in the last years of his rugby career. With the benefit of hindsight, he might well have been given a fairer shake, as he had played a big part in some of the Springboks' most impressive victories: 35-16 over the British Isles in the third Test at Ellis Park in his debut match in 1997; 61-22 over Australia at Loftus in 1997; 68-10 over Scotland at Murrayfield in 1997; and the game in which his name was indelibly written into the annals, 44-21 over England at the Stade de France in 1999.

The next day, also at Twickenham, an overconfident All Black team lost concentration, allowing the unpredictable French to snatch a dramatic victory in the other semi-final in a match rated as one of the all-time World Cup classics. It meant that the two great rivals of the southern hemisphere, South Africa and New Zealand, would have to play off in Cardiff for third place, with Australia and France going through to the final.

Had it not been for the fact that they were up against the Springboks, the shattered All Blacks might have had even less of an appetite for a game no one really wanted. As Rassie Erasmus remarked, 'The heart stays a little more sore than the body after losing a game like that.' But old antagonisms resulted in a keenly fought, albeit error-ridden game that raised another query about team selections.

Breyton Paulse produced a piece of individual magic to score the only try of the match, which begged the question why he had not been given a chance earlier in the tournament. And Montgomery got into the drop-kicking act to land two and help the Springboks to a 22-18 victory.

Could the Springboks have won the World Cup with a different team? Would Teichmann have made a difference? What if Honiball had been fit? But that's the trouble with hindsight: we may think the outcome could have been different, but we have no way of knowing for sure. The questions, however, remain. Gary Teichmann, for instance, once remarked that if Honiball had been on the field in the semi-final, Larkham, who was skittish when playing against 'Lem', might not have ventured so close to the forwards. He would thus have been too far from the posts to attempt a drop goal.

However, as the old saying goes, in everything there is something that pleases someone. With South Africa out of the final, the honour of refereeing was bestowed upon Benoni's André Watson, who by then had shaved off his moustache to avoid constant comparison to the actor John Cleese by his fellow arbiters. Watson presided over a one-sided match in which the French, typically, forgot the beautiful game they had produced against the All Blacks and instead resorted to nefarious tactics that Watson punished and the Wallabies exploited.

In the end, John Eales led his men to a one-sided 35-12 victory. The Wallabies thus became the first nation to win the World Cup a second time. The champions ended the tournament having conceded just one try, and the scorer of that try was a South African, Juan Grobler, playing centre for the United States.

With the Webb Ellis Cup lost, a changing of the guard was inevitable. But a momentous tectonic shift in South African rugby had also occurred in another foreign land. In the SANZAR/UAR Under-21 championship, held in Argentina in July, the junior 'Bokkies' had beaten New Zealand 27-25 in a pulsating final. The team was coached by Eric Sauls, and a man by the name of Jake White was his assistant. It was captained by a former Pretoria Boys' High pupil, playing out of KwaZulu-Natal, called John Smit. There were also many other players in the team who would become Springboks, as well as a lock, Daniel Vickerman, who would be capped for Australia.

White had actually been involved with the senior Springbok side on a number of occasions. He'd acted as a video analyst for Kitch Christie in 1995, and he was a member of Mallett's initial management team. However, on one occasion Alan Solomons, Mallett's assistant coach, dismissed White as 'only the video operator', a disparaging remark that caused ill-feeling between the two men. Mallett was eventually forced to appease his UCT buddy by jettisoning White.

Solomons' snipe prompted an 'Inside Edge' item in the *Sunday Times* warning him to be careful, as he could be described as 'just the man who puts out the cones at practices'* if he ever fell foul of the powers-that-be. He did, and in the end it was the 'video operator' who reached the greatest heights.

In 2000, Mallett would be in charge for eight more Tests, but, resenting that he did not have ultimate control, he was no longer the hard-bitten, forceful, committed driver who could whip a side into shape. The Springboks lost a significant Test in Bloemfontein to an England side led by Martin Johnson, signalling the beginning of England's climb to rugby's highest peak, which they would reach in 2003. The Springboks also went down three times to the Wallabies and once to the All Blacks, and in September

Mallett decided he could do it no more ... making way for the bizarre tenure of Harry Viljoen.

---

* *Plastic cone-shaped road markers used to mark the 'grids' players run in training drills.*

13

Shake and make up

Of the many unforgettable moments I have experienced as a recorder of the deeds of the Springboks, this was undoubtedly the most absurd – a tableau so bizarre that I had difficulty accepting that it was actually happening. We were in an office in the SuperSport building – five representatives of the television channel, the Springbok coach and me – and like naughty schoolboys who had clashed on the playing fields or in a rugby match, the coach and I had just been instructed to shake hands, apologise to one another and bury the hatchet. In fact, I had basically been told to say sorry to the coach for having made his life a misery, even though I had done nothing to apologise for.

I had known Harry Viljoen for a long time – ever since the late 1970s, when he broke into the Transvaal side as a robust and highly promising young scrumhalf. Viljoen hailed from Florida Hoërskool in Johannesburg's western suburbs and he was part of a burgeoning rugby set-up at RAU (Rand Afrikaans University). Even then, Viljoen was trendy and progressive. He caused quite a sensation in the Transvaal dressing room, which contained hard men such as Kevin de Klerk, Johan Strauss, Dave Frederickson, Richard Prentiss and Corrie Pypers, when he produced a hairdryer to ensure just the right styling for his cockscomb haircut, which was then in fashion.

Viljoen would almost certainly have been a Springbok had he not played in the years of apartheid isolation, but unlike those who simply drifted away from the sport, he found great stimulation and satisfaction in turning his keen mind to coaching.

I got on well with Viljoen. I enjoyed his serious, cognitive approach to playing the game and his enlightened outlook on how players should be managed and treated. In turn, when he became a coach, the players responded to someone who had their welfare at heart, and he had the distinction of taking Transvaal (1991), Natal (1993) and Western Province (1997) to a Currie Cup final before finally winning the cup with WP.

Viljoen was widely admired, in spite of an eccentric side to his nature. However, his habit of skipping from one province to another, a tendency to want things to go his way and a dislike of confrontation were indicative of his lack of staying power. This characteristic he demonstrated rather dramatically when he abruptly resigned as Springbok coach, a position he was meant to occupy until after the World Cup in Australia in 2003.

Viljoen took over from Nick Mallett in November 2000, and he resigned in January 2002. His tenure coincided with a big change in my career. Mike Robertson had taken over at the newspaper from Ken Owen, a man whose intellect I greatly admired. Unfortunately, Robertson and I did not get along. I thus decided to take up an offer from Russell MacMillan to join SuperSport as the name writer on their budding website, known as the SuperSport Zone. I had also been promised an opportunity to move into television.

It was the start of a saga of dissatisfaction for me at SuperSport. Their relationship with SA Rugby frequently – and exasperatingly, as I needed the work and could not simply find another job – tested the principles of transparency, impartiality and credibility in which I had been schooled. The scene I mentioned at the beginning of this chapter took place midway through Harry Viljoen's brief term as Springbok coach. I had been called to a meeting, ostensibly demanded by Viljoen but probably at the behest of Mark Keohane, his press officer, to discuss and sort out my supposed 'continued criticism' of and negativity towards the coach.

Some years previously, when Viljoen was coaching Western Province and I was with the *Sunday Times*, I was surprised to receive a call from him one evening as I was driving down Conrad Drive in Blairgowrie. It was such an astonishing call that I remember it vividly.

I pulled into a service station and listened for some 45 minutes as a distraught Viljoen complained about Keohane's writing in the *Cape Times*, saying that he was making his life a misery, upsetting his wife and negatively affecting the Western Province team. He said that the situation had got so bad that some of the players had suggested they arrange for Keohane to be 'sorted out'. He wanted my advice on how to handle the situation.

Needless to say, I told him to shelve any thoughts or talk of physical intimidation and explained that he did have recourse to the reporter's editor. However, I added that the editor, given that it was a sporting matter and that libel is very hard to prove under South African law, would in all likelihood support his reporter. 'Look, Harry,' I said, 'I know this is going to stick in your craw, but you need to go on a charm offensive; you need to make an ally of Mark Keohane. He wants a war with you, so don't give it to him. He strikes me as someone who needs recognition, so why not call him in for a cup of tea or coffee, or take him to lunch, and tell him how much you admire his writing and his knowledge of the game. Make an ally of him, confide in him. I have no doubt his attitude will change. You can't win against someone who is out to get you and who is known for not being objective.'

I did not hear from Viljoen again, but I was surprised to see that not only did he make an ally of Keohane, he made him a friend and house guest. By the end of the year, the coach and the writer went on the Springbok tour together, Keohane transformed himself from reporter to supporter, and the *Cape Times* banged a loud drum for Western Province.

Keohane, seemingly without a pang of conscience about journalistic neutrality, became involved in advising the team and producing motivational videos for them, one set to the tune of R Kelly's 'I Believe I Can Fly'. At the reception after Province's victory in the 1997 Currie Cup final, his sports editor, Louis Neethling, unblinkingly told me that if it hadn't been for the role played by the *Cape Times*, Western Province would not have won the cup.

In the meeting he demanded at SuperSport, Viljoen couldn't come up with anything specific I'd done to cause him such irritation and, to be frank, I was outraged that SuperSport had agreed to the meeting at all. You cannot write about rugby without upsetting someone, and whenever I had incurred the wrath of the coaches – Williams, McIntosh, Christie, Markgraff, Mallett – the issue had always been sorted out face to face. Enslin and Roets harped on about the need for SuperSport to have good relations with the Springbok team, and the meeting finally came to a bizarre end when Enslin said that Viljoen and I should stand up and shake hands.

When Viljoen was appointed to succeed Mallett, he had been out of the game since 1997, when he stood down from Western Province. Needless to say, his appointment raised a few eyebrows. One of his first decisions was to appoint the controversial Keohane as his media liaison officer. He then took the Springboks on a bizarre roller-coaster ride that was meant to end at the World Cup in 2003.

Keohane, of course, had crossed swords with many administrators, was unpopular with a lot of the players, did not have any PR experience and had a reputation for being rather subjective. Butch Watson-Smith, who had led False Bay to a famous Grand Challenge victory in the Western Province Club League and who had been my MD when I worked for PG Wood in the mid-1980s, had been pulled in by Viljoen as his team manager. Watson-Smith told me that Keohane had been appointed as media liaison officer 'to silence potentially [the Springboks'] most vociferous critic', a claim I found ludicrous.

During the 1994 Springbok tour to New Zealand, when Keohane was working for one of that country's Sunday papers, he earned the nickname 'Cowboy' because of his tendency to shoot from the hip. However, I nevertheless admired him for his energy, and the balls and bravery he exhibited when he broke big stories.

When Mallett departed, Viljoen was made the Springbok coach. It was indicative of how dynamic the times were that, alongside the notice in August 2000 that I had joined the SuperSport Zone, there was a column written by Keohane titled 'Why Mallett must stay'.

'Nick Mallett must stay on as coach of South Africa. He is the best man for the job. In addition to this belief, there are no alternative candidates ...' he wrote. Within less than three months, Keohane, always an amazingly malleable character with the ability to be completely oblivious to an opinion he might have held before (even one aired reasonably recently), had joined Viljoen and was singing his praises as the new messiah of Springbok rugby.

Viljoen had big ideas for the Springboks, but instead his era marked a time when South African rugby lost its way. I found my own career veering off course as well. As I've stated, at the outset I was determined that this book should not be about me, but my years at SuperSport lent a different perspective. They were intrinsically woven into the quest for the Holy Grail of rugby, of which I was a part, and thus warrant inclusion in this tale.

Viljoen quickly became a victim of the apparent dementia that seems to befall anyone taking on the job of Springbok coach. He wanted to control everything – from the way the players played and the clothes that they wore to what they read. He did have a bold vision for South African rugby, but sadly for him he had neither the time nor the personnel to bring it to fruition. As the pressure to win – the be-all and end-all of Springbok rugby – began to overwhelm him, he went from wanting to run the ball from every angle to fielding a side that contained two players not known for their speed or running capabilities – Louis Koen and Braam van Straaten – alongside each other in the Springbok backline.

Fans are passionate about rugby and they expect those who write about the game to comment on what's going on. I certainly was not the only one to express my opinion. However, it was not until Keohane fell out with Rudolf Straeuli, Viljoen's successor, and jumped ship that I realised the full extent of the paranoia one was dealing with.

In his book *Springbok Rugby Uncovered*, about one of the most turbulent times in Springbok history, to which he bore close witness, Keohane revealed that when I was made to shake hands with the Springbok coach and apologise, I did not know the half of it.

Keohane's telling exposé, which revealed his own astonishing volte-face, painted such a vivid picture of how the media was being controlled that I thought it would cause an uproar at the time it was published, but it made hardly a ripple. Far more important to the media were the controversial events that took place at a pre–World Cup training camp in Pretoria and at the notorious Kamp Staaldraad. In his book, Keohane accurately stated that SuperSport 'owns rugby as much as rugby owns the broadcaster', and he revealed how he had set about controlling how SuperSport and a newspaper like *Rapport* reported on rugby. It was an exercise in propaganda that would have made Joseph Goebbels proud.

As it turned out, the players were witheringly critical of me and Andy Capostagno. When I first read their comments in Keohane's book, I was surprised, as I felt I had had a good relationship with quite a few of the players from that era. But then I realised that I was ignoring an old fact – that players really don't like reporters, especially ones who ask straight questions and express candid opinions.

In the survey, some players mentioned that they only saw me at the games, which was not true. In fact, I was at loggerheads with the Super-Sport Zone because of *not* being sent to games.

Incredibly, in his book, Keohane claims that he knew that my (alleged) problem with Harry Viljoen indirectly stemmed from an issue I had with *him* (Keohane). Even though we had had our clashes and I had let him know he was very low on my radar, he wrote: 'Perhaps Dan felt Harry should have appointed someone more experienced to advise him ... someone like Dan Retief?' In fact, I *had* advised Viljoen, and no, I never wanted the job. On three different occasions over the years I was asked (by two coaches and an SA Rugby president) to make myself available as a sort of media Svengali, but never by Viljoen. At that point I was still hoping to break into television.

One thing Keohane was right about was the Catch-22 situation in which I found myself. When Viljoen fell on his sword he blamed the media, in particular SuperSport. Rian Oberholzer, with the help of his spin doctor, saw this as an opportunity to push Roets and the broadcaster into a deal. As Keohane wrote, 'SA Rugby and SuperSport would operate as a partnership and look after each other. Rian Oberholzer hoped to avoid a repeat of the Viljoen situation to protect Rudolf [Straeuli, the new coach]. He asked for Dan to be muzzled, which he was, much to the journalist's displeasure. Dan had two options: adapt to the new partnership, or leave. He chose to stay, and to be fair to him he did not have much of a choice. Media partnerships are stronger than independent voices. There was nowhere for Dan to go. SA Rugby bosses regarded the silencing of Dan as a small victory in the pursuit of turning the media into a friend and not a foe.'

Following Viljoen's exit, Keohane and Oberholzer, who was furious that he'd been let down by someone for whom he'd gone out on a limb, moved quickly to control the microphones at SuperSport. It was an astonishing about-turn from the most strident rugby critic in the South African media. Just as amazing was the new relationship between Oberholzer and Keohane, who had often presented himself as the judge and jury of SA Rugby and who had made his name because of his outspoken and highly critical columns. In his book, he claimed that good PR meant spin-doctoring rather than telling things truthfully, and that his job had been to control and manipulate the news rather than create proactive protocols to ensure positive public relations.

Interestingly, in May 2002 I had a meeting with Edward Griffiths, my former sports editor at the *Sunday Times*. Perhaps sensing my discomfort, and with his own background as general manager of SABC's Topsport, he explained that the reality of rights purchases and partnerships puts television stations on a completely different footing to print media.

He tried to convince me that sport on TV was actually entertainment rather than news coverage, and in time I began to grasp the difference. Interestingly, Griffiths also mentioned that Imtiaz Patel had told him that SARFU had insisted that SuperSport dismiss me.

In the end, they did not fire me and I stuck it out with SuperSport for 10 years. Perhaps they feared the fallout I might have caused with the help of the highly skilled labour lawyer to whom I was referred by my old friend Steve Mulholland. But mostly I suspect that Imtiaz Patel drew the line at being told who he could hire and fire.

In time I began to appreciate the differences between a newspaper and a television channel, which has to enter into joint ventures with rights holders, and learnt to toe the line. SuperSport's coverage of sport was arguably the most comprehensive in the world, its dynamism undeniable and it had a winning formula.

This period at SuperSport provided a key change of direction for me and is relevant to the World Cup story I am telling. I covered two World Cups for SuperSport (2003 and 2007), and the situation I was experiencing explains the detachment I felt as incredible drama unfolded around the Springbok team in 2003.

Although I always felt like an outsider at SuperSport, I was grateful for the opportunity to gain a grasp of the internet and to have had the chance to work in television – especially being part of the updated *Springbok Saga* series. For the 2007 World Cup, in France, I was SuperSport's man on the spot, which I still greatly appreciate, as the only way I could have been closer to the team was if I were a member of it.

As for Mark Keohane ... A few years ago we buried the hatchet over a steak and a few bottles of wine (one sent over by George Rautenbach). Perhaps I should have done the same years earlier with Mark, Rian Oberholzer and SuperSport.

Harry Viljoen had been in charge for 15 Tests (eight wins, six defeats, one draw) and, when he left, Rudolf Straeuli, with whom I had a good relationship from the 1995 World Cup and during his time as coach of the Sharks, was charged with taking the Boks to Australia in 2003. It was to be a period in which fact was often stranger than fiction.

14

Cloud Cuckoo Land

'Bizarre' is a word that has cropped up many times in this manuscript, but it's going to have to be utilised again to describe the quadrennial between Wales 1999 and Australia 2003. Living through some of the preposterous goings-on was strange enough, but arranging the incidents into chronological order for this book makes them all seem doubly absurd. These events made me marvel at the wonderful capacity of human beings to accept things at face value and to try to make some sense of them rather than screaming, 'This is madness! Stop the merry-go-round, I want to get off!'

The fifth World Cup, in Australia in 2003, was South Africa's worst up till then. The Springboks, competing in the tournament for the third time, lost to England in their pool and then got knocked out of the tournament by being beaten comprehensively by the All Blacks in the quarter-final at the Telstra Dome in Melbourne. The Boks headed home, and it is possible, as they flew west across the Indian Ocean, that they crossed paths with aircraft carrying South African fans east to Sydney to support their team, which they expected to see in the final four. It was a thoroughly disappointing end to arguably the most turbulent time in the often stormy history of Springbok rugby.

Looking back, it's easy to see that the Springboks had no chance of success in Australia, given all the challenges to which they were subjected over the preceding years. Three coaches with distinctly different methods held sway at one time or another, captains came and went, players were selected, discarded and rotated with cavalier abandon, the quota system and racial considerations created great conflict, and some of the episodes bordered on the macabre.

When Nick Mallett departed, he was replaced with Harry Viljoen, who arrived with a Gucci briefcase full of new ideas and high hopes. He wanted the Boks to be trendy in the way they dressed: black leather jackets instead of green tracksuit tops or blazers. He wanted the players armed with laptops and talked of 'empowering' them. He wanted them to play the game in a new, expansive way, and in his first Test in charge, he decided on a radical method that would shock them into the bright new future.

Viljoen's first international as coach was against Argentina in the River

131

Plate Stadium in hazy, sultry Buenos Aires. In the past, the Boks had played Test matches at the rickety Ferro Carril Oeste (the western railway) Stadium, and it was rather ironic that in Argentina's vast cathedral of football, Viljoen sent the Springboks out with instructions not to kick the ball at all. Viljoen wanted to move away from South Africa's traditional game, in which the kick was often employed, to a fast, ball-in-hand game that he believed would elevate them above other top sides and make them not only trendsetters in the game, but also the biggest and most exciting brand in rugby. Viljoen had ground-breaking ideas, and after his premature departure I often wondered whether he should not have been SA Rugby's manager in charge of future development rather than coach of the Springboks.

Viljoen started his tenure faced with the familiar problem of not having a settled flyhalf, and for this Test he decided to go with Percy Montgomery in the No.10 jersey, hoping that the man with one of the best boots in the game could use his pace and innate footballing skills to ignite the running game he envisaged. The upshot was a mad, helter-skelter game in which the Springboks scored five tries but left enough ball lying around to enable the Pumas to score three of their own.

The Boks ran up a big lead but ended up having to defend for their lives to win 37-33, Montgomery finally breaking ranks in the 72nd minute and kicking for touch. A significant feature of the game was that it marked John Smit's first start in a Test, but administrators, coaches and the media were aghast at this first sighting of the 'new' Springboks.

On tour with a cumbersome, over-manned party, Viljoen and his team then travelled to the British Isles to play Ireland, Wales and England. At Lansdowne Road, in conditions that were patently not suited to an expansive game, Viljoen's enthusiasm for running the ball was called into question, but the Boks nevertheless got home 28-18. In Cardiff, Viljoen was drawn into a spat, interestingly with Graham Henry who was then coaching Wales, over whether the Millennium Stadium's roof should be open or closed during the game, a situation that could have been avoided. Fortunately the Boks were determined to get back at the Welsh after the disaster of 1999, and they showed all their fighting spirit to get a win after Robbie Fleck was sin-binned in the second half. In the end the Boks came away with a 23-13 victory after a tactical decision by the Welsh, when they substituted Neil Jenkins with Arwel Thomas, went badly wrong.

Viljoen's tenure had thus kicked off with three wins, but in the final game of 2000, against England at Twickenham, he vacillated on an all-out attacking game, moving Montgomery to fullback and picking Braam van Straaten, a superb goal-kicker but not a pivot known for his running and distribution skills, at flyhalf. England, however, were an army on the march. They prevailed 25-17 in a Test that marked the second of an unprecedented run of seven successive victories over the Springboks.

The year 2000 had ended with a dismal record for the Boks: played 12, won 6, lost 6. Mallett's previously impressive win ratio had taken a serious knock, but with Viljoen making it three out of four on tour, there were high hopes that 2001 would see a resurgence that could peak in Australia in 2003. It was not to be. Instead the graph flattened out when only five of 11 Tests were won (and three of those were against Italy and one against the United States), with one draw. The Boks lost twice to New Zealand, twice to France and once to England, and Viljoen's only consolation was that he had gained the edge over the formidable Wallabies with a win in Pretoria and a draw in Perth.

An account of the year, under the sub-heading 'Reckless' in the *SA Rugby Annual*, had this to say:

Coach Harry Viljoen's uncertainty over his best combinations meant that 41 players were used in the season, four of them in the perennial problem position of flyhalf and another six in the centres where eight different permutations were tried in the 11 tests. The chopping and changing would probably have been minimised if Natal's Butch James had seized his chance after an outstanding Super 12 cast him in the role as the long-awaited successor to another Natalian, Henry Honiball. James's robust defence and excellent handling skills promised to free up the backline and answer a fervent prayer. But his reckless tackling style (for which he was twice suspended during the season) and an inability to immediately carry his provincial form into the test arena meant that he was no longer sure of a place on the end of season tour, even before injury and a six-week ban for dangerous tackling in a Currie Cup match prematurely ended his year. The pedestrian nature of South Africa's backline play meant that they scored only one try or none at all in eight of their 11 tests and their reliance on penalty kicks left them impotent against the best defences.

To be fair, Viljoen's plans had been adversely affected by a string of injuries, but the dazzling new world he had promised was just not materialising. He could at least point to bright young things emerging, for this was the year that a lanky young lock from the Blue Bulls called Victor Matfield started to rule the skies, and in which 20-somethings such as Conrad Jantjes, Adrian Jacobs, Joe van Niekerk, Lawrence Sephaka, Dean Hall and Lukas van Biljon made their debuts. But for all that, Viljoen was quickly discovering the old truism, and the only one the fans seem to believe in: 'The only good Springbok side is a winning one.'

The Springboks were in a downward spiral, and one of Viljoen's remedies, to bring in three Australian coaches in Tim Lane, Les Kiss and Mick Byrne, failed to pay off. Viljoen believed South African rugby was in need of an injection of novel expertise and different thinking. This was no bad thing, but the manner in which he introduced the *uitlanders* (foreigners) was too brazen, and it riled some of the players. Also, the administrators of the players' home unions were affronted by 'having Aussies teach us how to play the game'.

The trio of Lane, Kiss and Byrne was personable and most skilled. Lane had been a member of Mark Ella's famous Grand Slam Wallaby side in 1984 and had worked as Rod Macqueen's backline coach at the World Cup in 1999; Kiss was highly thought of and imparted some useful innovations from his background in rugby league; and Byrne (or 'Kiss & Burn' as Mallett dubbed them in a column) had such know-how on how to kick the oval ball that he was later contracted by the All Blacks.

At the outset of his term, Viljoen had also been either persuaded or forced to appoint André Markgraaff as his assistant coach, and the dark age/new age chemistry in the make-up of his auxiliary staff was unavoidably unstable. Interestingly, one of his other assistant coaches was Jake White.

For the first Test of 2001, France arrived with an inexperienced side, and with the Springboks sporting a run of five successive victories against *Les Tricolores*, the shock was great when they lost 23-32 at Ellis Park. *Les Bleus* had managed to maintain an unbeaten run at the Johannesburg stadium. Breyton Paulse scored a try within 20 seconds of the opening whistle, but instead of the expected slaughter, the French pack gained control (the Boks had erred by putting rookie tighthead prop Etienne Fynn up against the refractory old Jean-Jacques Crenca). With unheralded flyhalf Gerald Merceron kicking sublimely plus scoring a try for a match tally of 27 points, the French were full value for their victory over an over-confident Springbok side. What made the defeat even harder to stomach was the fact that one of France's better players was their tighthead prop, South African–born Pieter de Villiers.

I was by now office-bound at SuperSport, but by checking the dispatches, I could see that Viljoen was looking increasingly persecuted whenever he had to face the media. However, as so often in the past when they had their backs to the wall, the Springboks fought back for a face-saving 20-15 win in the next Test, in Durban. 'Fought' was the operative word, as both Mark Andrews and De Wet Barry were sent to the sin bin, while Butch James was later cited and suspended for two matches. A series defeat had been avoided, but Viljoen's next gambit, when he, too, decided that Bob Skinstad was The One, backfired, causing the demons to start playing pinball in his mind.

Skinstad's knee had flared up again after the 1999 World Cup, and he had missed all of the 2000 international season. He was back in the frame for selection in 2001, and made an appearance off the bench in both Tests against France. Viljoen had inherited gentlemanly André Vos as his captain and No. 8, but just like Mallett two years previously, he began to think that Skinstad, with his distribution and vision, might be the catalyst to spark the game he wanted to play. He convinced himself that the time to make the change was after a winning Test, ironically a Test in which Vos had been the Man of the Match.

It is said that there never is a right time to drop a Springbok captain, but the way André Vos was dropped remains one of the most awkward moments I have experienced in 40 years of covering rugby. The two players were informed of the coach's plans: Skinstad (who, never forget, did not pick himself) would be elevated to captain and Vos would stay in the team and take on a new role – that of fetcher flank. Vos and Skinstad would appear together on the dais at the press conference, clearly to soften the blow for the former captain, but the upshot was that most hearts at the event bled for 'Vossie'.

He looked grim and quite sick, and Skinstad looked down at the floor for most of the conference while Viljoen explained that he was looking for a different dimension at No. 8, and also that he had decided that Bob would skipper the side 'through to 2003'. Vos, although he must have been breaking up inside, maintained his dignity throughout. 'Like the coach says, it is a new opportunity for me now,' he said. 'I just have to focus on what happens out on the field and try to work my [way] back [into] the side. It would be unfair to compare myself and Bob. We play two completely different games and the style that the coach is looking for is what Bob has to offer.' Skinstad, who thus became his country's 50th captain, added tellingly: 'There's not a helluva lot out there that is fair.'

It was amazing how, yet again, controversy surrounded the man in the No. 8 jersey. In fact, it had almost become a Springbok tradition. At some stage or another, Doug Hopwood, Tom Bedford, Morné du Plessis, Wynand Claassen, Rob Louw, Tiaan Strauss, Gary Teichmann, Nick Mallett, Bob Skinstad and André Vos had been put through the mill, and often it involved the captaincy.

Like other captains before him, Vos's subsequent successful career – with Harlequins in London – left many rugby fans and experts wondering whether his enforced exit as Springbok captain had not been premature. Tiaan Strauss had likewise excelled for the Cronulla Sharks rugby league side in Sydney before returning to rugby union. He was capped by the Wallabies and played in the 1999 RWC. François Pienaar was part of Saracens' strong entry into professional rugby, and Gary Teichmann became a legend at Newport in Wales.

Nevertheless, Skinstad led the Springboks to a 60-14 win over Italy in Port Elizabeth, in a Test in which Victor Matfield made his debut as a sub. But a record of three wins (over Australia, Italy and the USA), four losses and a draw was never going to satisfy South Africa's demanding fans or convince them that Viljoen was the right man for the job. The fact that they were influenced by a rugby-writing corps who was never comfortable with the coach and his manipulative media officer ensured that sparks began to fly off the axes being ground.

In July, wet weather at Newlands militated against a running game, but the All Blacks had the more sound defence and the better goal-kicker in Tony Brown. They won 12-3 after Butch James and Percy Montgomery between them missed a number of penalties that might have swung the result. Victor Matfield got his first run-on cap.

Moving to the Highveld, the Boks got home 20-15 against Australia, illustrating once again Australia's inability to beat the Springboks in South Africa (unfortunately, the same could be said for South Africa on Australian soil). It was a fine win, as Australia was coming off a series victory against the British & Irish Lions. A young Conrad Jantjes shone on his debut at fullback and Joe van Niekerk made his debut off the bench.

The Loftus faithful could go home happy and Harry Viljoen could heave a sigh of relief.

In August, the away leg of the Tri Nations started promisingly. Returning to the scene of their last away win over the Wallabies – their home from home in Perth – the Springboks were confident. However, this time the Wallabies were able to score one more point and they forced a draw, 14-all. It was a Test the Boks should actually have won, but for the fact that Butch James and Bob Skinstad were yellow-carded by referee Steve Walsh. It was while Skinstad was in the sin bin that Nathan Grey found the gap through which to score the Wallabies' try.

It was the first draw in the Tri Nations series and the first draw in 47 Tests between the two countries. Mark Andrews, already the most prolific try-scorer among South Africa's forwards, got the Boks' try, while Viljoen had the satisfaction of being able to say that the all-conquering Aussies had been unable to beat his side.

Across the Tasman to New Zealand. The Springboks had not beaten the All Blacks at Eden Park since 1937, and the status quo remained in another lacklustre performance in more rainy weather. Just as at Newlands, the Boks failed to score a try. Discipline was again a problem, with Lukas van Biljon conceding a penalty try with an early tackle on Leon MacDonald, and the All Blacks pulled further ahead on the historic scoreboard. At least there was one highlight: Bob Skinstad preventing Jonah Lomu from scoring a try. However, the All Blacks triumphed 26-15 and another Tri Nations was down the drain.

The end-of-year tour was made up of four Tests: France, Italy, England and the USA. But the Springboks' first appearance, at the Stade de France, was nothing to write home about. France again pulled a little-known fly-half, François Gelez, out of the hat to torment the Boks, and even though they led 10-9 midway through the second half, thanks to Pieter Rossouw's 20th Test try, *Les Bleus* were the better side. In fact, their dominance was more emphatic than the score of 20-10 suggested.

The Stadio Luigi Ferraris in Genoa, home to football clubs Genoa FC and Sampdoria, was the next stop for the Boks, but a new venue failed to inspire them and press reports spoke of the same old dross as they won 54-26.

On to Twickenham, by now the least favourite ground of the Boks and their fans, many of them young 'Saffers' working in the UK. Fielding arguably one of the slowest backlines ever to take the field in a green-and-gold jersey (Van der Westhuizen, Koen, Van Straaten, Halstead, Hall, Paulse, Jantjes), the Springboks failed to score a try for the third time in the season as England registered their third successive victory. Yet again, poor discipline was the Boks' Achilles heel, and Jonny Wilkinson kicked them to kingdom come. The only positive was that it took an overwhelmingly dominant England side 79 minutes to score a try in their emphatic 29-9 win.

There was one more assignment: South Africa's second Test against the American Eagles. The first had been an amazing rugby event, staged in 1981 on a polo field in Glenville in upstate New York and played before fewer than 30 spectators, most of whom were players, officials and state troopers. The Boks were always going to beat the Eagles at Robertson Stadium in Houston, which they did 43-20, but there were a number of oddities from the team's barmy management. Six of the Boks were allowed to stay in England to play for the Barbarians, but this at least provided run-on caps for Adrian Jacobs and Deon de Kock and a debut for loosehead prop Lawrence Sephaka, the first player of Nguni descent to start a Test.

André Vos, in what turned out to be his last Test, stood in for Bob Skinstad as captain and did an excellent job, but the Eagles could feel justifiably proud of their game. Unbeknown to the Springboks, their crew and the media, this was also Harry Viljoen's last Test in charge.

In January 2002, Harry Viljoen cut and ran, disillusioned, he said, by the public criticism that accompanies the post and ending his contract almost two years early. Viljoen had quit coaching positions with Transvaal, Natal and Western Province for personal reasons, and this time he blamed media criticism for his decision, though he accepted that it was part of the job. 'I think the pressure on the coaches of New Zealand and South Africa is the most intense,' he said. 'You don't know the pressure until you're there yourself, and I've struggled to handle it. There's another two years to the World Cup, and facing that would have been a problem.'

Rian Oberholzer did a poor job of masking his fury at being let down. 'I'm very disappointed that Harry isn't able to see through the process he has initiated, but we're still on track and a lot of planning has gone into this team. We'll continue with that process.' Oberholzer had vociferously defended his coach and had appealed for Viljoen to be given time. He'd even volunteered that he, as chief executive, would carry the can if Springbok results did not improve in 2002.

Viljoen's sudden departure meant that SA Rugby was searching for its ninth national coach in 12 seasons. Rudolf Straeuli, then coaching the Natal Sharks, and Gert Smal, coach of Western Province and the Stormers, were the front-runners for the job. World Cup winner Straeuli, who had made a name for himself as a player/coach with English club Bedford, had taken the Sharks to three finals in his 18 months in charge – including the 2001 Super 12 final against the ACT Brumbies – but had lost them all.

Smal had won two Currie Cup finals (both when pitted against Straeuli), but he had a history with SA Rugby. When he was assistant coach to Carel du Plessis in 1997, the pair had sued their employers for breach of contract after they were sacked. Other contenders were London Irish coach Brendan Venter, Ulster's Alan Solomons, and Rudi Joubert, who was then with Cardiff. The hunt was on for the next poor sucker willing to drink from the poisoned chalice, and Australia's World Cup was less than two years away.

And as to bizarre …? There was more, much more to come.

15

Out of the frying pan and into the fire

A strange expression settled on the face of Louis Koen, the Springbok fly-half, as he said, 'Well, terrible things ...' The Springboks were in Fremantle, a coastal suburb which is to Perth what Kalk Bay is to Cape Town, at the start of Rugby World Cup 2003. I was chatting to Koen and an Australian journalist at a media jamboree where all the players were available to talk to the press.

It was an awkward gathering, however. Some players, such as skipper Corné Krige, scrumhalf Joost van der Westhuizen and the new shining light of South African rugby, 20-year-old Derick Hougaard, were crowded by writers holding out their tape recorders or scribbling notes, while others were left twiddling their thumbs. Having done the interviews I wanted with Neil de Kock and Stefan Terblanche, I stopped to listen to what Koen, the incumbent flyhalf, had to say to the solitary Australian reporter inter-viewing him. And that was the first I heard of it – the pre-tournament training camp that would gain notoriety as Kamp Staaldraad.

Koen was telling the Aussie reporter about the team's preparation and the training camp in the bush. When asked what sorts of things the team had experienced, his immediate response was, 'Well, terrible things ...' He quickly recovered to say that it had been an army-style survival camp in which the players had had to fend for themselves in rough conditions. He added that the experience had brought them closer together.

However, the fleeting look of horror on Koen's face piqued my reporter's inquisitiveness and indicated that there was more to the story than met the eye – especially given the alleged racial incident that had occurred between Quinton Davids and Geo Cronjé at the team's training base at Pretoria University's High Performance Centre. It had cast a pall over the squad even before it was named.

I made some inquiries but, given SuperSport's 'three monkeys' policy (see no evil, hear no evil, speak no evil), perhaps not as purposefully as I might or should have. I had a good relationship with Rudolf Straeuli, dating from the 1995 World Cup, when I was asked to advise the World

Cup players during their stand-off with Louis Luyt and Transvaal. As we, the press, were staying in the same hotel as the team – the quaint, old-fashioned, ballustraded Esplanade – it was easy enough to ask him about the training exercise. Also, Straeuli had earlier asked me to address the players on how to deal with the media and promote positive PR, and I was keen to discuss the content of my talk with him. In fact, shortly after being installed as coach, Straeuli had wanted me to act as the team's liaison officer during the World Cup, but had eventually come back to say that Rian Oberholzer had baulked at the idea.

In light of what had happened at the Tukkies training base (which I will cover in detail later), one of my messages to the Springboks was going to be, 'having a PR doesn't mean you have PR.' Another point I wanted to make was, 'beware of a question that contains a statement.' To illustrate what I meant by that, I was going to tell the tale of Kit Fawcett, who toured South Africa with the 1976 All Blacks. On the team's arrival in the country, reporter Viv Prince's eyes alighted on the good-looking Fawcett, and she approached him with the question: 'Bet you're going to score more off the field than on the field?'

Taken by surprise, Fawcett, as most young men would – especially one on an All Black rugby tour to South Africa – nodded in the affirmative. The boastful 'remark' was attributed to him and it ended up ruining his tour.

It was early days at the 2003 RWC. We'd just arrived in Australia, and I felt free to simply approach Straeuli. But it would not take long for the laager to be drawn tightly shut as the coach became increasingly guarded, seemingly under the spell of the rather sinister and overtly suspicious Adriaan Heijns, a former special branch policeman who was now the Springboks' security officer. Rather unsurprisingly, I never did give my PR talk. Straeuli, however, did explain to me that the camp Koen had been referring to was a commando-style team-building exercise, similar to those previously undertaken by other sports teams. These included South Africa's pool opponents, England, who were also in Perth, ensconced in a high-rise hotel in the inner city.

Straeuli's explanation was good enough for me, but word soon started filtering out about what had gone on at Kamp Staaldraad* and that some players had not enjoyed the experience at all. Former Springbok lock

---

* *Camp Steel Wire, although it was incorrectly translated as Camp Barbed Wire by the English media.*

Schalk Burger and his wife Myra had flown to Australia to support their son, Schalk Jnr, who, along with Hougaard and Jaque Fourie, was one of the three 20-year-olds in the side (interestingly, all three were born in April 1983), and 'Groot' Schalk hinted that it may be worth trying to find out more.

'Some of the guys are not happy at all,' he told me. Reporters are well known to the players and, in spite of Heijns's absurd efforts to try to isolate them, some hair-raising stories nevertheless started to reach us.

I must admit that at first I dismissed any claims made of players having to strip naked and spend hours in an ice-cold dam. Or of them having to fight each other in a boxing ring, or going hungry and being sleep-deprived. And sitting in a pit while recordings of 'Swing Low, Sweet Chariot' and the Haka blared from loudspeakers, or being forced to tackle bags draped in England shirts? What? In a Springbok side? You must be kidding! But how wrong I would turn out to be.

The mood in Fremantle soon changed dramatically, much to the frustration – and, sometimes, cynical amusement – of those of us whose employers had spent thousands of rands to send us to Australia to cover the World Cup and, in particular, the Springboks. Adriaan Heijns had been Rian Oberholzer's chief of security at the 1995 World Cup, but Oberholzer had now appointed him to keep an eye on the Boks, and he approached the job with the zeal the CIA reserves for the president of the United States.

Apparently a man with a persecution complex, Heijns found ready disciples in the Springbok management team, including Rudi Joubert, Gert Smal and Uli Schmidt. Some of the players, always edgy when the press was nearby, also got under his wing, and Straeuli, whom I had always considered an affable bloke and who had been one of the jokers in the side when he played for the Boks, had now become suspicious and guarded. We gaped open-mouthed at some of the stories we heard from the players when we bumped into them on 'Cappuccino Lane' (so named by us because of the many coffee bars to be found there).

Heijns had apparently had the team room swept for bugs and had hired extra security men to keep a watchful eye on the balcony that encircled the Esplanade Hotel. He would also position himself by the door of the team room and count the players as they entered the room – after which he would quickly shut the door, stuff a towel in the gap underneath and fill the keyhole with Prestik!

The players might have been exaggerating, but I had personal experience of the paranoia that was setting in. One evening a group of us visited a great eatery on the harbour front across the park from our hotel, the Little Creatures Brewery, where the tables are set among the stainless-steel beer-brewing tanks – talk about heaven for travelling sports writers! As we wanted an early night to try to sleep off our jet lag, some of us headed back to the hotel after dinner. As we reached the Esplanade, the team bus drew up. The squad had also been out for a meal. As Straeuli alighted, I walked to him and we started to chat. However, the next moment Heijns brusquely stepped between us, pushed me aside and dragged the coach away – as if I represented a threat to a man nearly twice my size and half my age.

I said as much to Straeuli, but it was clear that the laager mentality had well and truly set in. Around the corner and up the street from the hotel was an all-night fast-food outlet called Fast Eddy's – a boon to the travelling journalist working late or returning from some pub with an Irish name! On one occasion, a group of us was standing around waiting for our orders when Mike Greenaway, the Independent Group's chief writer and a good man to have on tour, nodded towards the door and whispered, 'We've got company.' We glanced outside just in time to see 'Inspector Clouseau' (our nickname for Heijns) jerk his head back from where he'd been peeping around a public telephone booth. We roared with laughter when we all caught him peeping again. A few moments later, a sheepish-looking Straeuli and Heijns came into Fast Eddy's. The coach had apparently been waiting across the street while Heijns had snuck up to check that the coast was clear. One of the more outlandish yarns doing the rounds was that Heijns had convinced Straeuli that Mark Keohane had taken out a hit on him!

As I've mentioned in passing, the World Cup campaign had started under a cloud after an incident between Geo Cronjé and Quinton Davids during training at the Tukkies High Performance Centre. This was before the naming of the 30-man squad that would travel to Australia. To my mind, the issue between Cronjé and Davids, how management handled it and subsequent events was the story that was going to feature once the World Cup was over – unless the Boks went on to win, in which case all would be forgiven and forgotten. As a result, I did not pay the Kamp Staaldraad story the attention it deserved.

In Pretoria, Geo Cronjé had apparently moved out of the room he and Davids were meant to share, which he was not allowed to do. Davids turned up late for a practice session at this time. As punishment, both players had to do a severe exercise drill. Soon, the incident erupted into a full-scale controversy when it was claimed that Cronjé had moved out of the room because he refused to share with a black man. And the management believed Keohane was responsible for leaking the story to Dale Granger of the *Argus*.

Next, Bolla Conradie was fingered. Apparently he had made a phone call home to his people in the Cape, who then leaked the story to the local newspaper. That Davids was a coloured from the Cape and Cronjé a white Afrikaner, his scraggly beard making him look like the archetypal right-wing 'boer', fuelled a situation that could have been handled better, but which instead got completely out of hand. Keohane, in *Springbok Rugby Uncovered*, categorically denied any involvement in leaking the story and provided a detailed account of how Granger had come to hear about the incident. Watergate brought down Richard Nixon, and in the end 'Geogate', followed by Kamp Staaldraad, would result in the rugby 'impeachment' of a number of people.

Dale Granger is an eccentric character whose late father, Viv, founder of the National Football League (NFL) and a real newshound in the days of the *Sunday Express* and the *Rand Daily Mail*, had imbued in him the bulldog qualities necessary to unearth a good story. His nickname among the press corps was 'Grave Danger'. Granger subsequently emigrated to Australia, where he recalled the incident as 'a big issue in my life'. According to him, the story came to him via rugby's fertile grapevine. His version of the rather sordid tale provides intriguing insight into how dysfunctional the Bok team's management had become.

'I was chatting on the phone to Martin van Schalkwyk [former WP hooker] about Currie Cup rugby when he asked me whether I had heard what was going on in the Bok camp,' Granger said. 'He told me the shit had hit the fan because Geo [had] refused to share a room with Quinton, who was very upset and wanted to "klap" Geo.

'Most of the WP players knew about it, but I decided not to phone the Boks [Keohane] or anyone at SARU until I had confirmed the story with one or two other sources. So I called a couple of WP officials who I knew would have contact with players at the Bok camp and who would either know or be prepared to make a few discreet phone calls and verify the information. The info that came back confirmed strife and tension in the Bok camp just before the World Cup, not only between Geo and Davids, but [also between] Corné [Krige, the team's captain] and Joost [Van der

Westhuizen, the former captain], because Bulls players were calling Joost "cappy" [South African slang for "captain"].

'Only once I had all the info – enough to write the story or at least confront the Boks with confidence in the facts – did I call Keo for comment. Keo stalled initially and wanted to know when I intended going to print. I said, "tomorrow," irrespective of what comment was forthcoming from the Boks. That was in the afternoon. I stayed up until 3 or 4 the next morning verbally sparring with Keo, who was only really interested in one thing: Who was the source of the story?

'The Boks were convinced the story had been leaked out of their own camp. They were paranoid and on a witch-hunt, trying to find the culprit. But I also wanted Keo to confirm the story. He was reluctant to do so without me divulging my source. Eventually I gave in. But I didn't trust Keo, so I bullshitted him a little, saying that the WP players were merely talking about it and that Davids was big mates with Bolla, had told him [about it] and the story had then spread at WP training and other players, like Van Schalkwyk, knew about it too. That was actually how I thought it *had* got back to WP. But I didn't know that for sure.

'Keo, instead of keeping this info confidential, as [we'd] agreed, ran straight to Straeuli. This was after he had relented and told me that our story was true. I still needed comment from SA Rugby and Keo seemed quite willing to bring Rian Oberholzer's comment into the story. At 4 in the morning, sensing that this story was going to unleash a storm, I decided to email it to Oberholzer and then get his comment. I did this to cover myself, because I was feeling a little uneasy about the reaction it might spark. I had no idea about the firestorm it would unleash. I was stunned when I spoke to Rian and he said both players had been suspended and SA Rugby would investigate. He had no issues with any factual inaccuracies in the story. Of course *The Star* ran the story the next day under a banner headline, "Racist Bok", above a picture of Geo that made him look like a neo-Nazi, even though the story itself was pretty straightforward reporting with no editorialising.

'It turned out that Straeuli didn't believe Keo [about] who I said the source was. Three or four days later, Straeuli phoned me on my mobile. I found this so ironic, because I did not have his number and my repeated requests for interviews up to that point had resulted in only one call some months earlier from "The Moose" [Straeuli's nickname among the press] and a nothing interview. He wasn't interested in any facts or details. I told him his management team was a joke and that they could have handled the whole Geo–Davids issue differently and avoided the crisis completely.

'He agreed, but [he] was only interested in trying to find out who my source was. He made it quite clear that Keo was suspect number one and kept probing. "There is no source," I told Straeuli. "Players and people in rugby talk and things get out. That's all!" Some years later, Joost made a speech in Port Elizabeth and told everyone that Keo was not only the source of the story, but had written it too and sent it on to me. But the truth is that Keo was not the source of the story.'

From a playing perspective, the build-up to RWC 2003 could not have been worse. The previous year's end-of-year tour had been an unmitigated disaster, with the Springboks stumbling through record defeats against France (10-30) and Scotland (6-21) before possibly the most humiliating juncture in their history when they were beaten 3-53 by England at Twickenham. The low point was a damning tape of incidents in the game aired by Sky TV, allegedly passed on by Clive Woodward from the England team's own footage. It showed the Boks committing all kinds of nefarious deeds, with skipper Corné Krige the chief culprit.

Straeuli's response was an attempt at bravado: 'See you in Perth,' he said to England, referring to the key Pool C game in Australia the following year. But in the end, bluster was all it turned out to be. The results earlier in 2003 simply did not provide the required momentum for a team going into a World Cup. The Boks made heavy weather of defeating Scotland in a two-Test series, and were then extremely lucky to beat a gutted Argentina 26-25 thanks to Louis Koen kicking a penalty deep into extra time.

There was some respite with a 26-22 win over Australia at Newlands in the Tri Nations, but then everything went pear-shaped. The Springboks were decimated 16-52 by the All Blacks at Loftus Versfeld (another un-wanted record and the heaviest home defeat since South Africa first took to the field in 1891). As the wags had it, 'The only other time 1652 was significant to South Africa was when Jan van Riebeeck landed at the Cape.' But worse was to follow. The Boks lost 9-29 to the Wallabies in Brisbane, and lost again, 11-19, to New Zealand in Dunedin. (This was the game in which Richard Bands scored arguably the greatest try by a prop forward in a Test match.) Three successive defeats going into the World Cup were not auspicious, and 'see you in Perth' was starting to have a distinctly hollow ring to it.

And if that was not bad enough, the 'Geogate' furore created the most farcical situation imaginable for a team preparing to play in a World Cup. If the team's management had hoped to put a lid on the accusations of racism, they were rudely disillusioned when Mark Keohane walked out, announcing that he could no longer condone the racial prejudice that existed in the team. Although the media officer left abruptly – so abruptly that he was said to have left a lot of his kit in his room – he produced a lengthy report containing damning accusations of racism in the squad.

An initial inquiry by SARFU found no conclusive evidence of racism, but disgruntled administrators ordered a second, independent investigation. However, its results would be overwhelmed by the sensational Kamp Staaldraad story, which Archie Henderson (*Argus*) and Clinton van der Berg (*Sunday Times*) broke just after the Springbok team arrived home in disgrace from Australia.

Much to the chagrin of Straeuli and team manager Gideon Sam, who felt they had not been given the opportunity to refute Keohane's 'one-sided, self-serving agenda', it was then decided that the media officer's report would form the basis of an investigation into the allegations of racism. The commission would be chaired by retired judge Edwin King, the man who had led the inquiry into the Hansie Cronjé match-fixing scandal in cricket.

Before the wholesale administrative changes that would take place as a direct result of the failed World Cup campaign – the simultaneous departure of the president, Silas Nkanunu, CEO Rian Oberholzer and coach Rudolf Straeuli – an internal investigation into events at the High Performance Centre and Kamp Staaldraad, led by Koos Basson, chairman of SARU's national judicial committee, was ordered. Typically, his report (of which I have a copy) was incoherent, obfuscated in legalese and did not culminate in a conclusive ruling. It is nevertheless quite instructive on how the seemingly straightforward task of preparing for a Rugby World Cup tournament could descend into such chaos.

It reveals that Keohane had sent a draft of Granger's article, which was due to appear in the *Argus*, to Oberholzer, who had then appointed former Springbok scrumhalf Christo Ferreira (general manager of policy and regulations at SARFU) and Adri Brand (SARFU's attorney) to investigate whether or not Geo Cronjé had breached the Code of Conduct.

Four days later, Ferreira and Brand delivered an interim report containing the following conclusions: 'We determine that there was no conclusive evidence to support or justify that a breach of the Code of Conduct [in respect of the *Argus* article] may have been committed by Cronjé and that disciplinary proceedings against him based on the acts of racism were accordingly not warranted or justified on the strength of the information at our disposal. More especially is this so where the alleged victim [Davids] himself disavowed any notion of acts of racial discrimination against him by Cronjé, and where none of the other persons interviewed could provide any support for any of the allegations made by Dale Granger etc.'

However, the plot thickened. According to Basson's report, Oberholzer was displeased that no form of racism could be linked to Cronjé's actions and felt that the investigation had not been thorough enough. It was claimed that he thought it was a 'cover-up'. Keohane's supposedly confidential memorandum was in the hands of virtually everyone who wanted a copy, and what it said did not make good reading for Cronjé and severely prejudiced whatever defence he might have had.

The upshot was that both Cronjé and Davids were removed from consideration for the RWC team (although this was not publicly announced), SA Rugby released a strongly worded statement in support of Oberholzer and announced that a new investigation would be held – the one by Judge King. This inquiry was meant to commence immediately but was postponed to allow the Bok team and management to concentrate on their preparations for RWC 2003. It is interesting that Cronjé, whose career as a promising lock off the Blue Bull conveyor belt was ruined by the controversy, has never publicly defended himself.

Straeuli, himself a lawyer, was deeply upset that Keohane's version of events was accepted as fact and that it would serve as the basis for the King Commission. He was willing to submit to whatever processes SARFU wished to pursue and wanted a public hearing in which everyone involved could be interrogated. His revelation that Oberholzer had appointed Heijns's Pro-Tect International organisation to run Kamp Staaldraad fell on indifferent ears.

I met with Straeuli in Durban in the hope that he might want his side of the story to appear in this book, but he declined on the grounds that a single interview would never suffice to cover all the facts contained in the documents he has kept. I respect his wishes, with regret. I believe he may have been able to shed some light on an extremely sordid side of South African rugby, which would have left certain key figures in the game – some of whom have tasted World Cup glory – cringing in shame. That said, when the full extent of Kamp Staaldraad emerged, I was disappointed that

Straeuli, a real rugby man with sporting values imposed on him by his father, Hans, a former provincial player, Doc Craven and Kitch Christie (his coaching guru), had not drawn a line and simply said, 'You do not treat Springboks in that way.' Why had he not? I expect he ponders that himself.

Although I admired Keohane's decision to leave his post out of principle, his departure and the furore unleashed by 'Geogate' left the Boks in a mess ahead of the World Cup tournament. Anthony Mackaiser was appointed to replace Keohane, and I found myself in yet another ludicrous situation when I was dispatched to Pretoria to conduct interviews for SuperSport.

Over the years one becomes sensitive to the mood in a team, and the squad that awaited me in Pretoria was certainly an unhappy one. There is always a natural barrier between the press and the players when the Springboks are in camp, but I found the players particularly furtive on this occasion. They seemed determined not to make eye contact and weren't keen to be seen talking to, or even greeting, a member of the media. Something had clearly gone very wrong; the group chemistry was disturbed.

This could largely be blamed on the decision to exclude both Cronjé and Davids from consideration for the World Cup. Davids' exclusion was unacceptable to the black and coloured players in the group and his Western Province teammates, as they felt he had done nothing wrong. For them, an example should have been made of Cronjé and the alleged prejudices he had not even tried to hide, in spite of interventions by Straeuli and Corné Krige. After all, the group had been told why the two men had been put through a punishment drill (known as 'opneuk' or 'opfoksessies' in team parlance): Cronjé had refused to share a room with Davids, and Davids had been late for a practice session. As such, Davids' punishment did not fit the crime.

And thus, in an effort to try to put an end to the media frenzy, the team decided to have an 'open day' for the press. They unfortunately also came up with the nonsensical idea of everyone assembling in the auditorium so that the reporters would be compelled to ask their questions 'in front of the whole group'. I suppose it made sense to them, as they sought to convey a sense of solidarity, but there was another implication. With everyone present, no one would be able to speak out of turn, and the reporters could be so intimidated, they might not ask tough questions. Corné Krige was a decent man caught up in an unholy mess. He would later give his autobiography the telling title of *The Right Place at the Wrong Time*. In it, he wrote that we journos were terrified by the prospect of such an inquisition, but frankly I was more embarrassed than scared.

I decided that if that's the way they wanted to do it, let's get on with it. I called out three of the black players – Breyton Paulse, Ashwin Willemse and Gcobani Bobo – and asked them straight out about the racism allegations and whether they'd experienced any racism themselves.

Unsurprisingly, they all denied that such problems existed. They were happy, they were not being treated badly and they were dead keen for the World Cup squad to be named. They were all looking forward to being in the team and excited about the prospect of packing for Perth. The whole event was a bit of a farce, and in time it would transpire that these three were fibbing, but what else could one expect? On the eve of the announcement of the World Cup squad, an opportunity that most players experience just once in their careers, it was hardly likely that one of them was going to say, 'these are a bunch of racist bastards and I want nothing to do with them.'

Given all the drama of the preceding weeks, it was inevitable that the team announcement would be a damp squib – literally. A stage had been erected on a field at the Pretoria University sports grounds, where the players were due to make a dramatic appearance on an old bus, bedecked in Springbok livery, which would break through a wall of cardboard boxes amid exploding smoke bombs and thunder flashes. But the device that was meant to make the wall burst misfired, the boxes toppled over most undramatically and whatever impact was intended, was lost.

At the event, my job was to interview as many players as possible, and I experienced a very awkward moment, which might have been indicative of the tension in the squad, on the balcony of the rugby club. Ashwin Willemse took up his place in front of the camera, and I thought I'd feed him a question that would allow him to talk about his inspirational life's journey, which had taken him from running with gangs to a World Cup tournament.

Willemse, who was in the midst of an outstanding season that would result in him being named the SA Rugby Player of the Year for 2003, misunderstood the gist of my question and took umbrage. 'What a stupid question to ask!' he snapped. 'Here I am in a Rugby World Cup team and you have to bring that up! What's that got to do with it? We should be proud of our team.' Or words to that effect. It was embarrassing, but great was my relief later on when producer Scott Seward revealed that the interview had been recorded and had not gone out live.

The atmosphere in the team was clearly poisoned. Early the next morning, the players would, in great secrecy, be spirited away to Kamp Staaldraad. As a build-up to Australia 2003, it is difficult to imagine a worse scenario.

16

Packing up in Perth

As the Springboks unpacked in Perth, they no doubt could not wait to put events in South Africa behind them. Their first practice session took place at the stadium of the Fremantle Dockers, a local Aussie rules club, but even here the bad luck followed them when hooker Dale Santon injured a hamstring and others pulled up a little lame. It was not a great lead-in to their first game of the tournament, against the lowly 'Los Teros' of Uruguay. All eyes, however, were already on the second pool game, against England, which had to be won if the Boks were to avoid playing a quarter-final against the All Blacks.

Nevertheless, the match against Uruguay was significant for marking the debuts of Jaque Fourie and Danie Rossouw, as well as Derick Hougaard off the bench. Joost van der Westhuizen scored his second Test hat-trick (the other occurred against Wales in Cardiff in 1996) to advance his try record to 38. Unfortunately, these would turn out to be his last tries, as he retired from international rugby after the tournament. Against Uruguay the Springboks eventually scored 12 tries to nil, winning 72-6.

And when the Springboks finally did 'see' the English in Perth, they were in for a big shock. The Western Australian capital had been described as the Springboks' home from home because of the large number of South African expats who lived in the city. Of this there was proof aplenty in the local telephone directory with its large number of surnames starting with 'Van'. But they had not reckoned on an even bigger group of English immigrants living in Perth, not to mention the significant numbers of 'Barmy Army' supporters who had travelled to Australia.

The Boks were expecting to play to a Subiaco Oval crowd mostly on their side, but instead were shocked to see a sea of white jerseys while a constant din of 'Swing Low, Sweet Chariot' rang out from the stands. Prince Harry was present, but the man who gave the crowd the most regal wave was England coach Clive Woodward, who acknowledged the fans while his team warmed up. Jonny Wilkinson was constantly cheered while he practised his kicks, which he did for a full hour. We were to become rather used to his stylised ritual as the tournament unfolded – four steps back, five steps to the right, tap the left toe twice, take up a golfer's stance with your hands clasped in front of you, then send the Gilbert sailing between the posts.

The prize of topping this pool, as I've said, was avoiding the All Blacks in the quarter-finals, but even before the game, one could gauge the different mindsets of the two teams going into the match. Martin Johnson was simply focusing on the match at hand: 'It's a huge, huge game – as simple as that,' he said. 'Bigger and more intense than anything that's gone before. I'm expecting a ferocious encounter and am looking forward to it.' Corné Krige, however, was forced to deal with matters other than rugby.

'We've put it ['Geogate'] behind us,' he said. 'Now we can focus on rugby. I feel it [the problems before leaving] made the team pull together.' Of course, the story of Kamp Staaldraad had not yet broken. Team manager Gideon Sam was asked for his comments on what he thought awaited the team once they got back home. He said, 'Fact is that when we come back, we're all prepared to go to the King Commission and answer questions. We'll not allow it to derail us [at the RWC]. We'll concentrate on our game. We'll come back and be part of the process and help try to solve the problems of transformation.'

In the match itself, the Boks put up a better showing than might have been expected. It was 6-all at the break, with Koen having missed some kicks, including two he probably should not have attempted at sea level. With 17 minutes left to play, the score was still only 6-12. The Boks had been unlucky to lose tighthead prop Richard Bands as early as the sixth minute, but the crucial turning point came in the 63rd minute, when Lewis Moody charged down a clearance by Koen some 40 metres from his own goal line and Greenwood was unopposed as he toed the ball through to score.

The score changed to 6-19, and Wilkinson sealed it 25-6 when he landed two drop goals. The Aussie press seized on the drop kicks while failing to notice how organised, confident and, in the end, dominant England had been. Afterwards, the Bok camp suggested that Bands might have been 'got at', and they were also livid about Dallaglio punching Delport in the last minute of the match. But the sins the Boks had committed at Twickenham the year before had come back to haunt them, and they decided not to kick up a fuss. Needless to say, officialdom also did nothing about the incidents, with the England No. 8 getting away with an offence that would almost certainly have resulted in a suspension had he been cited.

The Boks were thus a doubly tormented side as they headed to Sydney for their next match, against one of the minnows, Georgia, at what was then called the Aussie Stadium. With its fan-like roof, we had first come to know it as the Sydney Football Stadium (SFS) on the tour of 1993.

The most interesting thing about the Georgians was the proliferation of 'i', 'vili' or 'ze' at the end of their surnames: Kopaliani, Dadunashvili, Margvelashvili, Gujaraidze, Didebulidze, Bolgashvili, Tsiklauri, Chkhaidze, Jimsheladze, Kavtarashvili, to name but a few. We knew television commentator Hugh Bladen was going to have a hard time of it that evening.

The Georgians were up for the physical aspects of rugby and managed to register a good haul of points in going down 19-46. Their score included a try that had them celebrating as if they had won the World Cup. From a Springbok perspective, the match turned out to be hugely significant on two fronts: it was John Smit's first as captain, and Schalk Burger made his debut off the bench.

Smit thus became South Africa's 51st Test captain, and Burger, at that point the youngest RWC Springbok at 20 years and 193 days, also became the eighth son to follow his father into the Springbok team – lock forward SWP Burger, or 'Groot' Schalk as he is affectionately known. 'Klein' Schalk and Derick Hougaard, who had both played cricket (Schalk as a left-hand opening batsman and first-change bowler, and Derick batting at No. 4) and rugby for Boland from primary school to Under-15 and Under-19, marked the occasion by getting their first Test tries.

The final pool match was against Samoa at the Suncorp Stadium in Brisbane, and with the islanders having given England a pretty good go, there was much talk about what a fight they would put up against the Boks. But it was never a contest, with the Boks scoring exactly 60 points for the third time in four clashes against Samoa, to win 60-10. Joe van Niekerk scored a great try in the second minute, and the Boks went on to score seven more, playing arguably their best rugby of the year.

Derick Hougaard, in spite of having his bones rattled by 'The Chiropractor' (Brian Lima, competing in his fourth World Cup), scored in all four ways to cement his place in the side for the quarter-final. An odd incident occurred when a Samoan fan tackled Louis Koen, who had replaced Hougaard in the 69th minute, just as he was successfully kicking his final conversion of the match, thus ensuring the tackler a role in any future rugby quiz shows so popular in local pubs. His name was Tapumanaia Laurasi, and in the process he succeeded in knocking himself out, being carried off on a stretcher and later being fined R6 000 on a charge of 'interfering with a person engaged in a sport at a sporting facility'. Trust the Aussies to have a law for it!

The Boks were through to the quarter-finals, but the defeat against England had condemned them to having to take on the All Blacks at the Telstra Dome in Melbourne. Known as the cultural capital of Australia, Melbourne turned out to be filled with fillies for me, as it was the week of the famous Melbourne Cup horse race. On the same evening that I received an invitation from my old friend Richard Nurse to go to the races, the Springbok squad inexplicably and without prior warning invited the travelling press to a social gathering with the management. The races, however, were too good to be missed, as the Melbourne Cup is a truly unique event. The city literally comes to a standstill during the running of the race, and the atmosphere as you make your way to the Flemington racecourse has to be experienced to be believed. It's as though the entire population has dressed up for the occasion, and there's lots of laughter and fun in the air.

And the fillies? Not nearly as exciting as you might be anticipating. I was making my way through the throng at the back of the grandstand to a marquee I had been invited to in the inner ring of the track when I was suddenly halted by a phalanx of black-suited security guards. The arrival of the governor? Perhaps Prince Harry? No, the blonde flutter of Paris and Nicky Hilton, enjoying yet another moment in the limelight. They had been much in the news, and it struck me that there were celeb watchers who would have paid to swap with me right then.

It should have been an omen, but needless to say, I didn't pick the winner. The big race was won by a filly, Makybe Diva, who would go on to become the first horse to win the race three successive times, also triumphing in 2004 and 2005. Makybe Diva was owned by a wealthy South Australian tuna fisherman who had cobbled together the champion filly's name from the first two letters of each of his five employees' names: Maureen, Kylie, Belinda, Diane and Vanessa.

There was another clue that I should have wagered a few dollars on Makybe Diva: her dam was a horse called Tugela. But I missed that too. Instead I had a good party with a group of erudite English supporters who enjoyed a good laugh and an intelligent chat about rugby. One of them turned out to be legendary British Lions prop Fran Cotton, and it did not take him long to regale the group with the tale of how I had come to earn one of the cleverest nicknames ever bestowed on a rugby journalist.

When I was covering the 1980 Lions tour to South Africa for the *Rand Daily Mail*, my first major assignment, I drew the ire of the players in my first match report (of the EP game), in which I stated that this team would struggle to emulate the all-conquering 1974 British Lions. It was a provocative statement to make, more so because all rugby tourists to South Africa tend to read English newspapers while being quite oblivious to the harsh things said about them by Afrikaans writers.

The tour progressed to the second international, in the Free State. One morning I walked into the breakfast room of the old Bloemfontein Hotel. On my way I had to pass the tables set aside for the Lions (these days teams dine in private), and Ray Gravell, the powerful red-headed, red-bearded Welsh centre who had become a huge character in the team, looked up from the *Mail* and uttered the words, in his distinctive Welsh accent, that have stuck with me ever since: 'Ah, Dan Retief ... Dan Retief ... I tell you what ... from now on we're going to call you Hand Relief! It's a good way of calling you a fooking wanker!'

Such was the glint in Grav's eye that I knew he meant it in jest (well, a little), and we would become good friends by the end of the tour. In fact, I was hugely flattered when I was the only journalist invited to attend the team's famous 'Sunday School' gathering on the last Sunday in Kimberley – an experience which left me much the worse for wear but nevertheless proud to have been accepted into the inner circle.

As they say in the classics, a great day was had by all at the Melbourne Cup, but elsewhere in the city, the Springboks were in no mood for fun. I was told by my fellow scribblers that the media gathering had been entirely missable, as some members of the management team had been rather belligerent, Rudi Joubert in particular.

When the team for the match against the All Blacks was announced, it had *kragdadig* (forceful) written all over it – a team to batter the All Blacks into submission. The Springboks fielded possibly their heaviest pack in history in order to crush the life out of the All Blacks, but instead they were made to look like plodding dinosaurs being run off their feet by the speedy Kiwis. The All Blacks scored three tries to nil, with Carlos Spencer the matador slaying the South African bull. A cheeky back-pass between his legs set up Joe Rokocoko for the final try of the match to seal a 29-9 victory. It was Joost van der Westhuizen's 89th and final Test appearance, and his sentiments afterwards summed up the dejection we all felt.

'It's just so bad to finish like that. Yes I'm sad, not about ending my career, but sad about losing like that.' Thinus Delport had been flattened in a tackle by Jerry Collins, and he was more to the point: 'It felt like I [had run] into a brick shithouse.' The All Blacks thus went on to Sydney, while the Springboks slunk home, defeated.

When the final whistle blew, the closed roof of the Telstra Dome symbolically put a lid on arguably the most miserable period in Springbok history. In three years, Viljoen and Straeuli had been in charge of 38 Tests (ironically, exactly the same number as Mallett), producing a combined record of 20 wins, 17 defeats and one draw. Neither could boast a win over the All Blacks, which, interestingly, meant that New Zealand coach John Mitchell could claim a 100% record against his country's arch-rivals: seven wins in seven matches. His run included the Springboks' 16-52 drubbing at Loftus Versfeld in 2003 and their 9-29 defeat in the quarter-final of RWC 2003. And, astonishingly, as it turned out in the unforgiving world of the international rugby coach, that would end up being not good enough.

Rudolf Straeuli's plea, after the miserable end-of-year tour to the UK in 2002, that he should be judged on the Springboks' performances, had now come back to haunt him. But some things were worth rescuing and cherishing in the debris of the failed RWC campaign. Deeply disappointed South African fans, however, would take quite a while to realise that. A heavy pall had settled over the South African game, and everyone wondered whether the Boks were in an irrevocable decline. All the off-field controversies, including the 'Geogate' scandal, and exiting the World Cup in the quarter-finals meant the end of Straeuli. In a wider context, it also led to the departure of MD Rian Oberholzer and president Silas Nkanunu, with the controversial Brian van Rooyen taking over the top post.

Although South Africa's preparations for the tournament had been severely stunted by the 'Geogate' scandal, it was nothing compared to how the players had been affected by their experiences at Kamp Staaldraad. Details of this exercise in deprivation would start emerging shortly after the Boks returned home.

17

Sting in the tail

Sydney was a city swathed in the gold of the Wallabies, but pubs, restaurants and the famous picture-postcard backgrounds of the Harbour Bridge and the Sydney Opera House were overrun by the white of England. 'Swing Low, Sweet Chariot', the Negro spiritual English fans had adopted as their anthem, drowned out 'Waltzing Matilda', the Aussies' favourite ditty. For me (as I explained in the Prologue) it had become quite an 'English' World Cup. I frequently shared in their irritation when they were abused by the Aussie press; a local tabloid, the *Daily Telegraph*, was particularly bad. On one occasion the paper printed a picture of Jonny Wilkinson with instructions on how to turn the image into a voodoo doll so that you could stick pins into it!

The Wallabies had pulled off a stirring, and somewhat unexpected, win over the All Blacks to put them in line to become the first side to retain the Webb Ellis Cup, as well as the first to win it three times (a record within reach of the Springboks in 2011). New Zealand's defeat meant the end of the road for John Mitchell,[*] who was fired in spite of setting an All Black coaching record of 23 Test wins from 27 games, an 85% winning record, the highest of any All Black coach in the professional era.

England had dispatched a disappointing France to set up a dream final between Old Blighty and its former penal colony. Wallaby coach Eddie Jones joked in the press about the England players' ages – an old Aussie tactic that had worked before, notably for the 1991 final – and their reliance on Wilkinson, but this time 'Dad's Army' would have the last laugh.

In an epic final, England defied predictions that they would use a relentless kicking game and repeatedly ran the ball, while both sides showed exceptional ball-handling skills as the floodlights of the Telstra Stadium (Sydney's Olympic Stadium in 2000) turned showers of rain into a silvery sheen. A perfect cross-kick by Stephen Larkham, which Lote Tuqiri plucked out of the air above Jason Robinson, gave Australia the lead in the sixth minute. But three penalties by Wilkinson moved England into the lead

---

[*] *Mitchell next became coach of the Force Super 14 team in Perth, and in 2010 joined the Lions in Johannesburg.*

(9-5), before a well-worked try to the speedy Robinson on the left gave them a sizeable 14-5 advantage at the break. However, Elton Flatley, playing at centre, produced a nerveless goal-kicking display to reel in Johnson's men. He slotted a crucial goal in the 80th minute to force the game into extra time, and another in the 99th minute to possibly bring on the first ever drop-off in RWC history.*

Of course the Springboks were long gone, knocked out in the quarter-finals, but at this moment, a solitary South African found himself in the middle of a huge dilemma, terrified at the prospect of what he might have to do next. Before 82 957 people in the Telstra Stadium in Sydney, Australia's biggest live television audience in history (4 015 723), a worldwide viewership topping 3 billion and with just 24 seconds of extra time left in the Rugby World Cup final, he would have to blow his whistle and award a point-blank penalty which, with the world's best goal-kicker in their ranks, would in all likelihood hand the Webb Ellis Cup to England.

André Watson was that lone South African, refereeing his second World Cup final (he had also been in charge in the 1999 final between Australia and France), and he now admits that he was secretly praying for Jonny Wilkinson to succeed with a drop goal in order to win the trophy for England.

'When I coach younger guys,' Watson says, 'I always emphasise that you should try not to end the game on a penalty; that your decision should not influence the outcome. But in that instance, I had no option. I was shouting at the Wallabies to go on side as England drove up to their posts and I would have had no choice but to award a penalty. There was no doubt that the Wallabies had been offside trying to stop England. I was actually thinking, "Please drop, please drop" as the ball came out to Wilkinson. And then, "Oh shit, what are you doing?" when I saw him dropping it onto his right foot rather than his left. I've never been happier to see a kick go over, because if it hadn't, I would have had to award a

---

* *Had the match ended in a deadlock after extra time, the final would, for the first time, have been decided by a drop-kick competition involving five different players: the first from directly in front of the posts on the 22; the second from behind the 22 between the 15-metre line and the touchline on the left-hand side of the posts; the third from behind the 22 between the 15-metre line and the touchline on the right-hand side of the posts; the fourth from behind the 22 between the 5-metre line and the touchline on the left-hand side of the posts; and the fifth from behind the 22 between the 5-metre line and the touchline on the right-hand side of the posts. And if it was still tied then, the process would start all over again with five different players, until some poor soul missed. As Watson said, 'After 44 days and 48 matches, no one wanted it to end like that.'*

penalty – a penalty that would have decided who won the cup. Can you imagine what an anticlimax that would have been?'

Watson's dilemma provides some insight into the incredible pressure referees experience, which is very often not appreciated by those of us who watch from the sidelines. But when Wilkinson made Watson's wish come true and he slotted the drop goal that sealed England's 20-17 victory, he provided the most appropriate ending to what had been a glorious World Cup in a country and city that revel in staging great sporting events.

When England had beaten South Africa four weeks earlier in Perth, closing down the game with a pair of Wilkinson drop goals, the *Sydney Morning Herald* had set the tone for the rest of the tournament with a taunting headline: 'Is that all you've got?' In the end, it proved to be enough.

Wilkinson was a curious and strangely insecure character whose introspective press conferences made you feel as if you were eavesdropping on a session between him and a psychologist. But when he dropped the ball onto his weaker right foot to win the World Cup for England, he succeeded in not only ensuring a knighthood for coach Clive Woodward, but also OBEs or MBEs for himself and the rest of the squad in the New Year Honours list. He also relieved André Watson of the responsibility of awarding the most difficult penalty of his distinguished career, though Watson later said, 'I think I would have had the balls to do it.'

But then came the moment when Watson could blow the whistle on the sweetest drop goal (they call it a field goal in Australia) he had ever awarded. The mighty white pack had been trundling forward, Wilkinson was in the zone, but Matt Dawson made a break, taking play 15 metres closer to the posts. Fittingly, Martin Johnson hit the ball up one more time, which propelled the Wallabies into an offside position in order to block the England flyhalf, who dropped the ball onto his weaker right foot and sent it spiralling across the bar and between the uprights. There was not enough time left for another kick-off from the centre spot. England had won 20-17. For the second time, a World Cup final was decided by a drop goal in extra time, and it drew the curtain on what the Aussies were quick to proclaim 'the greatest ever World Cup final'.

And the Australians were magnanimous in defeat. The *Sydney Morning Herald*, whose coverage of the tournament had been superb, proved that they could take the punch (after having dished out a few during the tournament!) by posting the following notice on the front page of their RWC supplement on the Monday after the final.

PUBLIC NOTICE

To England and its sports fans

Regarding your magnificent football team's 20-17 triumph in the Rugby World Cup final on November 22, on behalf of all Australians, we would like to admit the following:

You were not too old (although we hoped you would be when the game went into extra-time).

You were not too slow.

You scored as many tries as we did.

You kicked no more penalty goals than we did.

You did it with one of your own as coach (even though he did spend some formative years playing for Manly).

You are better singers than we are (and just quietly, 'Swing Low, Sweet Chariot' is growing on us, as is Jonny without an 'h').

You played with class, toughness and grace.

You were bloody superior ... and

You are, for the first time in 37 years, winners of a football World Cup.

AS A RESULT:

We believe Twickenham is a most fitting home for Bill, though we humbly remind you that, unlike the Ashes, you have to hand it over if you don't win it next time.

We concede the time has come to forgive you for using Australia as a dumping ground for your poor, weak and defenceless – even if the practice continues unabated every fourth summer.

We'll stop including the Socceroos' victory on our boastful list of triumphs over you and concede, upon reflection, it was only a friendly and you substituted your entire team at half-time.

We will no longer characterise your fans as beer-swilling, pot-bellied louts or knife-wielding hooligans and try to remember the sporting and enthusiastic supporters who did so much to make the final memorable.

We will stop calling for the International Rugby Board to change the scoring system. In fact, if you guarantee us a final as good as that one again, we'll ask them to actually *increase* the value of penalty and drop goals.

Needless to say, these sentiments lasted for about a day!

As the curtain came down on the 2003 Rugby World Cup, preparations for the next one had already begun and were toasted with champagne at the Four Seasons Hotel in downtown Sydney: *Bienvenue* to the *Coupe du Monde* in France in 2007. What a time that would be! But as I headed home to South Africa, my thoughts were on whether Springbok rugby could find a way out of the hole it had dug for itself. Whether this would be possible was down to the administrators, but in the midst of the despair that had enveloped the Springboks, it would take some time before anyone noticed that Straeuli had at least got some things right.

For example, in the desultory quarter-final against the All Blacks, the pack had included five notable names: John Smit, Victor Matfield, Bakkies Botha, Juan Smith and Danie Rossouw. Jaque Fourie and Schalk Burger were blooded, and Smit captained the team for the first time. None of us knew how important that would be until four years later, on a marvellous night in Paris.

But long before that moment, South Africans would be treated to the disgusting sight of the Springboks, their private parts covered by rugby balls, sitting in a pit of water looking utterly miserable. Kamp Staaldraad would become a blight on the proud history of the green-and-gold jersey, and the controversy would rumble on for months, with some tragic results.

The story broke in the press on the Friday after the team's return to South Africa. Archie Henderson, then sports editor of the *Argus*, ran a piece detailing what had happened at the bush bash. On the Sunday, Clinton van der Berg, who had managed to speak to Schalk Burger Snr and Gcobani Bobo, added more particulars in the *Sunday Times*. Henderson recalled that he, like the rest of the rugby-writing press, had received information that some odd things had happened. 'I had got wind of it like everyone else, I suppose. Something was amiss, and I thought I should try to find out and write the story. So I made one or two innocuous calls … and then something interesting happened.

'I got a call from Alan Dunne in management, who at the time was working with SA Rugby on a big ads deal. He said he believed I was working on a story involving SA Rugby and asked me to make sure I got comment from Magna Carta (the PR firm who was handling SA Rugby's account at the time). Needless to say I was furious at being put under subtle pressure not to go too far. I made more calls, but I wasn't really getting anywhere … until I managed to speak to Adriaan Heijns.

'He adopted a wheedling, evasive tone and suggested that we should meet over a cup of coffee. I had a sense that he was stalling, and I asked him straight out: "*Meneer, waarvoor is julle bang?*" ("Sir, what are you afraid of?") That's when he confirmed what had happened, and I realised it was a helluva story.

'Next I got hold of Gideon Sam [the team manager], who was quite cagey but did not deny anything – other than to say that there had been no shooting! I also called Werner Greeff [the Springbok fullback who had allegedly been the only player to object strongly to the treatment dished out to the players at the camp] and he just said, "*Ek het geen behoefte om daaroor te praat nie.*" ("I have no desire to talk about it.") But I had enough for what I thought was a bomb of a story. At the *Argus*'s Thursday conference, I said I was working on a strong story and suggested that it could be the front-page lead. [Henderson explained that he was following the story because the rugby writer Dale Granger was on leave.]

'On the Friday we ran the story across the top of the back page, but our assistant editor decided to move it to the front page. I think of our sister papers, only the *Pretoria News* ran a small piece. After that, Clinton van der Berg, who had spoken to "Groot" Schalk Burger and Gcobani Bobo, went big in the *Sunday Times*.

'The following week I got a call from Dale McDermott (who had been the Springbok team's video analyst under Harry Viljoen and Rudolf Straeuli when Kamp Staaldraad occurred) to meet him. "I want you to see something," he said, and we arranged to meet in the House of Coffees across the road from the *Argus*. He was sitting furtively near the back with his laptop and he showed me the pictures of Kamp Staaldraad. They were sensational – from a newspaperman's perspective, there's no other word for it. Then Dale said he wanted to sell [the pictures].'

Mark Keohane, who had started to freelance for the *Argus*, claimed in *Springbok Rugby Uncovered* that he had assisted in the writing of the Staaldraad revelations and admitted that he had pressurised McDermott to release his images. He claimed that the catalyst to his decision was a video, with images, that Heijns had peddled to the *Carte Blanche* television programme. He makes no reference to McDermott wanting to be paid for his photographs.

Henderson, however, says that a payment was made. 'Newspapers often buy photographs, and we certainly paid for the pics Dale was offering us. However, I have no idea what the sum was. It might have been R50 000 (a claim made to me by someone who did not want to be named), but I don't know.' Henderson, who is now sports editor of *The Times*, told me that McDermott might have approached him in the hope that he could help him realise his [McDermott's] ambition to become part of the coaching team at UCT.

I was told that a certain high-profile rugby personality had also been involved in sending McDermott to the *Argus*, but I was unable to get on-the-record verification. The whole repugnant episode took a tragic turn in January 2005 when McDermott, allegedly in deep depression about his role in the Staaldraad saga and his inability to get back onto the Springboks' auxiliary staff, took his own life.

In September 2006, the boil flared up again when Adriaan Heijns and his partners tried to release a DVD of the camp, ostensibly to show that Corné Krige had not given a truthful account of events in his biography. On reading newspaper advertisements of the imminent release of the DVD, titled *Kamp Staaldraad: Die Ware Verhaal* (*The True Story*), Werner Greeff and five other Springboks brought an urgent interdict to halt the distribution of the DVDs. And the man Greeff turned to for help was Johann Rupert, who, not for the last time, would have to use his considerable clout to mount a legal defence for the Springboks.

Rupert recalls getting a call from Greeff on a Sunday morning and, unable to raise anyone at SARU, springing to work. 'We got a lawyer [Gerrie Swart] and brought an interdict that night. Richard Bands represented the players before the High Court, and we succeeded in obtaining an interim interdict against Heijns and his cronies. I told Werner to rally as many players as he could to stand together against this invasion of their privacy and, as far as I know, the only one who didn't want to [join in] was Joost van der Westhuizen.

'This was one of the most distasteful things I've had to deal with. I don't know how the guys involved with the DVD thought they could get away with it – to me it was one of the biggest scandals ever.'

A few days later, Swart, of the legal firm Adams & Adams, obtained a full interdict, restraining Heijns and his fellow respondents from disseminating the DVD in any format.

For Van der Westhuizen, there was an added sting in the tail. The scrumhalf had applied for membership at Rupert's exclusive Leopard Creek golf club near Malelane on the Kruger Park border, but so incensed was the business magnate with his actions (Van der Westhuizen was allegedly the focus of attention in the banned *Staaldraad* DVD) that he instructed a committee member to return his deposit and cancel the application with the message, 'We don't want members who are not loyal to others.'

Springbok rugby was as low as it could go.

18

A man with a plan

The fallout caused by the Springboks' failure in Australia led to a dramatic 'clear-out' at the offices of SA Rugby. The coach and chief-executive positions were left vacant, but Silas Nkanunu was challenged, and vanquished, for the role of president by Brian van Rooyen, the controversial Johannesburg official from the Eldoranians club. Van Rooyen had been instrumental in the putsch that had led to the end of Louis Luyt's iron rule.

Van Rooyen was an unashamedly ambitious man, unafraid of controversy and confrontation, and he quickly replaced Nkanunu's rubber stamp with a teak gavel of his own. He wanted change, he wanted it fast and, if he had his way, Chester Williams would succeed Rudolf Straeuli as the Springbok team's coach.

Straeuli's departure had triggered a search for a new man to be handed the 'poisoned chalice', and in spite of Van Rooyen's desire to display dynamic leadership, the process was as haphazard as anything that had gone before. It was announced that four candidates would be considered: Heyneke Meyer of the Blue Bulls, André Markgraaff, still scheming away in the background, the little-known Dumisani Mhani from Border, and Chester Williams, then the national Sevens coach. Markgraaff and Meyer, giving credence to the obvious lack of thought that had gone into the process, declared themselves unavailable almost immediately, and for once some of the provinces, stirred up by the Sharks, objected to the nominees and demanded that the net be cast wider.

This was done, and five more contenders were asked to apply. Three of these had previous experience with the Springboks: Carel du Plessis, Gert Smal and Rudi Joubert. The other candidates added were Pieter de Villiers (who then spelt his Christian name with an 'i'), Jerome Paarwater and Jake White, a young coach who had had a very good run with the Under-21s. He was employed as SA Rugby's technical coach at the time, but he seemed to have been added to the list as an afterthought, perhaps to swell the numbers.

The whole process was certainly a mess, and I posed this question in a column: 'How could one have confidence in a process that had started with four nominees, of whom two had immediately withdrawn, and which had then been increased to eight candidates, including one who had previously been dismissed from the post?' Nick Mallett, who I thought was the obvious coach to reinstate, was clearly *persona non grata* at SARFU and not even considered. I wrote: 'The whole business of finding a new Springbok coach is indeed a tragicomedy and certainly does not broadcast a message that the people in charge of South African rugby know what they're doing.' It was a line that certainly wasn't unique to that particular year!

The candidates underwent psychometric tests, their rugby know-how was tested and they were interviewed on their plan of action to pull Springbok rugby out of the doldrums. Eventually it was announced that the committee charged with appointing the new coach had reached a decision. The announcement would be made at a hotel near Paarl in the Western Cape. As with most decisions taken in camera by SA Rugby, it soon slipped out on whom the choice had fallen. Officials nevertheless went through with the charade, and Jake White had to wait out of sight in an adjoining room so that he could make a dramatic entrance when Van Rooyen read out his name to the media.

I was sent on one of my sporadic SuperSport assignments to cover the announcement, and that evening, while waiting to board my return flight at Cape Town airport, Brian van Rooyen and I spotted each other in the business-class lounge. I joined him at his table and we started chatting. Naturally, the talk turned to South Africa's ninth coach (not including Gerrie Sonnekus) in 12 post-isolation years.

'What do you think of the appointment?' Van Rooyen asked.

'Well, I have to say, even though I obviously knew who had been given the job, I was a little surprised. You know, I, ahem … I thought there might have to be, ahem, a nod to, you know … the transformation imperative,' I mumbled. This was the euphemistic term white South Africans used when talking about selections in sport that fell under the quota system. 'I was quite surprised that you decided to go with one of the least experienced of the candidates.'

Van Rooyen surprised me by being fearlessly candid. 'You know, if it had been down to me, it would have been Chester. I wanted it to be Chester. I thought the time was right for us to appoint a black coach. I thought it was a necessary thing to do,' he said. 'But you know, when we saw the results of the tests and listened to their plans of action, Jake's was far and away the best. When I saw the results and listened to him, I realised that he was the best man for the job.'

Back in Johannesburg, I ended up giving Van Rooyen a lift home because of a mix-up with his driver. This chance meeting would lead to the second time I was approached to act as a media consultant to either SA Rugby or the Springbok team, but more about that later.

It's a staggering thought that White, the man who would be at the helm for the next great episode in Springbok rugby and who would hold the job for a considerably longer period than any of his predecessors, came that close to *not* getting the job. Interestingly, the man who succeeded White as Under-21 coach was none other than Peter de Villiers.

Years later a tale would emerge that I have never been able to verify – for obvious reasons. The story goes that as SA Rugby's technical director, White had been tasked with drawing up the questionnaire the candidates would be asked to complete. Apparently this questionnaire was not changed once he was added to the list of candidates, so he ended up answering his own questions. As the person who conveyed this piece of intriguing gossip quipped, 'Jake got 60%.' A little puerile, I know, but could that have been the reason why White's replies were so impressive that they were able to sway Van Rooyen, a man determined to name Chester Williams as the next Springbok coach?

Whatever the reason, Jake White turned out to be an exceptionally good decision by a body not known for making them. When he took over, the Springboks were ranked No. 6 in the world, and by the time he left, they were not only No.1, but also the world champions. On the way, he created a golden generation of players who, if they don't end up being acclaimed as the best ever, will certainly be right up there with the great teams of 1937, 1951/52, 1960/61, 1995 and 1997/98.

White got things right from the start, and it was not until I collaborated on the making of SuperSport's *Springbok Saga* series, which covered Springbok rugby from one World Cup victory in 1995 to the next in 2007, that a pattern emerged that was quite astonishing in its prescience.

White, although not the righteous great white knight he and his chums in the press would often portray him as, was a man with a plan. His clarity of thought was obvious, although not generally appreciated, when he named John Smit as his captain long before the start of the international season in June. White also wanted to be able to select players who had gone to play overseas, which would eventually be of enormous benefit to the team. And he set about building a squad based on his conviction that the key to success in international rugby was players with size, speed, mobility and versatility.

White raised a few eyebrows with the faith he placed in John Smit, whose qualities as a player and a leader were often called into question, but his next move caused consternation among some of the dial-a-quote former Springboks, who foresaw more disaster ahead for the national team. White recalled Os du Randt after a four-year absence due to knee problems and, recognising the need for a reliable goal-kicker, sent for Percy Montgomery in Wales and Jaco van der Westhuyzen in Japan. Van der Westhuyzen was earmarked as the man who would solve the enduring problem at flyhalf, a plan that did not come off quite as well as White would've hoped. But with Du Randt and Montgomery, the new coach struck pay dirt – both would be enormously influential on the route he plotted to reach France in 2007 with a world-beating team of players.

Whereas White's immediate predecessors had become bogged down in their desire to win single Test matches, he had a long-term vision. His first Test in charge was against Ireland in Bloemfontein, and he astonished the squad he had selected by telling them that his aim was neither to beat Ireland nor to reverse an appalling record in the Tri Nations, but to win the Rugby World Cup in Paris in October 2007.

White's first Springbok squad contained only a few new caps – Fourie du Preez among them – displaying his conviction that there was little wrong with the quality of South African players. But it would not be until 2008, while I was working on *Springbok Saga*, that I noticed the amazing template he had created. For his first Test in charge, White picked the following set of forwards: Jacques Cronjé, Pedrie Wannenburg, **Schalk Burger**, **Victor Matfield**, **Bakkies Botha**, Eddie Andrews, **John Smit** and **Os du Randt**. Gerrie Britz replaced Cronjé and **CJ van der Linde** came on for Andrews. **Fourie du Preez** made his debut at scrumhalf, and **Jaque Fourie**, although not used, was among the reserves. That meant that six of the forwards and two of the backs who would be in the side that won the World Cup in Paris three and a half years later were in the first team selected by White.

Percy Montgomery had been unavailable for the first Test, but for the second, against Ireland, he was back (No. 9 of the 2007 RWC final team) and, with his new two-step kicking style, contributed 16 points to the Boks' 26-17 victory. This match also included an awkward postscript to the year before. With Bakkies Botha, the Man of the Match in the first Test, unavailable because of injury, the No. 4 jersey went to Quinton Davids, who was replaced by Geo Cronjé in the 71st minute – thus making Jacques and Geo Cronjé the first pair of brothers to appear together in a Test since Carel and Michael du Plessis in 1989.

The next Test, at Loftus, was significant, as it was the first attended by Nelson Mandela since the World Cup final at Ellis Park in 1995. Wales were thrashed 53-18. White was also making progress in the delicate area of representivity, with six players of colour – Breyton Paulse, Wayne Julies, Bolla Conradie, Hanyane Shimange, Quinton Davids and Eddie Andrews – the biggest number yet, playing in the Test. Three of them scored.

Next up was a trip to the antipodes for the Tri Nations, but before the start of the tournament, a match had been scheduled against the Pacific Islands, a team made up of representatives from Samoa, Tonga and Fiji, in Gosford, New South Wales, Australia. The match was part of the IRB's efforts to uplift the islands, but it turned out to be a significant occasion for Montgomery, as he broke Naas Botha's long-standing South African record of 312 points in Tests with a haul of 18 points, which took him to 313. The Boks charged into a 33-0 lead, but then were made to fight for it as the Islanders hit back. The Boks eventually won 38-24.

Four wins in succession under White meant that the Boks' downward graph had bottomed out, but the start of the Tri Nations brought him his first taste of defeat when the team went down 21-23 to the All Blacks in Christchurch. The Boks scored their first try within 23 seconds as John Smit surprised Justin Marshall at the back of a ruck and Jaco van der Westhuyzen and De Wet Barry put Jean de Villiers (playing on the wing) in.

Dan Carter, who would be the Boks' nemesis for many years to come, kicked the All Blacks back into the lead, but a great break by Fourie du Preez put the Boks back in front when Jacques Cronjé scored. Then Du Preez scored one of his own for the Boks to lead 21-12 at the break. In the second half, the Boks defended heroically to keep the black machine at bay, conceding just a pair of penalties to Dan Carter and Carlos Spencer. Smit's men were on the brink of the first Springbok win in New Zealand since 1998, only to have the match snatched away in the dying seconds after a botched line-out throw (a long one by Smit) allowed the All Blacks the attacking platform they needed to get Doug Howlett over in the corner. Carter nailed the conversion.

The next engagement was against the Wallabies at the Subiaco Oval in Perth, and lighting struck twice in the space of a week as a try by the opposition's right wing late in the game robbed the Boks of victory. What made it even worse was that the try was scored by Jake White's SA Under-21 captain, Clyde Rathbone! South Africa were outscored in tries (4-3) in a pulsating match that marked George Gregan's 100th Test cap, the Wallabies winning 30-26. There was despair that the Boks had been unable to break their hoodoo Down Under, but the two narrow defeats, by two and four points respectively, meant that they had collected two bonus points, which would prove to be crucial.

The first return Test was against New Zealand at Ellis Park, and finally there were signs that the Boks were on their way back. After being 0-10 down at one stage (thanks to a fine try by Mils Muliaina), the Boks recovered to produce one of their all-time great Tests. Marius Joubert scored a hat-trick (the first against the All Blacks since Ray Mordt in the 'Flour Bomb' Test in 1981), and the Boks ended a run of eight successive defeats against New Zealand as emphatic 40-26 winners.

In a memorable moment during the game, Joubert counted off the three tries on his fingers with Jean de Villiers. In size and looks, Joubert was a player reminiscent of the great John Gainsford, and he was earmarked to be one of White's key strikers. Unfortunately he would run into injury problems, which, sadly, meant that he was not part of the eventual 2007 winning team.

The finale of the Tri Nations series took place at the ABSA Stadium in Durban, with the Springboks suddenly finding themselves in a position to win the tournament for the second time since 1998. The confidence in the side was growing, and they built a lead of 23-7. But they then had to survive playing with 14 men for most of the last 11 minutes following the overlapping sin-binnings of Montgomery (69th min) and Paulse (78th min) by referee Paddy O'Brien.

The Wallabies scored two tries to cut back the lead, but the Boks managed to hang on to win 23-19 and claim the Tri Nations trophy. The bonus points for tries picked up at Ellis Park and the two on the road for finishing within seven points had seen them through to victory.

Victor Matfield turned in a Man of the Match performance by dominating the line-outs, making the scoring pass for Joe van Niekerk's try and then running in a superb touch-down of his own after Paulse had tapped back his own up-and-under. It was also picked as the Try of the Year.

The turnaround exceeded the wildest expectations of long-suffering South African fans, but the year-end tour to play all four Home Unions showed that White had not yet perfected the product. In the Test against

Wales at the Millennium Stadium in Cardiff, the Boks raced into a big lead (38-22) with 10 minutes to go, but then lost concentration and conceded two late tries, including an embarrassing pushover try right on the final whistle after White had become confused by the stadium clock and, thinking that time had expired, sent on a raft of replacements, including Tim Dlulane and Michael Claassens for their debuts. Fortunately, though, the Millennium Stadium timekeeper could not stop the clock altogether, and when the final whistle blew, the Boks were still 38-36 to the good.

The next stop on what White had embraced as a 'Grand Slam tour' would be Dublin. Their base was the Fitzpatrick Castle Hotel in the up-market suburb of Dalkey, a 35-minute train ride from Dublin, famous for being the home of Bono of U2. There, the new coach learnt a valuable lesson about how careful and guarded a Springbok coach needs to be. At a press conference, White walked straight into a leading question when he was asked how many Irish players he would include in the Springbok team. Without thinking, he answered, 'None.'

He could have qualified his answer by saying that as the Springbok coach he was being loyal to his own boys but, even though he said he might look at Ireland's lock pairing and centre Brian O'Driscoll, he managed to create the impression that he did not rate the Irish players. After all, his charges had beaten them in South Africa in his first two Tests. My former colleague Clinton van der Berg and I turned to each other and whispered, 'That will come back to bite him.'

Dalkey turned out to be a memorable stop. I found myself 'back on the beat', as it were, having travelled to the UK with the SuperSport team of Hugh Bladen, Kobus Wiese, Russell Belter and Jacques van Schalkwyk. We'd endured an unforgettable trip from Heathrow to Cardiff in a rental car that was much too small for the five us, especially for Kobus and his mighty suitcases. There was also Russell's camera equipment, so three of us crammed into the back seat with the cases piled up to the roof on our laps and absolutely no view of the surroundings.

On arrival in Ireland, the rental car booked at Dublin Airport was again too small, and I received a call from SuperSport saying that I was excess baggage and could I travel on my own. I was miffed at being pushed out, but it turned out to be the best call ever, because I linked up with the travelling writers and once again got to experience the hospitality, gentle humour and quaintness of Ireland. The press always find a pub to call home, and in Dalkey we discovered The Club, set in what appeared to be an old theatre, allegedly Bono's favourite port of call for a pint. We asked the barman if this was true, and he replied, 'That would be right, but ya wouldna recognise him if ya saw him. He's a fookin l'il roont!'

The Irish press rubbed their hands in glee at White's thoughtless comment, which made for great copy, but not nearly as much as Ireland's coach Eddie O'Sullivan, who fired up his team by allegedly having the newspapers delivered to their rooms and pasting the offending quote on the team-room wall.

Accustomed as they are to dry, warm weather, the Boks always struggle in the arctic northern conditions, and not only did they give a bad showing at rickety old Lansdowne Road, but they were also on the receiving end of an even worse performance by New Zealand referee Paul Honiss.

Listening devices or field ears (*veldore*), which can tune in to the referee, were for sale at the venue, and for once they worked really well. I was astonished to hear Honiss's monologue as he literally shouted the teams through the game. On television, the sound of the referee is more muted, and often blocked out, but when his is the only voice you're hearing, it justifies the view of a player like David Campese, who believes that refs should be taken off the mike because it makes them play to the audience.

With his fearless attacking style, Schalk Burger had made an impactful entry into Test rugby, but it did mean that he was often yellow-carded. In the first Test under White in Bloemfontein, again in Cardiff and on this afternoon in Dublin, it seemed as if the referee was watching only one player. 'Get out, No. 6!' 'Let go, No. 6!' 'Back, No. 6!' it rang in our ears as the flank with his striking blond mop hurtled around the field. It came as no surprise when he was eventually yellow-carded – when he was actually standing a few metres from where the offence had occurred.

However, the departure of 'No. 6' to the sin bin was not the worst of Honiss's errors. In the 20th minute, Joe van Niekerk was penalised to the left of the Boks' posts for handling the ball in the ruck, and Honiss told Smit to 'talk to your players'. Smit did his bidding, but while the skipper's back was turned, Ronan O'Gara tapped the ball to himself and scurried to the line for a try; Bakkies Botha was the only Bok to react, trying to make a desperate tackle.

In spite of Smit's vociferous protestations, the try stood, and it eventually made all the difference. An inspired Irish team put an end to the Springboks' Grand Slam dream with their first win, 17-12, over the Springboks in 35 years. With the mood as dark and sombre as a pint of Guinness, it hardly registered that Breyton Paulse had become the first player of colour to earn 50 Test caps. In the pubs around Lansdowne Road and on the train back to Dalkey, the sporting Irish, who win as well as they lose, helped us to lighten up. Spotting my partner Linda's Springbok scarf, an elderly gent leant over and said: 'You know, if we'd known how good ya were, we woulda played our best team!'

Breyton Paulse would be a central figure in the next debacle White had to deal with. It was an incident that upset the team, but which did not become common knowledge until White discussed the episode in his biography, *In Black and White*. For their next game, at Twickenham, White had selected Jaque Fourie on the wing instead of Paulse, because he feared that England would exploit Paulse's lack of height with cross-kicks. But then Brian van Rooyen forced White to include Paulse to comply with the quota demands.

It turned out to be another horrible day for the Boks. Up against the current world champions, the Springboks were simply outmuscled in the forwards, and flyhalf Charlie Hodgson, standing in for Jonny Wilkinson, played the game of his life. England won 32-16 – their sixth win in a row over the Boks. However, there were some significant moments for the Boks: **Bryan Habana** came off the bench to earn his first cap, scoring a try with his first touch of the ball, and **Danie Rossouw** was another significant substitution, replacing AJ Venter and playing at No. 8, with Van Niekerk moving to the flank.

Habana and Rossouw were pieces No. 10 and 11 in the puzzle that White was building for RWC 2007. However, at the time White was so upset by a second successive defeat that he used the post-match press conference to rebuke his players and send a sharp message to SA Rugby administrators about what he would require on the road forward. 'It was like Standard 8s against matrics,' he said. In his opinion, the Springboks had lost their traditional edge and the players had simply not been strong or tough enough.

There were two more Tests to be played in White's first year in charge, and both were won with some ease – Scotland were whipped 45-10 in Edinburgh, and then the Boks took the long way home to beat Argentina 39-7 at the Velez Sarsfield Stadium in Buenos Aires. At Murrayfield, the Scots were so bad that the Springboks were able to power to a big victory in spite of having locks Matfield and Botha simultaneously yellow-carded by referee Nigel Williams. There were debuts for Solly Tyibilika (who scored a try) and Gurthrö Steenkamp, some intercept magic from Habana, and three drop goals from flyhalf Jaco van der Westhuyzen, who probably had his best game ever in the Springbok jersey.

In Argentina, up against a Puma side stripped of most of its overseas players, the Boks started like a house on fire, scoring five tries in 30 minutes, to lead 36-0. But then they slipped into packing-for-home mode. Argentina scored their only try just before half-time, and the tourists were able to add just a penalty in the second period. The final score: 39-7.

The transformation in the Springboks' performances was phenomenal. The year's daunting programme of 13 Tests had yielded nine wins, a climb from sixth (the lowest the Boks had ever been) to fourth on the IRB's ranking list, and victory in the Tri Nations. Even so, White felt his makeover was far from complete. His efforts, however, were recognised when he was chosen as the IRB's Coach of the Year at season's end from a shortlist that also included Grand Slam–winning French coach Bernard Laporte, New Zealand Sevens guru Gordon Tietjens and Tomaz Morais, who had taken Portugal to European Nations Cup success and RWC Sevens qualification.

Schalk Burger, who had made a massive impact on the game and was still only 21, became the South African as well as the IRB's Player of the Year, and the Springboks scooped the Team of the Year award – fair recognition that not only South Africans but the rest of the top rugby-playing nations were pleased to see the Boks back.

You would have thought that with such achievements White would have been the flavour of the month at SA Rugby, but instead of the adulation he might have expected, the cracks were already beginning to show. Brian van Rooyen's abrasive and dictatorial style (ironically exactly what he used to criticise in Louis Luyt) was causing deep fissures in the administration. But White's insistence on being given carte blanche in the running of the Springboks was also getting up the noses of those officials who had their own political agendas.

The supposed solution – that White would report directly to Van Rooyen – was not well received by administrators who feared that he might become a law unto himself. Not for the last time, White was forced to demand that his contract be confirmed until after the 2007 World Cup.

In 2005, the Boks suffered losses to France, Australia and New Zealand, but they did have the satisfaction of being the only side to beat the All Blacks, who had whitewashed the British Lions 3-0, won the Tri Nations and closed out the year with a successful Grand Slam tour to the UK.

Significantly, the Boks also managed to get a monkey off their backs with their first away win in the Tri Nations since 1998. Two long-range tries by Bryan Habana helped them to a 22-19 victory over the Wallabies in Perth.

The Springboks arguably played a better Tri Nations than they had the year before, when bonus points favoured them, and they had the satisfaction of climbing to No. 2 on the world rankings – their highest placing since the rankings were introduced in 2003. White had often warned of the 'second-season syndrome', but he was certainly not afflicted by it. His belief in continuity and a settled squad was highlighted by the fact that he named only four new caps (Ricky Januarie, Tonderai Chavhanga, Gary Botha and Meyer Bosman) – the fewest ever in the post-isolation era – as he worked towards expanding the squad of internationally competent players beyond the match XV.

White insisted on the three Ss – size, speed and strength – and ingrained his so-called rush defence in the team. This entailed inside defenders coming quickly off the line and players on the outside going up fast (rather like the horns-of-the bull tactic employed by King Shaka of the Zulus) in order to compress the space and put opponents under pressure. One consequence was that they were regularly accused of being offside, but a rash of intercept tries, particularly by Jean de Villiers and Bryan Habana, meant that not too much heed was paid to what coaches Graham Henry (who had been named coach of the All Blacks in 2004) and Eddie Jones had to say.

The year got off to a record start – if the rugby equivalent of bludgeoning seals can be claimed as a record. Uruguay were the helpless pups, the Test was awarded to East London, and the Boks went on a 134-3 rampage, which also provided Zimbabwean-born Chavangha with the individual record of six Test tries. In the 52nd minute, **Juan Smith**, returning from injury, replaced Solly Tyibilika – he was thus player No. 12 of White's eventual World Cup–winning side.

During the rest of the season, three incidents seemed to substantiate South African fans' suspicions that officialdom was prejudiced against the Springboks. In the Test against Argentina, Jean de Villiers was yellow-carded for pushing Luis Borges, causing him to fall over advertising hoardings at the side of the field. But the Springbok centre, in fact, had had the presence of mind to grab the Puma wing's leg, saving him from a three-metre fall into a moat that surrounded the Velez Sarsfield Stadium field. In the next Test, Percy Montgomery, of all people, was shown a red card after his second yellow-card offence, a high tackle on Shane Williams. The card was expunged on appeal, as Montgomery had not been the guilty party when incurring the first yellow card.

The third incident occurred in the final Test of the year, a desultory 20-26 loss to France at the Stade de France. It was blighted by a shockingly unfair citing and penalty against John Smit, who was carrying the ball and charging forward when he thrust out his elbow to fend off his counterpart, Jerome Thion, making contact with his throat area. Later Smith was cited and given an unjustifiably harsh six-week ban for something that had clearly been accidental. The decision seemed to confirm that the French and the disciplinary tribunal had reacted to the fact that Thion had been injured (fractured larynx) rather than having judged the specifics of Smit's actions. They also had not taken into account the Springbok captain's flawless record.

White's third year in charge, 2006, was fraught with problems, many of them of his own making, but even though he railed at administrators and threatened to quit, parts of his long-term plan continued to fall into place. In July, he summoned **Butch James** from South Africa (ironically to replace a forward after Danie Rossouw was injured) to take over at flyhalf from Jaco van der Westhuyzen and André Pretorius. James had not played in a Test since he turned out at inside centre in that awful 3-53 loss to England at Twickenham in 2002, and was thus piece No. 13 of the developing RWC XV puzzle. And in September, **JP Pietersen** (No. 14) made his debut at fullback in a Tri Nations Test against the Wallabies at Ellis Park.

François Steyn made his debut at the age of 19, ironically on the wing, against Ireland in November, which meant that with just under a year to go to France 2007, all the players who would start the final had turned out for White. Of the seven reserves, **CJ van der Linde** (2004) and **André Pretorius** (2005) had featured in White's teams for some time, while he gave **Wynand Olivier** and **Johann Muller** their debuts against Scotland in June. **Ruan Pienaar** won his first cap off the bench against New Zealand in August, and the final pieces of the puzzle were the recall of **Wikus van Heerden** and debuts for the **Du Plessis** brothers, **Jannie** and **Bismarck**, on the Tri Nations tour in July 2007.*

---

* *The 22-man squad that took part in the RWC final at the Stade de France on 20 October 2007 consisted of: Percy Montgomery, JP Pietersen, Jaque Fourie, François Steyn, Bryan Habana, Butch James, Fourie du Preez, Danie Rossouw, Schalk Burger, Juan Smith, Victor Matfield, Bakkies Botha, CJ van der Linde, John Smit, Os du Randt.*
Reserves: Bismarck du Plessis, Jannie du Plessis, Johann Muller, Wikus van Heerden, Ruan Pienaar, Wynand Olivier, André Pretorius.

White's consistent selection practices and commitment to the players he picked resulted in another of his prerequisites for success – experience – becoming a feature of the team. Players built up an instinctive understanding of each other and grew confident in one another's abilities. As one victory followed another, new records were set for the highest number of caps in a team. There was no denying that White was a man with a plan.

19
Jake in the firing line

If ever proof were required of the old theatrical superstition that a bad dress rehearsal leads to a good performance, it was South Africa's rugby year of 2006 – the season before the 2007 Rugby World Cup in France.

In the introduction to my chronological framework for the *Springbok Saga* series, I described it thus: 'An eventful year that you would never have said was the precursor to South Africa winning the World Cup in France in 2007. In what was the 10th anniversary of the start of professional rugby, there was continued drama about the position of coach Jake White, particularly after a five-match losing streak that matched the worst in history and which included the second-worst defeat ever – 0-49 to the Wallabies in Brisbane. Schalk Burger seriously injured his neck, Bakkies Botha sat out for the Test season with Achilles tendon problems and the Springboks, by losing to France at Newlands, surrendered their undefeated home record under White.'

That was just a brief summary of what had happened to the Springboks, because there was more, much more. Quietly spoken Oregan Hoskins, the president of the Natal Sharks, brought the tumultuous reign of Brian van Rooyen to an end by challenging for, and winning, the role of president of SA Rugby; Jake White misguidedly mentioned that he might apply for the job of England's director of coaching; and a carbuncle of SA Rugby's own making, the Southern Spears, headed by the maverick Tony McKeever, threatened to burst, with disastrous consequences.

It was the first year that the Super Rugby tournament was extended to the Super 14, but it was business as usual when the title was claimed by New Zealand for the ninth time in 11 years. The Crusaders beat the Hurricanes in a final rendered almost unwatchable on TV, as well as from the far reaches of the stadium, when a thick fog settled on Christchurch. The Bulls finished a distant fourth behind the Waratahs, narrowly edging the Sharks on points-differential, but were well beaten in their semi-final by the Crusaders. Their glory years would coincide with the revival that would also carry the Springboks to World Cup glory.

Springbok duties commenced with an unofficial Test match against a World XV at Ellis Park, the most significant facet being the return of André

Snyman from overseas and a start for Hanyane Shimange. The Boks scored a streaky win, 30-27, thanks to 10 successful penalties, nine by Percy Montgomery and one by Gaffie du Toit.

Scotland, the next visitors, were pretty much overpowered by a vastly experienced Springbok side. André Snyman, on the wing, returned to Test rugby for the first time since 2003, Wynand Olivier made his debut, replacing Jean de Villiers, and Johann Muller made his debut replacing Victor Matfield. Montgomery continued his outstanding form with a contribution of 21 points from a try, two conversions and four penalties to take the Boks to a 36-16 result in Durban.

The second Test, in Port Elizabeth, was far more eventful, but there were few indications of the behind-the-scenes machinations in which Jake White was involved. Montgomery was once more the driving force – again scoring 21 points (seven penalties) – in a disappointing Bok performance some notches down from the previous week. It was made much worse by a neck injury to Schalk Burger, which, at the time, was thought could end his career.

Part of the problem might have been a rejigged backline, with Olivier (making his first start) and Snyman moving infield to accommodate Bryan Habana returning from injury. Scotland put up a spirited performance and might have run the Boks even closer had some refereeing decisions not gone against them. Montgomery's burst of points took him over the 600-mark in the 29-15 victory.

The next Test, against a supposedly tired French side containing many players who had just participated in their national club finals, exposed deep fissures in the relationship between White and his employers. Before a press conference ahead of the match, White was filmed in deep conversation with Mark Keohane, who had launched an extremely successful website (www.keo.co.za) following his resignation as Springbok media manager in 2003. Keohane was no longer on the rugby beat full time, but when the press conference started, his was the first question.

He asked White whether the upcoming Test would be his last as Springbok coach. This line of questioning was surprising, given that while there had been grumblings about White, there was no indication that he was ready to quit or on the verge of being dismissed. The whole thing seemed orchestrated (administrators and the other writers in the room certainly thought so), and White used Keohane's question to reveal that he had asked for, and been given permission, to talk to the RFU about England's vacant director of coaching position.

It reeked of a set-up and was not a clever thing to do. White had over-estimated his own importance. He was not a Springbok and had misread how his statement would be received by former Boks, who thought he showed little respect for the position he filled. Frik du Preez, for instance, was quoted as saying: 'If the Springboks are not good enough for you, Jake, then get on your bicycle and go to England.'

I had been flown to Cape Town to be part of the Chris Burger/Petro Jackson Players' Fund banquet, and was able to have a memorable meeting with one of my heroes, former Springbok fullback HO de Villiers. Joel Stransky and I had set up a game of golf with another former Bok flyhalf, Lance Sherrell, at Steenberg, a round in which the two No. 10s between them threw 10 birdies at me, and then we went for tea with HO, who was recovering from knee-replacement surgery. HO's appraisal of the forthcoming Test match turned out to be spot-on.

He declared that he would have loved to play against a rush defence, such as the Springboks', and that if he had been advising the French, he would have told them to chip from inside centre into the hole behind the Bok backline and to line up deeper, wait for the fast-approaching defender, and then beat him with a jink.

As it turned out, it was almost as if French coach Bernard Laporte had had a microphone hidden on HO's veranda as *Les Tricolores* overturned an 11-23 deficit after 50 minutes to win 36-26. Vincent Clerc scored one of their tries from a chip over the top, and Yannick Jauzion sidestepped the rushing De Wet Barry on his own 10-metre line, ran clear and linked with Florian Fritz to provide Clerc with his second try and France's fourth. With the French likely to be the Springboks' semi-final opponents in France the following year, White's honeymoon was well and truly over. After the next Test match, some administrators were determined to sue for divorce.

Having not travelled regularly with the team, I was not as *au fait* with rugby affairs as I had been on the *Sunday Times*, but for a brief moment it seemed I might be right in the thick of things. I was attending an SA Rugby Strategic Planning workshop convened by SA Rugby President's Council member Jannie Ferreira, the president of the Golden Lions, ostensibly to help draft 'a strategy for SA Rugby (2006–2015)' at a conference centre in Muldersdrift. I was surprised to be included on a panel with, among others, President's Council members Ferreira and James Stoffberg (Leopards), Barend van Graan, CEO of the Blue Bulls, national selectors Peter Jooste and Ian McIntosh, age-group coach Eric Sauls, Cape administrator Yagya Sakier and former Springbok Owen Nkumane (Toby Titus,

Avril Malan and Gerrit Pool could not attend), but I was utterly unimpressed by the process. Ferreira did not seem to know where to start or what he wanted to achieve, so we ended up doing a SWOT analysis of SA Rugby.

During the lunch break I took the messages on my cell phone, and one of them was to urgently call Gert Roets at SuperSport. His query was short and sweet. 'Can you go to Australia and New Zealand with the Springboks as their media liaison officer?' This was on the Monday. The team was leaving on Thursday.

'I'll have to check that my passport is in order and sort out a few things, but if the team needs me, I'll do it,' I replied. Roets then asked me to meet with Oregan Hoskins the following evening at the Sun International Hotel at Jan Smuts Airport (it would be renamed OR Tambo a few months later), where a media session on SA Rugby's Transformation Charter was due to be held.

The next morning I made preparations to fly off for five weeks (the Tri Nations had been expanded to include an additional game for each of the teams), but then got a call from Hoskins saying that my services would no longer be required. 'We'll get together soon and I'll explain it to you,' he said, but we never did have the meeting.

I was further taken aback some time later when Hoskins told me that I would be 'surprised to hear that it was Ali Bacher [who had spent a year as the sponsor's representative on the SA Rugby Board] who was against your appointment'. I'd had a few meetings with Bacher and had provided him, and the new chairman of the board Mpumelelo Tshume, with quite a bit of background information, invariably involving the extent of rugby transformation, they had asked for. I don't know whether Jake White was ever asked what he thought about me joining his team.

That was the second time I was approached to link up with SA Rugby. The first had been equally unsatisfactory, as would be the third, soon after Peter de Villiers was appointed. One evening in April 2005 I was at Parkview Golf Club when my phone rang. It was then president Brian van Rooyen, who told me that he needed me to come and work for him as his media consultant. Van Rooyen said he had discussed my being seconded to SA Rugby with SuperSport's CEO Imtiaz Patel and asked that we set up a meeting. We ended the call and my phone rang again almost immediately – this time it was Patel to tell me to expect a call from Van Rooyen, adding that if we could come to an arrangement, he was in favour of my linking up with SARU.

It was a rock-and-a-hard-place situation for me, and I said that if SuperSport wanted me to do it I would take it on, but with reservations. So I met with Van Rooyen at his business premises, Labat in Constantia Park near Roodepoort. Apart from SA Rugby's PR apparatus, the rugby boss had also retained the services of rugby journalist André Bester, whom he claimed had helped him to swing certain key votes in his election campaign. I was aware, though, that Bester's role was a point of contention with a number of unions and mentioned this as a potential conflict.

Van Rooyen said he had identified the problem and that he would be cutting ties with Bester. I also said that I was concerned about the ethics of working for Van Rooyen/SA Rugby while I was being paid by SuperSport, and that the media might take a dim view of such an arrangement. Revealingly, Van Rooyen kept repeating, 'You will be attached to the office of the president,' as though he really liked the ring of it.

We scheduled a follow-up meeting the next week to sort out the details, including remuneration. I reported to Patel on the progress we were making, but I remained unconvinced that the arrangement was practical or that I was committed to making it work. On arriving at Labat the following week, my phone rang while I was still in the car park. It was Van Rooyen, who said that he had thought about what to do about André Bester and that he had a role for him. To my surprise, when I arrived at Van Rooyen's boardroom (he would later try to get SA Rugby to pay an extremely high rental for the same offices), Bester was present and proceeded to virtually run the meeting. One of the key concerns turned out to be Van Rooyen's campaign to be re-elected president of SARU. I tried to make it clear that I would not be a spin doctor, and it soon became apparent that we were at odds about what the job required.

So I wrote a letter to both Van Rooyen and Patel stating my concerns:

Following additional discussions with my superiors at SuperSport, Imtiaz Patel and Ray Moore, it has become clear to me that because of conflicts of interest any role I could play could work on only two levels:

1. That I am employed by SARU as a full-time media/ communications/public relations manager on a proper contract with all benefits. In this capacity I would be responsible for all SARU's public relations in an executive capacity to formulate a communications policy, to manage staff and agencies concerned

with communications, and (in all probability) act as the union's spokesman. In short, I would cease to be an employee of SuperSport and be employed by SARU.

2. That my services be provided (on secondment from SuperSport) on a limited basis as a 'consultant' to perform various tasks or oversee various projects – i.e. to be attached to the Springbok side (for a limited time, such as a tour) to draw on my experience to guide and assist SARU's current employees in formulating and effecting a communications and public relations strategy.

As explained to you, I have reservations about certain circumstances in place at SARU and how they would impact on my ability to do a proper job; about how my role would be perceived and accepted by the media and the public if I were to remain in the employ of SuperSport; and my ongoing security of employment given that I would be working for one organisation while being paid by another.

Even though SARU and SuperSport are partners, it would lead to a breakdown of the credibility of both organisations if we were seen to be 'conspiring' together and make my position as a rugby journalist untenable.

The letter ended with the usual assurances of goodwill, but I did not receive a reply from either Van Rooyen or Patel and never again heard about 'joining the office of the president'.

And it was just as well, because there was not much anyone could have done to put a positive spin on the next Test the Springboks played. White was clearly a man wrestling with his own demons, and if there was ever any doubt over whether a coach's lack of focus could adversely affect the form of a team, the Test against the Wallabies at the Suncorp Stadium in Brisbane confirmed it. The Springboks went down 0-49, their worst defeat against Australia, the heaviest ever Tri Nations defeat and the second-worst defeat in Springbok history.

The Wallabies, like the French in their previous Test, exposed the Springboks' defensive system to score six tries without reply, had the match wrapped up by half-time, leading 30-0, and provided Pierre Spies and Akona Ndungane with nightmare debuts.

For his part, White was at war with some members of the press. Some Afrikaans reporters were calling for his head, and he was most displeased with Dale Granger of The Independent Group, even threatening the reporter with physical harm. Granger related how White had asked him whether he knew Nigel McGurk, and warned him that if he was not careful, he would get said McGurk to 'deal' with him.

When Granger told me about the threat, I was amazed that the newspapers he worked for had not come to his defence more strongly. Being bullied by an angry rugby player or administrator is part of the territory for a rugby writer, but being threatened with physical violence by a known tough in Johannesburg club and pub circles was something altogether more serious – a fact emphasised when McGurk was implicated in the 2005 contract killing of mining magnate Brett Kebble.

The next week the Springboks put up a more spirited performance against the All Blacks at the Westpac Stadium in Wellington, but were nevertheless well beaten, 35-17. Montgomery played his 78th Test match to become the second-most-capped Springbok, and Matfield got his 50th cap, but these landmark events could not prevent the Boks from sliding to their third defeat in a row.

John Smit's men were forced to sit out the next weekend because of the new protracted format. They were then denied a miraculous turnaround from the 0-49 defeat against the Wallabies when Mat Rogers scored a late try to give the Australians a 20-18 win at the Telstra Stadium in Sydney. That made it three out of three defeats on the road and four in a row as the Boks headed home to prepare for the return leg of the tournament – and more opprobrium for White.

Those of us who had questioned the wisdom of adding more games to the Tri Nations on the basis that too many clashes were killing the mystique of Test rugby, particularly those between the Springboks and the All Blacks, received some validation, because the Kiwis arrived in South Africa with the Tri Nations already in the bag. Graham Henry was by now well into his rotation policy, which would be cited as one of the reasons for the All Blacks' eventual World Cup failure, and he made 11 changes and a positional switch. It made no difference to the Springboks, though, as the All Blacks were still too good.

Yet again there were debuts not to be cherished, this time for Chiliboy Ralepelle, BJ Botha and Ruan Pienaar, all of whom came on as replacements, as the Boks were thumped 45-26. The Loftus Versfeld crowd can be vociferous and merciless and, even though it was the Springboks' fifth defeat in a row, they let themselves down that day by loudly booing John Smit during his post-match interview. It was hurtful to Smit, but one has to wonder whether that was the moment the spark was lit that would flare into a flame in 2007.

The revival started at the most unlikely of venues – the Royal Bafokeng Stadium in Rustenburg. Rumours were rife that White was on the verge of being sacked (in fact, some Afrikaans newspapers confidently predicted it), but a Springbok win that ended a run of 15 successive Test-match victories for the All Blacks put paid to that. The Springboks fielded a side that showed five changes from the previous week and turned in a spirited performance – but it still needed a late penalty by André Pretorius to get them home, 21-20. Pierre Spies, playing at open-side flank, turned in a Man of the Match performance.

Then, bringing the curtain down on the Tri Nations, the Highveld bogey once again struck the Wallabies as they slid to a 16-24 defeat at Ellis Park against a Springbok side clearly buoyed by the victory over the All Blacks. JP Pietersen made his debut at fullback in a game that left the Wallabies winless on the Highveld for 43 years. It also allowed the 0-49 thrashing of two months earlier to start fading into memory as the focus shifted to the year-end tour and 2007's Rugby World Cup in France.

However, White took the calculated risk – advocated by SA Rugby's world-renowned expert on matters of physical fitness, Prof. Tim Noakes – to rest the likes of Fourie du Preez, Victor Matfield, Os du Randt and Percy Montgomery, and fielded three new caps – François Steyn, Jaco Pretorius and Bevan Fortuin – in the first match, against Ireland at Lansdowne Road.

The Test was played in a special strip to commemorate the first Springboks who had toured the UK under Paul Roos in 1906. But on a wild and windy day in Dublin, the Boks did not do their legacy justice as they suffered their heaviest defeat, 15-32, conceding the most points and tries against Ireland, and also for the first time losing two games in succession to the wearers of the shamrock. Steyn, playing on the wing, announced himself with a debut try, but it was a poor performance by the Springboks. They had underestimated the Irish, and Ronan O'Gara taught them a lesson in how to play the prevailing conditions.

Yet again White was under fire as he tried to hold the line between ensuring that he had his best players ready, rested and fit for 2007 while still getting Test victories. But then his charges, in the first of a historic double-header against England, contrived to squander an 18-6 lead to succumb to a late try by Phil Vickery. John Smit led the Boks for the 37th time to become South Africa's most-capped captain (surpassing Gary Teichmann), but it was South Africa's seventh consecutive defeat against England.

It was arguably Butch James's best Test, but sadly he would be injured. It was a mishap that, for a while, also impacted on the embattled White. It appeared as if he had made an unwarranted and unnecessary substitution in the 57th minute when he sent André Pretorius on to replace James. Pretorius struggled to find his rhythm and, as a result, the critics blamed White in part for England's 23-21 win. François Steyn made the rugby world sit up and take notice with a massive drop goal, but the seventh defeat in a calendar year equalled the previous lowest point of 1965.

Ahead of the second Test at Twickenham, White had to contend with another issue that had raised its ugly head. Luke Watson had had an excellent season for the Stormers in the role of specialist fetcher flank. Aficionados, particularly in the Cape, contended that he was exactly the kind of player the Bok set-up needed, and there was a clamour for White to pick him. But White resisted, declaring rather crassly, 'The only fetchers I know are my two sons who fetch me a beer on a Sunday.'

White had lost Schalk Burger to injury and had used four other players in the No. 6 jersey – Joe van Niekerk, Solly Tyibilika, Danie Rossouw and Pierre Spies – while for this Test, Lucas 'Kabamba' Floors was flown to London and put straight into the match. It was accepted that another defeat would have put paid to White, but 13 points in the seven minutes up to half-time and four drop goals by André Pretorius (three in the second half) finally ended South Africa's nightmare run against England. Danie Rossouw, presaging 2007, was a revelation at No. 8, CJ van der Linde scored a great prop's try and the 25-14 win provided a significant psychological boost ahead of the World Cup, as the two sides were due to meet again in their pool in France.

In a development that would have been difficult to believe had it not actually happened, White was then forced to return to South Africa to face a motion of no confidence (lodged by the Blue Bulls' former players' group, headed by former Springbok scrumhalf Piet Uys) and address the President's Council while his team prepared for the next match, against a World XV in Leicester, without him. The win against England was clearly crucial, but in his autobiography White revealed that Johann Rupert had rallied support for him among administrators and sponsors, while John Smit also weighed in with a strong appeal: 'The worst thing SA Rugby can do is fire Jake. What he does best is deal with people and coach rugby, but this year's been so much more. It's incredibly sad and, as captain, I feel partly responsible. We all feel terrible for Jake. He turned the darkness of 2003 into light. I know it hasn't been easy, but not once did he let on to us the pressure he's been under. All I can plead is not to fire him – which other coach has beaten New Zealand, Australia and England in a single year?'

As it turned out, common sense prevailed, and White survived the motion against him quite comfortably.

No caps were awarded for the final match of the tour, in aid of the SA Rugby Players' Association, against a handy World XV at the Walkers Stadium in Leicester. Chiliboy Ralepelle, the first black player to captain a South African senior side, led the Boks to a season-closing 32-7 victory.

White was still in charge, though barely, and the dream he had kindled in June 2004 was still intact. The year of the *Coupe du Monde*, 2007, was upon us.

20

Madiba magic

Le Meurice hotel in Paris is situated at 228 Rue de Rivoli, the street that runs alongside the fabulous Louvre museum and terminates at the Place de la Concorde. Entering its rococo portals, all gilt-edged mirrors and furniture, heavy drapery, intricate panels, crystal chandeliers and ornate *objets d'art*, is like stepping back in time to when the French aristocracy, in all their finery, swanned around the City of Lights.

The Meurice, in other words, is not the kind of place the average person would normally think of visiting, especially regarding rugby matters, but Russell Belter (cameraman, editor, producer and skilled operator of all things electronic) and I were there to record an event that had a prophetic feeling: Nelson Mandela meeting John Smit's Springbok team on the day before the start of the 2007 Rugby World Cup tournament.

Madiba had inspired the 1995 team to their triumph, and Jake White and his players genuinely believed in his magic muti. Mandela was staying at the hotel, purportedly in the Belle Etoile Suite, said to be the most expensive hotel room in Paris at a rate of some €8 000 a night. Apparently, this suite was always reserved for South Africa's most revered statesman when he visited the city. Mandela was due to meet the Boks and receive an award from the IRB in a ground-floor reception room. Belter and I arrived early to scout out the room and establish where Mandela would be entering (for on-the-shoulder camera shots), and to set up the tripod in a good spot in front of the chairs that would be used in the group photograph.

Ann-Lee Murray, well known to us as the Springbok team's liaison manager but who was working for the IRB at the tournament, was the first to arrive, along with a concierge carrying a reinforced aluminium suitcase, which was placed on a side table. Murray stepped forward, clicked open the clasps, and slowly lifted the lid … to reveal, glittering snugly in its cut-out bed of foam rubber, the Webb Ellis Cup! A pair of white cotton gloves was in the case and Murray pulled these on before gingerly lifting rugby's Holy Grail and placing it on a table. It was a moment of wonderful drama, created by the inanimate golden cup which had for months been the focus of attention for the 20 teams now gathered in France.

A little-known fact is that the World Cup has a sister – and perhaps a cousin or two. An 80%-accurate replica of 'Bill'* – the name the Wallabies had bestowed on the original after they won the cup in 1991 – was created to protect the original from any damage. Legend has it that 'Bill' was taken on a country-wide celebration around Australia, and on one occasion was used as a ball in a boisterous pub game. As a result, the IRB decided to take protective action. The 'imposter' is not a true copy – the difference being a garish yellow colour as opposed to the deep golden glow of the original. Also, the winners' names are inscribed in capital letters on the original, but in upper and lower case on the reproduction.

It is rumoured that there might also be a few 'Willies' and 'Winnies' in circulation, but an inquiry to the IRB for some clarification did not elicit a reply. However, the fact that at least two cups existed was revealed when the Aussies made an unfortunate error on the cover of the match-day programmes (spelt program) of the semi-finals and final at the Telstra Stadium in Sydney in 2003. The cover consisted largely of a picture of the grand and golden prize, but the names of the winners on the cup were not in capital letters!

That moment in Paris was the closest I had ever been to the Webb Ellis Cup, and I quickly stepped forward to check which one Murray had brought to the 'audience' with Madiba. I was pleased to see that it was the real McCoy, the names of the previous winners being inscribed thus: 1987 NEW ZEALAND, 1991 AUSTRALIA, 1995 SOUTH AFRICA, 1999 AUSTRALIA, 2003 ENGLAND.

Soon enough the Springboks arrived, and their reaction on seeing the cup was curiously amusing. Although they glanced furtively in its direction, none of them touched it. No one had their picture taken with it. While waiting for Mandela to arrive, John Smit explained that 'the boys' were superstitious about handling the cup. 'It still belongs to England,' said the skipper. But he added prophetically, 'It is not yet ours.'

Madiba kept the team, the IRB dignitaries and the media waiting for an hour, and when he finally appeared, a ripple went through the room. By now, it was brimful with hotel staff and guests who had snuck in to catch sight of Mandela. Many who have met Madiba speak of the mystical quality he exudes, and you could see it reflected in the awe on the faces of

---

* *Short for William, even though the cup does not have 'William' engraved on it. It is known as the Webb Ellis Cup. See full description in Chapter 1.*

the players, even those who had met him before. Youngsters like François Steyn and Bismarck du Plessis were wide-eyed as camera flashes went off around them.

I felt it too, but I couldn't help but notice how frail South Africa's former president was. Journalistic detachment allowed me to notice how far away his mind seemed to be. He was chaperoned by Zelda la Grange, his personal assistant and devoted protector, and he asked her, 'Where's Hansie [Cronjé]?' La Grange gently answered, 'You mean François [Pienaar], Madiba.'

Once Mandela was seated, the players, introduced by Jake White and John Smit, filed past to greet him. By now they were feverishly working each other's cameras, but the only name that brought a glimmer of recognition to Mandela's eyes was that of Os du Randt. 'Ah, Os, he's a very good player!' Mandela called out. He then made a speech, but its impact was largely felt because it came from him rather than because of its content.

Also present were Dr Syd Millar and Mike Miller, chairman and CEO respectively of the IRB, who took the opportunity to present Mandela with a specially commissioned award in recognition of his contribution to rugby. The inscription read: *Presented by the IRB to Mr Nelson Mandela who, during Rugby World Cup 1995, united his nation under the banner of rugby. Paris, September 6, 2007'.*

Jake White said that the players would be inspired by having seen Mandela. On that morning, the 'most defining moment' in Rugby World Cup history had been announced. Those who voted on this event included John Eales, Martin Johnson, Joel Stransky, Zinzan Brooke and Philippe Sella in their roles as ambassadors for one of the World Cup sponsors. The winning moment? Mandela wearing François Pienaar's No. 6 jersey at the 1995 Rugby World Cup final.

'The stars are aligning themselves,' said White, borrowing a phrase uttered by Bob Skinstad shortly before the team left South Africa. 'It is amazing that he [Mandela] is in Paris, that he held the Webb Ellis trophy [in his lap when the picture was taken]. He's had it in his hands before. The speech he gave ... what more do you want? I don't think we need to do any more team talks now. It's an unbelievable experience. The players can't wait to start now. Everything has been so professionally run and to have the added bonus of meeting Madiba and listening to him talk, and being so close to him and seeing how genuine he is about South Africa and the Springboks, is amazing – you can't help but be moved. All we can do now is make sure we deliver on the field.'

White pointed out that the Boks had never lost a Test after being in the company of former President Mandela. Skipper John Smit presented Madiba with one of his No. 2 jerseys and asked him to keep it with him as a good-luck charm.

This was on 6 September 2007. The next day would see the start of the 2007 Rugby World Cup. And the stars were indeed aligned for the Springboks when the opening game, between hosts France and Argentina, provided a shock upset. It would set John Smit's team on a yellow-brick road to ultimate glory.

Right from their arrival in France, there were positive portents for the Boks. Their hotel, the Marriott Rive Gauche Hotel, which Jake White quickly noted was situated on the Boulevard Saint *Jacques*, was the same hotel where the Springboks had stayed in 1999 when Jannie de Beer kicked five drop goals to defeat England in the quarter-final of that World Cup. And their first match of the 2007 tournament, against Samoa, was to be at the Parc de Princes where, in 1997, they had scored a fabled 52-10 victory over France.

And the most conspicuous omen of all became apparent when night fell on Paris and all of us South Africans noticed that the Eiffel Tower was lit up in green and gold and not in the red, white and blue of France. Acceleratesport, the company owned by the former SA Rugby CEO and tournament director of the 1995 World Cup, Rian Oberholzer, had been awarded the contract to set up Rugby Town on behalf of RWC Ltd. as the official gathering place and party zone for rugby fans. It was situated in the gardens of the Trocadéro, across the Seine from Paris's imposing landmark, and we suspected that Oberholzer might have had a hand in bathing the tower in Springbok colours.

Oberholzer, however, said that it was mere coincidence: 'It was not our doing at all. I wish I had that much influence and [it] would be great to take credit for it, but it was not our doing. It was a true omen. The area in front of the Trocadéro has often been used for exhibitions and the like, and the first time I noticed [that] the tower was lit green and gold was when the IRB staged a launch at Rugby Town.'

The Springboks had adopted the maxim 'Now Is the Time', and what a time it turned out to be! My role for SuperSport was to write for the Zone website and to provide daily reports for the television station's *Blitz* sports-news programmes. This last job meant that Russell Belter and I had to link up with the team every day to compile reports on their activities and, even though access to them was strictly controlled by IRB regulations, I was provided with a peephole into their changing moods as the drama ebbed and flowed and eventually culminated in a wonderful finale.

Each morning Belter and I would set out from our base in La Défense, the city's modern, high-rise business centre with its striking upturned horseshoe of an office block called the Grande Arche (a modern take on the Arc de Triomphe), either to link up with the team at their hotel or at their training ground in Noisy-le-Grand, a satellite village on the eastern outskirts of Paris. At first we attempted the trip across town on the metro, but heavy equipment, including the tripod bag on wheels that I nicknamed 'my dog', made this a bit of an obstacle course. So instead we hired a left-hand-drive car, which Belter expertly guided through the bustling streets with the aid of a GPRS. He would become highly skilled at entering and exiting the hair-raising roundabout around the Arc de Triomphe.

On occasion we tried to keep up with the Boks' team bus, which was always escorted by a team of policemen on big motorcycles with sirens wailing in that distinctive 'wha-ha, wha-ha' French way (these same gendarmes had been assigned to the French football team during the 1998 FIFA World Cup), but it was impossible to keep pace on the frenetic *Périphérique*, or ring road. Sometimes the mobile cops would be so determined to get the Boks through the traffic quickly that they would kick out at cars to get their drivers to move while two hung back to prevent someone from tailing the coach too closely.

The Springboks were touched by the wonderful welcome laid on by the pristine community of Noisy-le-Grand. The town was covered in rainbow flags wishing the Boks *bienvenue* (welcome), the club rooms at the Stade Alain Mimoun, named after France's Algerian-born gold medallist marathon runner at the 1956 Olympics in Melbourne, was decorated in Ndebele murals by three women flown to France to complete the task, and the practice field was sporting manicured new turf. The townsfolk called it *L'Effet Springbok* – literally, the 'Springbok effect'.

Vusi Kama, the team's seemingly perpetually harassed media officer, had omitted to tell the travelling media of an official welcome that had been arranged for the team in the city hall, but it was probably just as well. Players later told us how manager Zola Yeye, a man given to theatrically delivered speeches, had dramatically introduced the Boks. 'Ladies and gentlemen, I give you … Wynand Claassen [Wynand Olivier]!' And later, 'Ladies and gentlemen, I give you Gysie Pienaar [Ruan Pienaar].' This prompted Jaque Fourie, one of the wits in the side, to call out on the bus, 'Ladies and gentlemen, I give you the Springbok manager … Zola Budd!'

France was truly in the grip of World Cup fever. Whole buildings were 'wrapped' in friezes and banners fluttered around some of the most recognisable monuments in the world. Some of the most striking were giant projections onto buildings (for instance, both legs of the Grande Arche) of All Black players proclaiming their Adidas slogan: 'Impossible Is Nothing'. While the grim and menacing visage of France's *l'homme des cavernes* (the caveman), Sébastien Chabal, glared at the passing throng from the top of the Champs-Elysées, bar and café menus offered a variety of *le rugby* specials. And millions of words were being written about the tournament, with dispatches coming in from every corner of the land – the All Blacks holed up in Marseille, the Wallabies lurking in Montpellier and the English in the opulent surrounds of Versailles. We did not know it then, but neither the All Blacks nor the Wallabies would get to Paris.

Pre-tournament predictions would be turned on their heads through-out the tournament, and it started when Argentina scored one of the greatest upsets in Rugby World Cup history by beating France 17-12 in the opening game at the Stade de France. After a vibrant, happy and colourful opening ceremony, which was meant to launch France on a tri-umphal march to the 20 October final, the Pumas played with great heart and spirit to achieve a supreme victory in the annals of their rugby history.

The match started to a rousing rendition of 'La Marseillaise', but with the chants of *Allez les Bleus* ringing around the vast stadium, it was the pale blue of Argentina that held sway in the opening exchanges. The French were clearly feeling the pressure of expectation as their passes went astray, balls were dropped and turnovers conceded in the face of the Pumas' swarming defence and hard, driving tackles. True to their reputation for excellent forward play, the 'Gauchos' had the French on the back foot from the start, often profiting from high balls, launched by flyhalf Juan-Martin Hernández, dropping into the space behind the French forwards.

Argentina's Felipe Contepomi, playing in the centre with his brother Manuel, had the honour of opening the scoring in the sixth World Cup with a penalty after four minutes and 50 seconds, but this was soon can-celled out by a three-pointer from French flyhalf David Skrela.

The flow and territorial advantage was with the Argentines, however, and the crowd went silent as Contepomi kicked two more penalties to make it 9-3. French coach Bernard Laporte's worried face was flashed up on the big screen and his expression seemed to say, 'This can't be happening!' But it would soon get worse as Argentina scored the first try of the tournament in the 26th minute and, as it turned out, also the only one of the match. At first it had seemed as if centre Damien Traille might turn the Pumas' high-ball tactics to France's advantage when he leapt into the air to claim the ball and then broke free, only to flip the ball to one of the Pumas and watch in horror as the flying yellow boots of fullback Ignacio Corleto carried him to the goal line on a glorious run from 40 metres. Contepomi's conversion hit the upright, but at 14-3 up, soon to be 17-6 at half-time, the positive energy was with the men from the pampas.

France came back to play a better second half, but a key moment occurred in the 45th minute when a rousing line-out drive up to the Pumas' try line from fully 22 metres out, followed by 10 pick-up-and-goes, was repelled. It was probably then that Agustin Pichot and his men began to believe that they could win this game. With Skrela, who had a horror night, missing a point-blank penalty and his replacement, Frédéric Michalak, completely duffing another, the French failed to get close enough to really rattle a Puma side which, eventually, seemed to be running out of steam.

In the end the Pumas made twice as many tackles as the home side, but they kept their line intact. The match ended with Contepomi kicking, and missing, for posts rather than France staging one of their great escapes. It was the wrong ending to a perfect beginning, but one thing was for sure: no one was crying for Argentina! We joked that the French had named a metro station after Jonny Wilkinson – *Invalides* – but also one that drew mutterings from the late-night stragglers returning from Stade de France on the metro: *Argentine*.

France's defeat sent out shock waves that were most keenly felt in Marseille. At their hotel on the Mediterranean, Graham Henry, Richie McCaw and the rest of the All Blacks had watched the Pumas' up-and-unders unsettling *Les Bleus*. They were due to play the hapless Italians in the second game of the tournament the following afternoon, but you can be sure that France's tame demise had caused hairline cracks in their confident facade. Even more so than the distraught French, this was definitely not the result the All Blacks had expected.

As almost certain winners of Pool C, the All Blacks' expected route to the final included a quarter-final against the runner-up in Pool D – either Ireland or Argentina, as France were expected to top their pool. The new scenario was not nearly as favourable, for if the French were to finish second in their pool, it would provide the most bizarre situation – a quarter-final between France and New Zealand at *Cardiff's Millennium Stadium* on 6 October: the only play-off match scheduled outside of France.

Still nursing the traumatic memory of their famous implosion against *Les Bleus* at Twickenham in 1999, the All Blacks unexpectedly found themselves in a situation where they might have to travel to face a team hell-bent on victory to ensure that they remained alive in *their* World Cup. An added irony of the draw was that the All Blacks also had to travel to Murrayfield in Edinburgh to play Scotland in another pool match. Their other two matches were against Portugal and Romania, which meant they would not face tough opposition until the quarter-finals – a factor that went unremarked at the time but which would later be seen as a key reason for their eventual failure.

However, France's defeat contained positive portents for South Africa. The Springboks had attended the opening match in a private suite at the Stade de France, but whether by design or because it took some time for the implications of the result to sink in, Jake White and John Smit's post-match comments made no mention of the new scenario. It might have been that the Boks were too focused on their opening game against Samoa, but, having predicted that the Boks would play (and lose to!) France in the semi-finals, I was immediately aware of the consquences of the host country's defeat.

In a column titled 'Prepare for the Unthinkable', I listed the permutations. With bonus points up for grabs in the World Cup for the first time, France could still top Pool D, described as the 'pool of death', on points difference, or even fail to qualify for the knock-out stages. It meant that the clashes between the hosts and Ireland, at the Stade de France on 23 September, and Ireland and Argentina, on the last day of pool play on 30 September, had effectively become play-offs to decide which two of the three went through. While logic had initially dictated that the Springboks could expect to play France in their semi-final, they might now end up playing Argentina or Ireland. And the unthinkable? That New Zealand might go out in the quarter-final.

The stars around *La Planète Ovale* were indeed aligning for the Springboks. Most of the attention was on France, New Zealand and England. In fact, the South African team secretly enjoyed how British newspapers (many of which were available at their hotel or on newsstands) attached so much importance to the Springboks' troubles in their build-up to the tournament and that they had again finished bottom of the Tri Nations table.

It was a case of fact masking substance. Yes, there had been controversy en route to France, but it had only unified the team and made it stronger. For this, Jake White's consistent team selections could be thanked.

As Andy Colquhoun wrote in the *SA Rugby Annual*, 'the case of Luke Watson [had] threatened to unhinge the whole Springbok year'. White had made no secret of the fact that he neither liked nor rated the Western Province and Stormers captain, while Watson had said some scathing things about White in a magazine article.

The Springboks had opened the year with two one-sided wins against an under-strength England touring side, victories that nevertheless were good for morale ahead of their key pool match in France, and an additional Test had been arranged, against Samoa in Johannesburg, ahead of the Tri Nations. White had signed off on his side for this game, but was then compelled, by decree of SA Rugby president Oregan Hoskins (allegedly under pressure from government officials), to include Luke Watson. It was a highly unsatisfactory situation, and I was surprised that Watson was willing to accept his selection under such circumstances. Still, he joined the squad.

I got an inkling of the acrimony that existed between coach and player at a Chris Burger/Petro Jackson fund-raising banquet in Kyalami. At this event, the players manned a battery of telephones, taking down pledges from callers-in. When it was Watson's turn to sit at one of the phones, he took off his jacket and hung it on the back of the chair, prompting White, who was waiting to be interviewed on air, to say to me, 'Look at that prick. I suppose the Springbok blazer is not good enough for him.'

As it turned out, the Watson saga resolved itself. Watson started the Test against Samoa but suffered an injury in the 51st minute and was replaced by Pedrie Wannenburg. He was thus unavailable for the Tri Nations, and by the time of the World Cup selection, he had slipped out of the frame. Other back-up loose forwards, notably Wikus van Heerden and Bob Skinstad, had by then staked their claims.

White's next gambit had the Australians in a right old froth and the New Zealanders peeved, but they were unable to do much about it. Concerned about player fatigue, especially after losing the home Test 21-26 to the All Blacks in Durban, White decided to take a virtual B-team on tour. He was being advised by Prof. Tim Noakes[*] of the Sports Science Institute

---

[*] *Author of the bestselling bible of road-running injuries and their treatment,* Lore of Running.

in Newlands, and when a number of players were injured in the home leg of the Tri Nations, White announced a touring squad sans approximately 20 household names, including those of John Smit, Victor Matfield, Fourie du Preez, Bryan Habana, Os du Randt, Bakkies Botha, Percy Montgomery, Jean de Villiers, Butch James, Pierre Spies, Juan Smith, Schalk Burger and Jaque Fourie.

In another masterstroke of selection, White then brought back Bob Skinstad to lead the touring side. The coach had realised that the team would need another leader in the World Cup squad, someone who could rally the rearguard while the assault troops were charging out of the trenches; someone who could stand in for John Smit because the first side could not play every game. Skinstad, back with the Natal Sharks, had risen to White's challenge and resurrected his career.

In Sydney, the Aussies were incensed, blustering about South Africa being in breach of the SANZAR contract, which made provision for the three members of the triumvirate to tour at full strength. The Kiwis, however, were more equable. Graham Henry had, after all, pulled 24 All Blacks out of the first half of the Super 14 tournament. White argued that he had no choice but to tour with a B-team if his players were to be at their peak in October. Greg Growden, rugby writer of the *Sydney Morning Herald*, quoted an old antagonist of South Africa, David Moffett, who was one of the architects of SANZAR and a former CEO of the Welsh Rugby Union and Australia's National Rugby League, in one of his articles. Moffett made the preposterous suggestion that South Africa should be kicked out of the southern hemisphere triumvirate.

I was back on tour for SuperSport (for the first time since 2004) and enjoyed appearing on Fox TV's rugby show – anchored by Greg Clark and with Phil Kearns, Greg Martin and Rod Kafer – to rebuff Moffett's nonsensical proposal. I pointed out that South Africa was hardly a junior member of SANZAR, and that Australia and New Zealand would be the big losers if SARU sought more income and better time frames by joining northern hemisphere competitions. After years of getting the thin end of the wedge from officialdom and having to suffer through longer tours than the Aussies and Kiwis had to undertake, there were many who believed that SARU should, in fact, take a leaf from Cecil John Rhodes's book and start looking north.

As it turned out, the Aussies soon wished that they had not saddled up their high horse. After just 16 minutes of the Test at the Telstra Stadium, the Boks led 17-0, thanks to tries by Wikus van Heerden and Breyton

Paulse and successful goal kicks by Derick Hougaard. Unfortunately, they were unable to maintain the momentum. Spurred on by the fact that the match marked Stephen Larkham's 100th Test and the last on Australian soil for him and George Gregan, the Wallabies mounted a strong rearguard action. With Larkham giving a master class in the art of the well-timed pass, the Wallabies drew level soon after half-time, and eventually forged ahead to a 25-17 victory.

The Springboks suffered a blow when Bob Skinstad sustained a rib injury (which would end his tour) and had to be replaced by reserve hooker Gary Botha. Insult was added to injury soon afterwards when referee Paul Honiss sin-binned Botha for kicking a ball, which had emerged from a ruck, into touch while lying on the ground. Four minutes from time, Johann Muller was also shown a yellow card, for an alleged punch. Afterwards Skinstad could not help having a sardonic dig at the Aussie press, who had predicted a landslide victory for their team: 'I thought we did very well for a B-team.'

Skinstad's injury meant he had to return home, which opened the way for Johann Muller of the Sharks to become his country's 53rd captain in the Test against the All Blacks at the Jade Stadium in Christchurch. I found that the nuances of reporting in New Zealand and the mood in the All Black camp were quite different to what we had experienced in Australia. Graham Henry was his usual hostile self towards South African journalists, but instead of knocking an under-strength Springbok touring side, the All Blacks were as focused on beating their keenest rivals as ever. To the Kiwis, the Springboks were the Springboks, no matter which team they picked, and they had to be beaten.

And a makeshift Bok team showed that they deserved this respect by putting up a decent performance. In a Test in which the Du Plessis brothers, Bismarck and Jannie, became the second set of brothers to pack down in a Springbok front row – after Boy and Fanie Louw in the 1930s – the Boks trailed by just six points (6-12) going into the last 10 minutes. However, Pedrie Wannenburg had been harshly sin-binned by referee Stuart Dickinson in the 52nd minute, and playing one man short (especially a loose forward) proved to be the undoing of the Boks. The All Blacks scored three tries to race to a lopsided 33-6 win that did not fairly reflect the efforts of the tourists. Muller was incensed at what he perceived as double standards, saying, 'If Richie McCaw had blond hair and wore a green jersey or had dreadlocks and wore a yellow jersey, he would never finish a Test.'

And so the Springboks tumbled to the bottom of the Tri Nations log. When they also battled to beat Connacht, Ireland's weakest province after Munster and Leinster, on a pre–World Cup tour and were said to be dour and unimaginative in beating Scotland 27-3, their chances of lifting the Webb Ellis Cup were by and large written off.

Write-offs: it was exactly how Jake White and John Smit wanted their team to be perceived. They, however, knew that the senior players were injury free, fully rested and confident in their ability to pull off any challenge, and that most observers had missed a key indicator as to their real potential.

In May, the Bulls had beaten the Sharks 20-19 in the Super 14 final at the ABSA Stadium in Durban. Bryan Habana had snatched it for the Bulls with a glorious solo try in the dying seconds in as dramatic a game as you will ever see. It was South Africa's first win in the Super 14 after 12 years of trying, the first time a South African team had topped the log (the Sharks) and the first time two South African teams had contested the final.

With Graham Henry having withdrawn the bulk of the All Blacks from the opening rounds, South African teams scored more overseas wins than ever before. The players' confidence was sky-high and, as White and Smit realised, it made them virtually unstoppable. If White selected a team consisting of the best of the Bulls and the Sharks players, joined by the likes of Os du Randt, Juan Smith, Schalk Burger and Jaque Fourie, they would be able to beat the very best in the world.

In Paris, one just sensed that the chemistry was right. Ahead of their opening game against Samoa, White had asked Morné du Plessis to present the team's jerseys and say a few words of encouragement, and the former Springbok captain and manager of the victorious 1995 side also felt the positive vibe.

'I was impressed by the professionalism and attitude in the team,' he told me at the time. 'I feel, as do a lot of the people around me, that it is time to move on from the great chapter of 1995, which will always remain folklore in our country. We love it and we're part of it, but it is time for a new story, and it is up to this team to go out and write a new chapter. I think they feel it too. Looking at Os [du Randt],* I could see him nodding his head and agreeing; he's been part of both [teams] and I can sense there is a yearning for a new chapter as great as the last one.

---

* The taking of the team photograph was preceded by a hearty rendition of 'Happy Birthday', sung for Os du Randt on the occasion of his 35th birthday.

'You've got to be ready for the unpredictable; but at the moment everything is falling perfectly. I just see how comfortable the team is ... they look at ease and organised, the management's organised, they look good and healthy; nobody's injured, while other teams are battling a bit. Their challenges will come; there's no doubt about it. However, I certainly think it's looking good for us. At the moment, there's very little mention of the Springboks in the papers, and it's good to be under the radar, but I have a feeling it's soon going to be a lot more green and gold.'

Du Plessis was right about that – and also about the challenges the Springboks would face.

21

The law is an ass

Seven steps to glory: that was Jake White's formula for winning the World Cup. The first of these steps presented itself in the form of Samoa on 9 September at the Parc des Princes on the southern edge of the Bois de Boulogne in Paris. The next step would be England at the Stade de France in Saint-Denis on 14 September, followed by Tonga in Lens on 22 September, and then the USA in Montpellier on 30 September. After that – the quarter-finals. Although the dates were known – 7 October in Marseille, 14 October in Saint-Denis (Stade de France) and 20 October in Saint-Denis – the Springboks' likely opponents were still in the hands of the gods. White had picked up quite a bit of Kitch Christie's pragmatism, and he hammered home the message that 'if you win seven matches, you win the World Cup'.

The Springboks had been overwhelmed by the warmth of the welcome they had received from the French (it probably helped that they had names such as Du Preez, De Villiers, Fourie and Rossouw in their line-up), but in their first game it quickly became apparent that the local crowd would side with the underdog and that the Boks would just have to get used to it.

With Samoa's strip a near replica of France's blue and white, cheers of *Allez les Bleus! Allez les Bleus!* rang out when the teams took to the field and reached a crescendo when the islanders, after as ferocious a period of play as I had ever seen, rattled the Boks by scoring the first try of the game to make the score 7-9 after 18 minutes. The scorer was Gavin Williams (son of the great All Black Bryan 'BG' Williams). The Samoans, always prone to high tackles, adopted an overly aggressive approach to upset the Boks, and with referee Paul Honiss failing to stamp it out, tempers quickly frayed.

The heavy hits kept on coming, and when I trained my binoculars on the Bok coaches' booth, the expressions on the faces of Jake White, Gert Smal and Allister Coetzee told a tale of a match starting to go horribly wrong. (Eddie Jones, as always, looked the picture of an inscrutable little Buddha.) In the 10th minute, Schalk Burger flattened Samoan scrumhalf Junior Polu when they both leapt for the ball, and I scribbled down that he might get into trouble for it. The crowd bayed for action to be taken against the Springbok flank. At the start of the tournament, referees' chief Paddy

O'Brien had announced a 'zero-tolerance' approach to dirty play, and this, coupled with the disproportionate punishment often meted out to South African players, made me think that this incident would be revisited.

The temper of the match continued on 'overheated', but John Smit kept his men focused on trying to control the ball in the pack, a sound tactic. Their line-out was supreme, as it would be for the rest of the tournament, and the Boks were gradually gaining the ascendancy in the scrums. What was needed was a spark, and it was provided by Bryan Habana with a dazzling piece of individual brilliance. Put away in the tramlines on the 10-metre line, the speedy left wing zigzagged this way and that, seemed to lose his footing, regained it and then powered through the grasping hands of the Samoans to dive over.

Although Percy Montgomery missed the conversion, the score changed to 14-7, and now there was steam in the Bok engine. Their next try was one for the ages. Setting a bridgehead on the Samoan line after JP Pietersen had been held up, the Boks bashed and mauled the hapless islanders through seven successive scrums (referee Paul Honiss refusing to award the penalty try) and, when they finally let the ball out to the left, Montgomery was able to sprint over.

This made the score 21-7 at the break, and the Springboks returned to play a pretty impressive second half, sparked in no small measure by François Steyn after he replaced Jean de Villiers. Poor De Villiers had again fallen foul of the injury hoodoo that dogged his career. Sadly for the blond Western Province centre, he had sustained a badly torn bicep muscle that ended his participation in the tournament.

Samoa were furious when a possible try by lock Joe Tekori was disallowed because he had been offside when he snatched up the ball at a ruck near the Boks' goal line. After that, the fight noticeably went out of the abrasive islanders, and South Africa strode to a 59-7 victory.

Bryan Habana, also wearing the No. 11 jersey, emulated Chester Williams' feat by scoring four tries against the Samoans. Williams, the talisman of South Africa's Webb Ellis Cup triumph in 1995, had scored his quartet of tries against the Samoans in the quarter-final at Ellis Park. Now Habana contributed his four to the Springboks' second successive 50-plus scoreline at the Parc des Princes – the last having been their 52-10 win over France in 1997.

The match also provided an apt example of a biter being bitten. Samoa's Brian Lima, whose reputation for bone-jarring tackles had been enhanced by a 'king hit' on Derick Hougaard in Brisbane in 1999, ran on in the 60th minute to become the first man to appear in five World Cups, having made his debut as a 19-year-old in 1991. Four minutes later, he was led off in a daze – the result of mistiming a head-high, no-arms in-tackle on André Pretorius (who had replaced Butch James in the 58th minute). It was a recklessly dangerous manoeuvre, but Pretorius, instead of being flattened as Hougaard had been, managed to duck, raising his elbow at the same time and knocking 'The Chiropractor' unconscious.

After tries by Jaque Fourie and Montgomery, Habana added three more to his opening try. It happened in the space of 20 minutes: first he sprinted in from the 10-metre line for his second in the 55th minute, then he tapped a penalty quickly to himself to dive over for his third in the 65th minute, followed by a glorious free sprint down the left-hand touchline for his fourth in the 75th minute.

Ahead of their crucial Pool A clash against England at the Stade de France six days later, the Boks could feel well pleased with their opening statement. They had managed to suppress difficult opponents by sticking to their tactics, had found some rhythm in the backs and, at the end, were able to give all their reserves a run. It was certainly a performance that would have resulted in some worried frowns in the England camp in Versailles. I decided to pick up on Jake White's theme by ending my match report with the following phrase: *One down. Six to go.*

If only it were that simple! There might have been six more matches left, but soon the Springbok camp was embroiled in a drama that left them incensed and feeling victimised. The Samoa game had been played on a Sunday evening, and for two days the Boks were on tenterhooks as the citing deadline loomed. As mentioned, Burger had felled Junior Polu in the air, and Juan Smith was caught on camera lashing out, after having lost patience with Samoa's truculent approach. Would two of their key players be cited?

Rules for the World Cup differed from those of the Tri Nations, where the citing deadline is 12 hours. At the World Cup, the citing officer had 48 hours following the completion of a match to cite a player. With the Springbok/Samoa match having ended at around 6 on the Sunday evening, it meant that the citing officer (whose identity was not revealed) had until Tuesday evening to cite the Springbok loose forwards. The fact that England captain and prop Phil Vickery and Eagles centre Paul Emerick were cited after the England/USA Pool A match in Lens and were subsequently handed suspensions by commissioner Steven Hines raised the overall temperature.

Although England (South Africa's next opponents) would have been unable to wangle a citing against the Springboks – had they wanted to try – their pressmen were nevertheless stridently condemning the alleged failure of RWC officialdom to sufficiently punish other incidents of foul play. In their articles, they made numerous references to the events in the Springbok game.

The clock ticked on, and it seemed as if Burger and Smith might be in the clear. But with less than two hours to go to the deadline, White got wind that a citing had been lodged. RWC officials were obliged to provide a DVD of the incident to accompany a citing, but instead of the DVD being delivered to Springbok manager Zola Yeye, as protocol dictated, the package was addressed to Jake White and could quite easily have gone astray. Burger was cited to appear before a judicial officer for having committed a dangerous tackle, but Smith was off the hook.

If White was furious at the delay in delivering the citing, he was 'catching snakes' by the time the judicial officer's decision was handed down: a four-week suspension. The Springboks, who had maintained Burger was going for the ball when he knocked down Polu, were confident he would get off. They were shattered that they would have to make do without the robust flank – whom White had often described as his most valuable player – in their next three pool matches and the expected quarter-final in Marseille.

Those were the bare facts, but behind the scenes an incredible tale of legal manoeuvring, which would have done John Grisham proud, was unfolding. I first heard about the goings-on late on the Tuesday night while working in my hotel room in La Défense. I received a call on my cell phone from Johann Rupert, who was in Geneva, where he was attending a Richemont board meeting.

'They've banned Schalkie for four weeks,' said an angry Rupert. 'You won't believe how incompetent SARU has been on this and what we've had to do to defend him. The whole thing is scandalous. We will be appealing.'

It transpired that after receiving a call from the player's father, 'Groot' Schalk, Rupert had to rally his immense resources to ensure that Burger was properly defended at his hearing. Apparently Springbok manager Zola Yeye did not have a RWC tournament 'participation agreement', which sets out disciplinary processes, accommodation details and other arrangements, in his possession, and neither did national teams manager Andy Marinos, who was in Paris. While England had a QC as part of their squad (they had one in Australia in 2003 too), SARU's lawyer was not even in France.

Burger Snr called everyone he knew with any clout, including Eddie Jordan of Formula 1 racing fame, while Rupert got hold of his contacts, calling in the counsel of a lawyer friend, Frederick Mostert (an expert in intellectual property rights), to help find someone to handle Burger's defence. Mostert, in turn, called on John McCaughran, a British-based QC, while another of Rupert's associates, Rob Hersov, head of an executive jet company, arranged to transport the barrister to Paris.

Burger's hearing before Australian judicial officer Terry Willis did not go well. Willis, allegedly, was rather arrogant, at one point saying that he had been a No. 6 flank himself and knew for a fact that Burger had not been going for the ball (referring to the player's defence). The four-week ban handed down was two weeks more than any other for a similar offence after the first weekend of fixtures. For his part, McCaughran allegedly told Rupert that he had never seen such a stitch-up in his life. The obdurate Willis had apparently not considered a single argument in what Rupert called a 'kangaroo court'.

On appeal, McCaughran was able to successfully argue Burger's plea for a reduction in sentence (to two matches). This ruling was a bit of a slap in the face for Willis, coming as it did from an organisation not known for backtracking. The Appeal Committee, comprising chairman Justice Wyn Williams, Bruce Squire QC and Judge Guillermo Tragant, determined that

> the Judicial Officer [Willis] had made an error in his first instance decision, in that he was wrong to find that the player was not at any time during the incident intending to win the ball. On the basis of the video evidence and the transcript of the initial JO [judicial officer – don't you just love the abbreviation!] hearing the Appeal Committee decided that the player was attempting to win the ball for a significant part of the time involved.
>
> However, the Committee found that the player ultimately realised that he was not going to catch the ball and instinctively adjusted his approach to tackle the opposing player. The Committee concluded that the tackle was a dangerous tackle but noted that the arm of Mr. Burger was withdrawn following contact with the opposing

player. The committee decided the offence should be categorised as a lower level entry offence rather than a mid range offence. The entry point for such an offence is a two week (or two match) suspension. The Appeal Committee confirmed that there were no aggravating factors but considered that the player's previous disciplinary history should be taken into account.

I wrote a column I titled, 'Average JO must go', which I rather liked, and pointed out that the implications of this about-turn were significant. It basically conceded that the disciplinary process in the tournament was seriously flawed and open to human prejudice and official injustice, and I called into question the competence of the JO concerned. To make matters worse, and to the annoyance of the Springboks, Brian Lima, who had knocked himself out trying to make a reckless and potentially dangerous head-high tackle on André Pretorius, was not cited at all.

Burger was thus out of the crucial Pool A game against England, opening the way for a most competent replacement in Wikus van Heerden to wear the No. 6 jersey. The Springboks had been settled, confident and happy at the start of the tournament, but the aggravation caused by the handling of the Burger affair exposed some of the anger and dissatisfaction in Jake White that I had not known existed up till then. White had not been pleased when Zola Yeye was appointed team manager, a feeling he did not try to hide in the often snide remarks he made. His feelings would only grow in intensity and become an interesting sideshow as we got deeper into the tournament.

England loomed large, however, and the players were focused on what was arguably their biggest match since the RWC quarter-final in Melbourne in 2003. On the day, one could feel the enormous tension in the air at the Stade de France. The great stadium's ramparts looked as if there had been a snowfall with the myriad England supporters in their white jerseys, but here and there one could spot an outcrop of South African fans wearing the green and gold. I had been to so many Test matches that I had become quite blasé during the singing of the anthems, but on this night I got choked up and felt tears filling my eyes as the outnumbered Saffers responded to 'God Save the Queen' by booming out 'Nkosi Sikelel' iAfrika'. They sang it with such fervour, it felt as if they were trying to win the game with their singing.

And how Smit and his men responded. Emulating the team of 1999, when Jannie de Beer and his teammates had annihilated the English, the Springbok class of 2007 gave an immense Rugby World Cup performance in the French cathedral of sport, stacking up a 36-0 victory that was more emphatic than even their boldest fans could have hoped for.

With Fourie du Preez proving himself the best scrumhalf in world rugby, the Boks sent out a blazing message of intent to the rest of the contenders. The amazing victory made them favourites to top their pool and obtain an easier quarter-final. Apart from a period late in the second half (with the game already won) when Martin Corry's men dominated possession and territory, the Boks were never really extended in shutting out a shabby England.

They rose magnificently above the setback of losing Schalk Burger (albeit against an England side who had to endure even more problems, including the loss of Jonny Wilkinson) in what was their best perform-ance on foreign soil since early 2004, when Jake White stepped onto the bridge of a listing ship and set sail for the distant *Coupe du Monde* in France in 2007.

The Boks were calmly focused, clinical in execution and unwaveringly composed as they set about blasting England's sweet chariot right off the park. England captain Martin Corry had talked about winning the collisions, but against faster, stronger and more determined opponents, his side was never in it. Not only did the Boks dominate the contact situations, but with Bakkies Botha and Victor Matfield dominating the landscape like a pair of Eiffel Towers, they created a wonderful platform in the line-outs, were always more explosive in the tackle and quicker to the turnovers.

The Boks' early domination seemed almost too good to be true, and one wondered whether the tension of the long build-up to this match would constrict their attacking nous. But it was a fleeting thought. In the sixth minute, Botha jumped to win a front-end line-out ball on his own 10-metre line, Du Preez worked the short side to JP Pietersen, who sped clear before sending the ball back to the scrumhalf. When Du Preez was hemmed in, he jinked infield before popping the ball up for a charging Juan Smith to carry over the line. Montgomery added the conversion, and he soon kicked a penalty to take the score into double figures. With the Boks playing from left to right in front of me, their dominance was such that I seemed to spend the rest of the half hunched forward in order to see past a steel pole that obscured my view of the England 22.

The Boks had a distinct advantage kicking the ball out of hand, the likes of Du Preez and Percy Montgomery making Mike Catt and some of the other England kickers look like inept beginners. But it seemed as if they might let the chance slip to wrap up the game by half-time. That thought soon evaporated, though, as Montgomery's smooth two-step took them to 13-0 before the unrelenting pressure again told on the English.

It was Du Preez who once more cracked the whip when he quickly countered with a turnover ball, sprinted up to fullback Jason Robinson before neatly letting the ball go to JP Pietersen, who was cruising clear on the outside. The conversion made it 20-0 at the break, and, in truth, that was it – you could not see the demoralised England outfit coming back from there.

Smit's men kept their intense focus after the restart, using the high ball to great effect and maintaining the field position to allow Montgomery to kick two more penalties (26-0). These were primal but necessary tactics, and the brave Jason Robinson was having such a torrid time of it that he left the field bleeding and in pain when his hamstring finally gave way. He had valiantly tried to spark life into his shell-shocked teammates, but had simply run into and been bowled over by a rampant Springbok once too often.

The *coup de grâce* was delivered after a crooked line-out, which gave the Boks a scrum. From there, the ball spun into centre-field to a crash-balling François Steyn. The ball was rucked back quickly, and Du Preez looped back against the flow, broke clear and again presented JP Pietersen with a try on a plate. Montgomery, who kicked all seven of his place kicks for a contribution of 18 points, did the rest, and not a soul in the crowd of 79 900 could say that the Springboks had not demonstrated that they were very real contenders to lift the Webb Ellis Cup. They had, after all, just demolished the current cup holders.

At the end, the Springboks enjoyed a lap of honour, an expression of gratitude for the ardent support of their fans. They might have been out-numbered, but they had provided an unceasing crescendo of support. It was a good night to be South African, and I was swept up in the euphoria. The closing lines of my match report read: 'The dream is crystallising, taking a tangible shape; one has a feeling it won't be the last time the Boks go from end to end to wave to the crowd at this venue. *Two down. Five to go.*'

Seldom has a stadium announcement sounded as glorious as it did at the Stade de France in Paris on that Friday night. 'Souss Africa, sirty-seex; Eengland, neel!'

The England fans, who had no idea then that they might have to return to the venue, immediately found a new name for the Stade de France: Ground Zero. It was quite apt, as so many of them were dressed in the white jerseys with the logo of the team's sponsor, O_2. South African fans had in seasons past endured the gloating on the tube back from Twickenham to London, but now it was music to their ears when they heard the Poms lament, 'I wanna go home, oh how I wanna go home' on the metro!

England's defeat was their first in Rugby World Cup action since going down to the Boks at the same venue in 1999. The 36-0 whipping also heralded a couple of other humiliating stats. England joined Côte D'Ivoire (1995), Canada (1995), Spain (1999) and Namibia (2003) as only the fifth team in World Cup history to finish a match scoreless. They were also the only reigning champs to not trouble the scorekeeper in RWC history. And the defeat was also England's heaviest at a World Cup. To add insult to injury, the 79 900 people present at Stade de France to witness England's loss topped the 79 312 who had showed up at the same ground for the RWC 2007 opener between France and Argentina exactly one week earlier, making it a new record attendance for a Rugby World Cup match in Europe.

Two South African–born players had turned out for England. The 2003 World Cup winner Mike Catt had a nightmare standing in for Jonny Wilkinson in the England No. 10 jersey. Facing him across the park was François Steyn, a young man who was just seven years old when Catt became Jonah Lomu's road kill at Newlands in 1995. And Os du Randt's direct opponent, Matt Stevens, was only 12 when the big Free Stater anchored the Springbok scrum in the 1995 Rugby World Cup final.

Beating England meant that the Springboks were well and truly on the high road, and then, almost as if planned, it was time to leave Paris for the next game, against Tonga at Stade Félix Bollaert in Lens, in the north of France. The team were given their own train (a high-speed, bullet-shaped TGV engine hooked up to a couple of luxury coaches) for the 300-kilometre trip, but any thoughts of a smooth passage were soon rudely dispelled by the Tongans.

The team were billeted at the Hôtel du Golf d'Arras, a golf resort situated between Lens and Lille, which greatly pleased the golfers in the group (of whom Fourie du Preez, a sometime scratch player, was easily the best), but there were more signs of White's increasing edginess. The coach had decided to rest most of the players who had negotiated the first two games so that the dirt-trackers, or second stringers, could have a run, with Bob Skinstad as captain.

White had asked rugby commentator Hugh Bladen to present the players' jerseys prior to the match, and after the team photograph was taken, Russell Belter and I were waiting for the coach while he talked to Anton Snyman of the SABC for the obligatory one-on-ones. We noticed that White seemed to be upset about something. He and Zola Yeye were staring daggers at each other and, as he came over to us, he called back to Anton, 'When this is over [the World Cup], *I'll* have the microphone and then you'll hear about the fucking shit I've had to put up with in this job!'

White seemed adamant that he would leave the Springbok coaching job and that in all probability he would be joining SuperSport. 'It will all be in my book,' became a regular refrain. That's why it came as a surprise to me when, in his bestselling autobiography *In Black and White*, he maintained that he had wanted to stay on after the World Cup but that SARU had wanted him to go. And in terms of Jake working for SuperSport and 'telling all', I could just smile. As mentioned earlier, SuperSport does not permit its commentators to indulge in criticism of national sports bodies, so Jake would most certainly not have been allowed to hang out his and SARU's dirty laundry.

But back to the World Cup. An amazing confluence of circumstances had given three of the Springboks who were to play against Tonga a chance to appear in the Rugby World Cup which, just months previously, had appeared unlikely. As late as early August it seemed André Pretorius might not make it to France, while for Bob Skinstad and Wayne Julies it seemed as if unhappy performances in the 1999 tournament would be the sum total of their World Cup memories.

Skinstad owed his 'resurrection' to White's faith in his enduring skills, and Julies got his break because of the injury to Jean de Villiers in the opening game against Samoa; but the real 'miracle man' was Pretorius.

In the first week of August, with the team due to fly out for the tournament on 3 September, Pretorius's continuing battle with injuries seemed likely to cost him his dream chance. In desperation, he then decided to consult a German doctor with a reputation for curing sportsmen (including sprinters Asafa Powell and Maurice Greene) with chronic hamstring injuries.

German physician Hans-Wilhelm Müller-Wohlfarth (the club doctor at Bayern-Munich FC) pinpointed the source of Pretorius's ongoing hamstring problem as being in his lower back and commenced his unorthodox treatment to try to make the little Lion better. It was a long shot, but scepticism turned into amazement when Pretorius's injury began to heal.

'The big problem was coming from my back,' Pretorius said when I interviewed him at Golf d'Arras. 'Apparently most of the guys who see Dr Müller-Wohlfarth turn out to have back problems. He normally needs a bit longer, but I only had a week with him. I saw a chiropractor every day, and I got injections – like 17, 18 injections a day, which was a double round. He leaves the needles in your back and then comes back with new syringes of his muti. It actually worked a miracle. The big thing about the doctor is that he is so passionate about what he does. He's really such a humble person. He still calls me to see if I'm fine. If I battle with my back, I can just get on a plane, get on a train and he would be willing to see me.'

'It's been quite an experience,' Pretorius added with a good deal of understatement.

Julies possessed a remarkable Springbok record, having earned just 10 caps in an international career that started with the match against Spain in Edinburgh in the 1999 World Cup. Interestingly, however, he had only once tasted defeat – when the Boks went down to France (26-36) at Newlands in 2006. As it turned out, the Test against Tonga would be his last.

Skinstad's involvement in the tournament also felt like a godsend. His participation in 1999 was clouded by Gary Teichmann's axing, and his own performance was adversely affected by not being fully fit following his knee injury. It was common cause that he should not have gone to Wales, and before the next tournament, in 2003, he suffered the disappointment of being part of the team in the build-up before missing out on selection for Australia.

His 40-Test career (up to then) showed an incredible four-year gap, between June 2003 and June 2007, and he nearly missed out again when he injured his ribs while captaining the Boks against the Wallabies in the Tri Nations in Sydney in July. However, Skinstad's acute intellect made him an important component in the Bok mix and he would fully justify the faith White had in him.

In Lens, the Springboks once again felt the full brunt of a crowd rooting for the underdog as the Tongans pushed them to the brink of a shock defeat. The Springboks survived an anxious, heart-stopping game before clinching a 30-25 victory. In a wild, roller-coaster encounter of brutal hits and vicious collisions, the Boks were at one point down to 13 men as the valiant Tongans made a stirring bid for victory after being 10-27 down.

Referee Wayne Barnes's final whistle sounded with the Tongans right on the Boks' line, after the bouncing ball had just eluded Tevita Tu'ifua for the try that would have tied up the scores. Skinstad summed up the relief of his team and scores of fans when he said, 'To be honest with you, we were lucky to get our four [log] points today.'

Skinstad was spot-on in his assessment of his team's performance. The Boks had been lucky ... extremely lucky. If flyhalf Pierre Hola's chip to the corner had bounced infield instead of into touch, the Tongans would almost certainly have scored.

Fielding a team with many players who had not had much rugby, the Boks were sloppy and inaccurate from the start, with Pretorius having a particularly bad day (he missed four penalties that might have made all the difference, and many of his kicks out of hand did not find touch). These mistakes allowed the Tongans to gain in confidence and take the initiative.

With poor control in the rucks and mauls the Bok forwards failed to set a platform, and the backs played into the hands of the Tongans with poor alignment, by taking the ball too flat and attempting reckless wide passes.

It was a sobering outing, and in White's mind the reality hit home that the Bok second stringers were just not on a par with the first XV, who had so emphatically accounted for England. It was stop-start stuff, with the Tongans getting a surprising amount of ball. This possession was cleverly put to use by flyhalf Pierre Hola with a variety of kicks, and only a piece of quick thinking by Ruan Pienaar got the Boks into the lead by the break. Tonga had conceded a penalty, and Pienaar produced a mercurial touch the islanders were probably not expecting from a South African side. Playing in the No. 15 jersey once sported by his father, Gysie, Pienaar waited for the ball to be returned to him on the far side of the field after the Boks had been given a penalty, giving the impression that he was going to kick for posts. However, he quickly tapped it to himself and sprinted in from 37 metres.

Skinstad's men reached half-time 7-3 up, but any thought that the coaches' exhortations during the break would bring an improvement quickly disappeared when the Boks conceded a penalty immediately after resumption of play and allowed the Tongans to go on the attack. White had taken the precaution of having a powerful bench, and up in the stands, he had had enough. He stomped down to the field and ordered his heavy artillery to be sent on – John Smit, François Steyn, Victor Matfield, BJ Botha and Bryan Habana arriving in a rush. Juan Smith came on when Danie Rossouw was stretchered off.

Soon Percy Montgomery was also part of the cavalry, earning a record 90th cap. He was just in time to goal the conversion of a try by Smith from a deep break-out that had started with a line-out steal on the Boks' own 22. From the kick-off after Smith's try the Boks again moved the ball wide to the left and then back over to the right, where Skinstad dived over. The try was not awarded for a good few minutes while the match officials sorted out an altercation that had broken out between Bakkies Botha and replacement Inoke Afeaki.

The Boks were frustrated, tempers were fraying and the upshot of the squabble was that François Steyn, who had been a peacemaker, was yellow-carded along with Joseph Vaka, who had, in fact, been the instigator, having run in and hurled Steyn to the ground. With order restored, the inconsistent Barnes awarded Skinstad's try, and at 22-10, after Montgomery missed the conversion, the Boks were in a position to push for the bonus point. They had found the Tongans' weakness by attacking wide from deep. The pattern of the ball travelling to the left touchline before being transferred back again with the forwards joining in resulted in a superb second try for Pienaar.

This time Montgomery raised the flags, and at 27-10, with the Tongans starting to look bedraggled and substitutes coming on in droves, it seemed as if the Boks might finish off in a blaze of scoring. But the complexion of the match changed dramatically when Bryan Habana was also yellow-carded, for killing the ball near his try line – cutting the Bok complement to 13 men with Steyn still off and the bench cleared.

The Tongans needed no second invitation to take advantage of the situation. A deft cross-kick by Hola created a try far out on the left for Sukanaivalu Hufanga. The conversion was missed, but at 27-15, the Tongans were a team with a new zest, bolstered by deafening support from a crowd who sensed an upset.

The Boks were vulnerable to the kick over the top, and the Sea Eagles made superb use of this tactic. When Montgomery raced back to stop a gap, the ball bounced off his foot and straight into the hands of prop Tevita Tu'ifua, who ran clear before cross-kicking for the hard-working flanker Viliami Vaki to win the race to the touchdown. Hola's conversion cut the margin to five points (22-27), and it stayed that way into the nerve-wracking last few minutes as an exchange of penalties (25-30) between Montgomery and Hola kept the islanders in with a chance of snatching at least a share of the spoils.

Hola's kick to the blind side might have worked the trick, and seldom has a Bok side been so relieved to see a touch judge's flag go up and to hear, moments later, the shrill blast of the final whistle, accompanied by jeers from the crowd. The Boks had their victory, and there would be no lifeline for France. It was quite fitting that it was the Tongans, many wearing Springbok jerseys they had exchanged with the Boks like the spoils of war, who went on a lap of honour to acknowledge the warm applause of the Pas-de-Calais crowd.

Three down. Four to go.

I wrote my match report wedged into the back seat of our car, along with Hugh Bladen and John van Rensburg, as we raced back to Paris, and filed it via 3G. It was a while before we discovered that the Springboks had incurred another citing and were faced with having to run the legal gauntlet again.

The Boks' final pool game was against the United States in Montpellier in the south of France, but we were not due to travel there until later in the week. It was a time to do some feature material in Paris. On the Monday evening (again stretching the 48-hour citing window to the limit), we heard the news that François Steyn had been cited by French citing officer Jean-Claude Legendre, allegedly for having bitten Tongan wing Joseph 'Sefa' Vaka's finger.

Steyn was to appear at a judicial hearing on the Tuesday afternoon at the offices of legal firm Clifford Chance in Place Vendôme, the square in the heart of Paris's richest arrondissement, which is also home to the Ritz Hotel (where Princess Diana had had dinner before getting into the car for her last journey to the nearby Pont de l'Alma tunnel).

The citing was patently ridiculous, but the possible suspension of the team's youngest member was an enormous worry for White. Steyn, after all, had replaced the injured Jean de Villiers with aplomb, providing rock-solid defence and the bonus of a prodigious boot.

Being part of a television crew meant I had access to video footage, and we immediately started to dissect the tape in extreme slow-mo – especially as the RWC had asked SuperSport to provide any footage of the incident we had. The video showed that Steyn had nothing to worry about, but

Left: Former President Nelson Mandela holds up the Springbok jersey prior to the start of the 2007 Rugby World Cup, in Paris, France

Below: Nelson Mandela and the Springbok team at Le Meurice, Paris, France, on 6 September 2007

@ Tertius Pickard / Gallo Images

I knew I'd get my hands on it one day ...
With the Webb Ellis Cup at Le Meurice

Working in front of the Eiffel Tower, which sported the Springbok colours of green and gold during the 2007 Rugby World Cup

The Grand Arche in La Défense adorned with laser images of All Blacks Richie McCaw and Mils Muliaina

Below: Working with cameraman Rudi Nel outside the Stade Vélodrome in Marseille after the quarter-final against Fiji

Above: In the press box at the Stade de France ahead of the semi-final against Argentina

Above: With my SuperSport colleague Xola Ntshinga in front of the Eiffel Tower

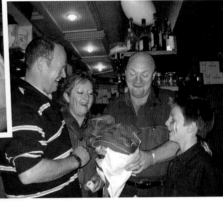

Below: My French friends. Presenting Didier Bongain with a Springbok jersey at his restaurant Au Village des Ternes in Paris, while his son Jimmy and wife Fabienne look on

Above: A jolly night out for the SuperSport crew: from left, Russell Belter, me and Hugh Bladen in Paris

Left: A unique photograph of the 2007 World Cup–winning Springbok squad with five members of the victorious 1995 squad: Joel Stransky, Morné du Plessis, François Pienaar, Chris Rossouw and James Small

In the press box prior to the start of the 2007 Rugby World Cup final at the Stade de France. John Smit is being interviewed on the big screen in the background

Below: The best scrumhalf in the world – Fourie du Preez

@ Gallo Images

Above: Bryan Habana scoring one of his two tries in the semi-final against Argentina on 14 October 2007. Habana equalled Jonah Lomu's tournament record of eight tries

@ Gallo Images

@ Gallo Images

The master of the line-out – Victor Matfield

Raising the flags – Percy Montgomery slots another goal

Above: Jake White (coach) and John Smit (captain) hold the Webb Ellis Cup after South Africa's 15-6 victory over England in the 2007 Rugby World Cup final

Above: President Thabo Mbeki congratulates John Smit after the trophy presentation. France's President Nicolas Sarkozy stands behind President Mbeki

What a difference a few years make ... It is clear from these two pictures that a Springbok coach and his captain suffer a great deal of pressure. The top photo was taken in June 2004, and the one immediately above in October 2007

Left: Percy Montgomery and Bryan Habana celebrate South Africa's victory with their fans during the victory parades the Springboks undertook throughout the country in 2007

@ Gallo Images

Above: With four Springbok captains at the launch of *Springbok Saga* in September 2008. From left: Gary Teichmann, John Smit, André Vos, me and Bob Skinstad

Right: Beating the British & Irish Lions in 2009. Tendai 'Beast' Mtawarira hurtles over Lions captain Paul O'Connell while Jean de Villiers (left) and Victor Matfield (right) look on

@ Gallo Images/Duif du Toit

Left: Interviewing for this book: With Dr Louis Luyt at the Luyt Lager Brewery in Ballito, KwaZulu-Natal, in July 2010

Below: With Gary Teichmann at his civil-engineering business in KwaZulu-Natal, July 2010

With Fourie du Preez at the Palazzo Montecasino in Sandton, August 2010

Below: Schalk Burger Snr and Daniel Brunnier on his estate Domaine du Vieux Telegraphe in the Châteauneuf-du-Pape region of France

Above: With Joel Stransky in Bryanston, Johannesburg, June 2010

Rugby brought me Linda, and it has provided us with some great times. Here we are at the 2010 Super 14 final at the Orlando Stadium in Soweto

then I discovered that the judicial officer was going to be none other than the Boks' favourite JO, Terry Willis.

The incident in which Steyn was meant to have bitten Vaka took place just moments after Bob Skinstad had dived over for one of the Springboks' four tries. This meant that it took a while for the cameras to swing back to the altercation that had broken out between Botha and Afeaki during which, in 'real time', Steyn jumped between the combatants and kept them apart. By the time Steyn came into shot on the match footage, he was already on the ground – the result of being thrown there by Vaka, who had run in a good few metres to 'attack' the Springbok.

The video footage confirmed my reading of what had occurred. Steyn had been attempting to separate Bakkies Botha and Inoke Afeaki when Vaka came running in from the left wing, grabbed Steyn and hurled him to the ground. Steyn retaliated by pulling Vaka down.

At the time I was astounded when Steyn, along with Vaka, was yellow-carded. In my opinion, the aggressor had been Vaka (it was not unlike the ruling against James Dalton in Port Elizabeth in 1995) and he alone should have been sent off – if any of the officials had actually spotted the incident. The video footage then showed Vaka walking away from the melee and kneeling down to fiddle with his sock or shoe. At that point he did not seem very concerned about any niggles he might have picked up from the incident.

Both teams then went into a huddle, and it was only when the referee called out the captains and the 'culprits' that Vaka started to fiddle with his hand. Referee Barnes announced his decision to yellow-card both players, and only then did Vaka start complaining about a bite to his finger/s. The soundtrack revealed Tonga captain Nili Latu inquiring whether the match official was going to 'look at the bite'.

Steyn's response, in Afrikaans, was graphic. *'Fok of! Ek het jou nie gebyt nie. Fok of!'* he shouted furiously as he strode off to the sin bin.

Reporter Xola Ntshinga and cameraman Dawie Janse van Rensburg were dispatched to the Place Vendôme to await the outcome of the hearing and get shots of Steyn and the rest of the Springbok management team in the black suits and lime-green ties they wore as their 'step-outs' during the tournament. This time the Boks were better prepared and had with them lawyer Nick Usiskin, who had appeared for them before (notably to defend John Smit in the 2005 incident with Jerome Thion).

Xola and Dawie waited at the archway leading to the lawyer's chambers, and after an hour or so we got a call from Xola. 'I think Fransie has got off,' he said.

'How do you know?' I asked.

'I've just overheard Anton Snyman [of the SABC] on the phone with Zola Yeye and he immediately phoned the SABC newsroom to alert them that the story was coming.' Yeye, whose day job was being the regional manager for the SABC Eastern Cape, was in the meeting and keeping an eye out for the corporation!

Steyn's hearing turned out to be the farce I had thought it would be, and he was cleared to continue playing. It transpired from the ruling that the citing had been initiated by the Tongan team's management. After hearing the evidence, the JO 'accepted the explanation by Steyn that the sequence of events was such that he could not have been involved in the contact that led to an alleged mark on Vaka's hand and accepted the evidence from the Tongan player that it may have happened by accident during the melee'.

The Springboks were furious. The Tongans had all but admitted that their accusation against Steyn had been concocted by Vaka because he had feared being red-carded (he had already received a warning), and that management went along with it because they didn't want tit-for-tat citings from the Springboks. White was happy to have his man back, but he was livid that no further action would be taken against Tonga who, at the very least, had brought the game into disrepute.

But the coach's problems were about to get much bigger ... and a lot more personal.

22

Invitation to a (war) dance

Montpellier proved to be an interesting and relaxing stopover for the entire South African touring group – other than Jake White. Situated in what is known as the Languedoc-Roussillon region of southern France, the main focus point of the city is the Place de la Comédie. On this vast square we did our intros for our SuperSport programmes or sat in the many cafés, just shooting the breeze.

One day a worried-looking Christo Kotzé, *Rapport*'s excellent sports photographer, approached me and said, 'Do you know what Jake White's girlfriend looks like?' I was quite taken aback.

'Girlfriend?' I said.

'Yes,' he replied with a pained expression on his face. 'Apparently he has a girlfriend who is here with him and I have been told to get a picture of them together.'

Kotzé explained that his editors at *Rapport* had received information about this woman who was with White in France and the newspaper was quite hot for the story. I was not that close to Jake and was surprised to hear these claims, as he had always seemed a close-knit family man to me. My heart bled for Kotzé, though. What an awful job to be lumbered with, especially for a specialist sports photographer who had to stay on good terms with the team so that he could take the daily human-interest pictures the newspapers needed.

Fortunately it was not something I had to be bothered by, and I immediately put it out of my mind as a hang-dog Kotzé shuffled away, mumbling, 'I'm not a bloody paparazzo.' There might have been something in the rumour, given how oddly White behaved subsequently (of which more later), but years afterwards Kotzé told me that he had been so upset by the incident that he was physically ill at dinner that night. The long-range picture he took was never published.

As explained, Montpellier was a gentle stopover and a chance for everyone to catch their breath. I always try to see the sights when I am on tour, and I had planned to visit the ancient fortified city of Carcassonne, location of many movies set in medieval times. But then we ran into 'Groot' Schalk

Burger,* and he invited me, Kobus Wiese and Russell Belter to join him and his family on an excursion to the wine-growing regions of Provence, an easy road trip away. As the match against the US Eagles was not until the Sunday, it was good to take a day off, and what a memorable experience it turned out to be.

Jake White and whatever problems he might have been having were soon forgotten as we headed for Avignon, where Schalk managed to navigate the minibus through hair-raisingly winding, cobbled streets I didn't think we would fit into. Then we headed for the world-famous wine region Châteauneuf-du-Pape, an area immersed in papal history. At one time, the seat of the Roman Catholic Church was based in Avignon, and Châteauneuf-du-Pape translates into 'the Pope's new castle'. The vines are literally planted in fields of stone.

I watched with great amusement each time we stopped at a cellar and Schalk and Kobus unfolded themselves from the vehicle. People always comment on the size of South African forwards, and you could just see the expressions of the French winemakers, who must have been thinking, 'Jeez, I'd heard these guys were big, but not *that* big!'

Meanwhile … there was a Rugby World Cup on. South Africa's match against the USA at Stade de la Mosson was the last of the pool games, No. 40, and as the Boks were expected to win comfortably, there was more interest in the preceding games – Wales vs Fiji, Scotland vs Italy, France vs Georgia and Ireland vs Argentina – as they would all have a bearing on who would play in the quarter-finals.

On the Saturday night, Fiji shocked Wales in Nantes to earn a quarter-final against the Springboks in Marseille. Scotland beat Italy, and France got the big win over Georgia that they required to put pressure on Argentina, log leaders in Pool D.

Thus Argentina's match against Ireland at the Stade de France – the second last of the 40 pool matches – was infused with massive importance, not only to themselves and the Irish, but also crucially to the French and the All Blacks. If the Pumas beat Ireland, they would definitely top the log and knock Ireland out of the tournament – a result that would mean France ending up as runners-up in Pool D. They would then have to play a quarter-final against the All Blacks in Cardiff.

---

* *Burger Snr and his family own a wine farm in Wellington; the highly regarded Burger & Sons Welbedacht estate.*

Interestingly, given how it panned out, at that point the southern hemi-sphere was well up on the north, with the trio who made up the Tri Nations – South Africa, New Zealand and Australia – already having qualified for the knockout phases.

So by the time the Springboks ran out in Montpellier for what would be Jake White's 50th Test in charge, they already knew that they would face the unlikely opponents of Fiji in the quarter-final, and that their semi-final opponents would be either Argentina or Scotland. Argentina had comfortably accounted for the Irish, and Scotland had seen off Italy to advance to the last eight. The other two quarter-finals would be between the Wallabies, who had not been much in the news, and England, while France were condemned to play the All Blacks in Cardiff.

White's amazing milestone of 50 Tests, given the rate of attrition among his predecessors, elicited a warm tribute from John Smit. 'I've known Jake since I was 16 years old, the first time I played for my first team [Pretoria Boys' High] was against his first team [Jeppe High School for Boys], and we've walked a long road together. And I tell you what: I don't think people will ever realise what an achievement it is for a coach to be in charge of South Africa for 50 Tests consecutively. In fact, I wonder if it will ever be done again. It is something that I would have said is impossible. It's a job that can be quite rigorous, with a huge [number] of demands, and the way Jake's coped – how he's kept his management team together, how he's stuck to his team, how he's kept us insulated from some of the problems – has been incredible.

'He's had to travel some rocky roads. I think it's three times harder to get 50 Tests as a coach than it is as a player, because there's just so much pressure. For us, the one thing that he's dedicated himself to since the day he got involved is that first speech that he gave us about winning the World Cup in 2007, and perhaps Jake's 50th Test will be irrelevant compared to the kind of gift we can give him on 20 October [the day of the World Cup final]. That's what everyone here has worked towards. Jake certainly has given every inch of his life, every hair on his head [smiling], has been dedicated to the fact that this team must be well prepared and able to win the World Cup in 2007. That would be better than any possible gift we could give him.

'The scariest moment was when Jake asked me to be captain even before the team was announced, but the best is what followed. That was one of the most impressive speeches I've ever heard. I sat down as this captain who was terrified and not too sure of what was coming and expecting him to tell us how we were going to beat Ireland, and before we'd even had a training session, he was telling us we were going to win the World Cup.

'We've had our highs and lows since then, but that's certainly what stands out for me. It was only when I was injured [Smit hurt a hamstring in the Tri Nations in the Test against Australia at Newlands in June, and did not see any action until the start of the World Cup] that I realised how emotional he gets during a Test match, how he lives every one of the 80 minutes with the guys out there. The Springboks are really a big part of Jake's life and I'd much rather be playing than listening to him shout and scream for the 80 minutes.

'The dressing room, however, is probably where Jake is best. He always says the right thing at the right time. I've never heard him lose his cool; when he's had to get a point across that the guys have neglected to do, he's always been calm and firm.'

Concluded Smit: 'In 50 Tests he's never panicked, or shouted, or gone beserk. Some guys can really lose their temper, but Jake's always been calm and collected and always given us the right information that's relevant to the Test we're playing. I think the guys are all aware that the best way we can repay him is by doing the job he gave us in June 2004.'

In the subsequent Test against the Eagles, the Springboks stuttered to a 64-15 victory against a side who had little to offer except a well-drilled maul, a big heart and a willingness to try to play attacking rugby. The Boks, on the other hand, knowing that their path ahead was already plotted, were distracted and inaccurate. Nevertheless they scored nine tries to two, but the match will be remembered for another African, the Zimbabwean-born Takudzwa Ngwenya.

The wing had first caught the eye against Samoa with a stunning, swerving try. Against the Springboks, he intercepted the ball near the half-way line, stood up to none other than Bryan Habana and beat him for pace on the outside to score a brilliant try. It was one of those moments that made the World Cup worthwhile for the minnows. Later it transpired that Ngwenya, who hailed from Harare and went by the nicknames of 'Zee' or 'Speedo', rated Habana as his hero.

The Eagles' other try, by fullback Chris Wyles, was also a good effort, and the warm applause the Americans received when they bade the tournament farewell was testimony to the fact that they had won the respect of the crowd. Two of their best players were South African–born Chad Erskine (scrumhalf) and Owen Lentz (hooker), while a third of their number, Todd Clever (loose forward), had made enough of an impression to be given a Super 14 contract with the Lions in 2009.

Schalk Burger, making his return in the No. 8 jersey after his enforced lay-off, deservedly won the Man of the Match award. *Four down, three to go.* Next stop, Marseille.

The Springboks were booked into the incongruous-sounding Palm Beach Hotel in Corniche Kennedy, which has a panoramic view of the Bay of Marseille (including the island that houses the prison of Château d'If, made famous by Alexandre Dumas' novel *The Count of Monte Cristo*). The Fijians were in a less fashionable establishment nearer the port, and big was my shock when I attended their first press call. *This* was not a team intent on taking prisoners. They were *huge.*

An unrecognised fact of the World Cup is that the three Pacific Island sides are at their strongest and most dangerous during the RWC tournament, as it is the only time they are at full strength. At other times many of their players are contractually obligated to provinces and clubs and unable to get leave to play in internationals. But during the World Cup, all other rugby is on hold and they are able to form into powerful units.

France's shock loss against the Argentines had thus not only put the Boks on a freeway to the final, but given them a set of matches against the cluster of islands that is unlikely to be repeated. Of course it came with the attendant expectations of facing three, possibly four, different 'invitations to war': the ancient rite performed by the Polynesian people before battle commences.[*]

---

[*] *Thanks to an article on the online site of the* Fiji Times, *I was able to glean that the Boks would have to link arms and accept a challenge from the Fijians by way of their* cibi *(pronounced thimbi) in the quarter-final. Fiji's* cibi *has been performed on the rugby pitch since their first tour of New Zealand in 1939. When returning from battle victorious, warriors would sing the* cibi, *brandishing their weapons and flying flags, one for each enemy slain. Fijian flyhalf Nicky Little (who was out of the forthcoming match because of injury) told a reporter that the* cibi *fired up the team: 'It's a tribal psyche-up for war. I think it makes a few people crazy,' he said. The Samoan war dance is the* siva tau, *first composed for RWC 1991, while Tonga's* sipi tau *is considered by some to be the most aggressive of the war dances, as the players advance towards their opponents. This resulted in an electric moment at RWC 2003, when Tonga and New Zealand faced off with simultaneous war dances. New Zealand's call to war is, of course, the Haka (first performed by the New Zealand Native (Maori) team in an overseas representative match on the 1888/89 tour of Britain). At that stage of RWC 2007, everyone was anticipating that the Boks would face the Haka in the final: either the 'Ka Mate' version made famous by the All Blacks, or the newer 'Kapa O Panga', with its provocative throat-slitting motion.*

However, in the city where a large part of the 70s movie *The French Connection* was shot, there was plenty of underground activity. On the Wednesday I received an SMS from Mark Keohane (who had established a hot line to Jake White's Blackberry) to say that he, Gavin Rich and some other pressmen were meeting White for drinks, and why did I not come along. But I couldn't join them, as we were taking Ann-Lee Murray, who had always been most helpful to SuperSport, to dinner, along with a producer from Australia's Fox TV.

Making my way back to my hotel later on, I ran into a group of supporters from Johannesburg, and they imparted the following interesting piece of *skinder* (gossip). 'Jeez, we've just seen Jake White, and he was absolutely hammered!' Apparently White had been making his way along the waterfront in the direction of the team hotel and, according to these fans, was distinctly worse for wear.

On the Thursday, Rich confirmed that the boys had, in rugby parlance, 'gone big'. No problem there – it happens on rugby tours, and given my own love of a good get-together, I was certainly not going to judge them. However, in the course of the day, we (the media) received an SMS from Vusi Kama, the team's press officer, inviting us to a cocktail party with the team's management at their hotel. This was strange, because while the team had been cordial and cooperative in terms of dealing with the media, they had tended to stick to RWC protocols – much to the annoyance of Russell Belter who, as a constant and inoffensive recorder of their deeds on many a tour, was accustomed to freer access.

A 'what's up?' flag went up in our minds, so there was a good turnout at the Palm Beach Hotel, although some might say the free drinks had something to do with it! Hugh Bladen and I were chatting to White on the terrace, and I was surprised when he told us a confusing tale about how he had gone out for a drink the previous night, met up with an Australian bloke who insisted on buying him rounds, and had had one too many. Why did he not just say that he had been with Keohane, Rich and the press gang?

Afterwards, White welcomed us and then made an impassioned speech about the team being in the quarter-final of the World Cup and how they needed all the support they could get. He appealed to us not to write or say anything that could upset the team. 'We're all in this together,' he concluded. Needless to say, Christo Kotzé felt the speech was directed at him! But a junior member of the management team (whom it would be unfair to name because he is still involved in rugby) remarked, 'It's a worry. This is starting to be more about Jake than the team.' When it came to rugby, though, White was his usual frank self, saying, 'If the Springboks can't beat Fiji and Argentina to reach a World Cup final, they don't deserve to be here.'

Eight teams left. Four matches. Three venues. On the Saturday afternoon it was England up against the Wallabies in Marseille, followed by France against the All Blacks in Cardiff. On the Sunday it would be South Africa's turn in the Stade Vélodrome furnace against Fiji, with the game between Argentina and Scotland in Paris deciding the fourth team that would advance to the semi-finals.

The Stade Vélodrome's capacity is 70 022, and every seat was sold for the Springbok match, thanks mainly to the many England supporters, and a good many Welshmen, who had travelled to the Côte d'Azur expecting to see their team up against the Boks. There was also a smattering of Aussies, but none of them would be cheering for South Africa. The Stade Vélodrome is a famous hunting ground for French teams who bank on the support of one of the most fervent crowds in sport, and the Springboks knew that about 65 000 of them would be providing a cacophony of sound to egg on the Fijians.

White, however, felt that his team's pool games had prepared them well for the hostile reception they could expect. 'It will be most important to keep our structure and hold onto the ball, not allow them any momentum and silence that damned trumpeter!' laughed White in reference to what had become a feature of the tournament. The trumpet refrain that is part of bull-fighting (and introduced to rugby by the rugby-loving Basques) had been adopted by World Cup supporters in France, and whenever the trumpet sounded, they would respond with a jolly 'Olé!'

As I had seen the Fijians up close and was familiar with their Sevens skills, I knew it was going to be a difficult game, but none of us had anticipated quite how difficult. And this in the light of the first two quarter-finals, which had produced massive upsets.

England had managed to pick themselves up after their heavy defeat against South Africa and their bulldog spirit was too much for a Wallaby side starved of the ball. Jonny Wilkinson once again broke Aussie hearts by kicking four penalties, cancelling out a try by Lote Tuqiri and a conversion and penalty by Stirling Mortlock, allowing England to take a 12-10 win.

And then France produced an inspired performance in the Millennium

Stadium in Cardiff to knock New Zealand out of the tournament. On a quarter-final day in which the form book was turned upside down, the French fought back from 0-13 down to hand the highly favoured All Blacks yet another crushing World Cup disappointment. Afterwards, the Kiwis complained bitterly that a pass from Damien Traille to Frédérik Michalak, which led to Yannick Jauzion scoring the winning try, had been forward by miles. They also found it incomprehensible that referee Wayne Barnes had not penalised France once in the second half, even though they'd spent most of it on defence.

But in truth they had paid the price for Graham Henry failing to settle on his best team, for playing the wrong kind of rugby and for the bad luck of ending up in a pool in which they were never tested.

During the game, Henry had made the almost unheard-of decision to substitute Dan Carter with Nick Evans, and in the stands the flyhalf's sick expression reflected a New Zealand nightmare.

The exit of the two southern hemisphere favourites was an immense shock, but a couple of hours later an inspirational John Smit would use their defeats to galvanise a Springbok team in danger of suffering the same fate.

In an atmosphere that had to be experienced to be believed, the Springboks survived a massive scare when the Fijians hit back from 6-20 down after 51 minutes to level the score in the 59th minute. The South Africans' game plan was to force the Fijians, who prefer free-wheeling rugby, into a forward battle. And the plan worked to perfection as possession and structure translated into tries for Jaque Fourie, Juan Smith and JP Pietersen. François Steyn had opened the scoring with a long-range penalty, while Montgomery kicked a conversion. Fiji could only respond with a pair of penalties by Seremaia Bai.

With less than 30 minutes to go, it seemed as if the Boks had effectively thwarted the threat of Fiji's big runners, and they eschewed their safety-first tactics and started leaving the ball exposed. Bad mistake. In the space of eight minutes, long-range tries by wings Vilimoni Delasau and Sireli Bobo, both converted by Bai, tied up the score at 20-all. Suddenly, the unthinkable – that we may lose – hit home.

It was a terrible moment. I had watched (with a tinge of pleasure, I admit shamefully) the horror on the faces of the Kiwis in the press box when they bombed out at Twickenham in 1999, and I had seen the grey pallor of the Aussies the day before in the Stade Vélodrome when they realised their team was going home. But now I started wondering how I would write *my* match report. In my mind I had been ready to wax lyrical about 'marching to Paris', echoing the passionate French anthem 'La Marseillaise' – *Formez vos bataillons, Marchons! Marchons!* (Form your battalions, Let us march! Let us march!). But suddenly all the signs indicated that the Springboks were heading for defeat.

However, cometh the hour, cometh the man ... This was the moment when John Smit once again displayed true leadership and found the words to rouse his team. It is not known exactly what he said, but he certainly climbed into his team while Bai was taking the conversion of Bobo's try, and the words hit their mark. With expletives removed, it went something like this: 'Look, there's still 20 minutes to go. Remember the look in the eyes of the Aussies yesterday; remember the look in the eyes of the All Blacks ... I don't want to see that look in your eyes! Pick yourselves f****g up!'

Soon Percy Montgomery restored the lead with a penalty (23-20), but it took an amazing tackle by JP Pietersen to keep the Springboks' dream alive. It was arguably the key moment of the Boks' entire World Cup campaign. Just as the much bigger, 120-kilogram lock Ifereimi Rawaqa was diving over the line for a try, which would have given Fiji the lead, the Sharks winger managed to clamp his arms over the ball and turn Rawaqa to prevent him from touching the ball down.

I was sitting in the press box with many of the UK writers, and they were stomping their feet and banging the desks, willing the Fijians on. The din from the crowd was deafening, and the instinct born of many years of rugby reporting told me that the Boks were done for. Slowly, however, they regained control of the ball, kept it in the opposition half and sucked the fight out of the Fijians. A succession of powerful scrums provided the platform from which tries for Juan Smith and Butch James were created, both converted by Montgomery, and the Boks clinched a 37-20 win that felt much less emphatic than the score reflected.

Flushed by what I felt was a heroic effort, turning what had seemed like certain defeat into victory, I started my match report as follows: 'The Springboks played like world champions to beat Fiji 37-20 in their RWC quarter-final ...' Later, at the airport, as I waited to catch a flight to Paris, I was amazed that my feelings were far removed from what some former Springboks were thinking. Joost van der Westhuizen and Kobus Wiese, who were both part of the SuperSport team of commentators, were scathingly critical. 'If they play like that [again], we can forget about winning the cup,' said Van der Westhuizen. And when Rassie Erasmus, accompanied by his long-time associate Frikkie Erasmus, came by, he was equally disparaging. I wondered whether I was becoming too much of a fan.

And yet: *Five down, two to go.*

Back in marvellous Paris, the SuperSport team had to split up due to a lack of accommodation, but I had the extreme good fortune to be booked into a hotel just down the hill from the Arc de Triomphe (my nearest metro was Charles de Gaulle-Étoile, right under Napoleon's great arch). For me, the last two weeks of the 2007 World Cup stand out as the best time I'd had in a reporting career spanning more than 40 years. My partner Linda had flown over, so our days were spent catching up with the Springboks and then rushing to take in the experiences of the truly majestic city: Monet, Manet and Van Gogh at the Musée D'Orsay, the Mona Lisa at the Louvre, Notre-Dame, a baguette, some cheese and wine for lunch on the lawns of the Eiffel Tower, the basilica of Sacré-Coeur shimmering on the hill, a romantic dinner while cruising down the Seine on one of the *Bateaux-Mouches* (river barges) … so much that appeals to the senses.

Up the street from my hotel I noticed a rugby-themed bar, Au Village des Ternes, and one day I went in for a meal and a glass of wine and ended up making wonderful friends in the proprietors Didier and Fabienne Bongain and their son Jimmy. Even though my French consists of no more than a few words, they took me in and introduced me to their friends, and we enjoyed many a memorable occasion. Late one night we even set an England flag alight with cognac on the pavement and did a war dance around it while singing the 'Marseillaise'. Well, what little I knew of it. These things happen. Didier is a cordon bleu chef with one proviso: you eat what he makes. And he makes the best lamb shank and *confit de canard* (preserved duck leg) anywhere in the world.

The Springboks were in Paris facing two more steps to glory. The All Blacks and the Wallabies never even got there.

23

Vive le Bokke!
C'est magnifique!

France against England in the first semi-final at the Stade de France on Saturday 13 October stirred up ancient rivalries. It meant that South Africa and Argentina, due to meet in the second semi-final, on the Sunday, temporarily dropped off the radar.

Media attention was instead focused on Lionel Beauxis (who had become Bernard Laporte's preferred No. 10) and Jonny Wilkinson, allowing Jake White and his good friend Marcelo Loffreda to prepare their teams in relative peace.

The Springboks, by dint of the fact that they'd never been beaten by the Pumas (not counting the famous 21-12 win by Hugo Porta's South American Jaguars, Argentina in all but name and political sanction, in Bloemfontein in 1982), were overwhelming favourites, so White's biggest task was to keep his players' feet on the ground. White talked up the Pumas, highlighting the power of their forwards and the great skill of *El Mago* (the magician), Argentina's flyhalf Juan Martín Hernández.

Possibly because of Argentina's undervalued status in world rugby, Hernández was not a 'name' in the sense that Jonny Wilkinson was in 2003, but he was considered one of the best players in France on the strength of his performances for Stade Français. He was initially listed as a fullback, but Loffreda moved him to flyhalf. (Loffreda, incidentally, had played centre for the Jaguars in that win over the Springboks.) As flyhalf, Hernández had played a key role in guiding the Pumas to the highest base camp they had ever reached in their ascent of rugby's Everest.

His kicking out of hand had exposed France in the opening game, and in the Pumas' last pool game he dropped three goals as Argentina disposed of Ireland, again at the Stade de France, an arena with which Hernández was obviously familiar. There were cries of *Maro! Maro!* – comparing the 25-year-old flyhalf to Maradona – and White pointed out that with his skipper, Agustin Pichot, Hernández had formed a halfback combination that had captured two French championships. Puma coach Marcelo Loffreda had clearly opted for the motto, 'When in Paris, do as the Parisians do.'

The announcement that Hernández and his teammate Felipe Contepomi, a flyhalf for Leinster but at inside centre for the World Cup, had been nominated for the IRB's Rugby Player of the Year award, the first time two Argentines had been included, simply confirmed why the Pumas were considered one of the four best sides in the world. The Argentines had always been renowned for their steamroller *bajada* scrum, but the class of 2007 had something else – backs who could hit on the counter and score long-range tries. One of their strong runners was, in fact, Contepomi's younger brother, Manuel, who had the distinction of joining his elder sibling in the centre.

White did such a good job of punting the opposition that he nearly turned the Pumas into the favourites, but come the match, Argentina's positives turned into negatives. Their greatest moment on the world stage was undone by the abject failure of Hernández and Felipe Contepomi.

In the end, the Springboks won through to the final comfortably – 37-13 – thanks to their ferocious defence, which unsettled and roughed up the Pumas, the slide-rule kicking of Percy Montgomery, who kicked seven out of seven place kicks successfully for a contribution of 17 points, and two moments of Bryan Habana's special magic.

Referee Steve Walsh had his hands full dealing with the remonstrations of both captains, as there was plenty of off-the-ball stuff going on, but the Boks' passage to the final was effectively booked by half-time, when they led 24-6.

The Pumas had advanced this far with a simple game plan based on plenty of pick-and-drive, high kicks from Hernández and Contepomi, and blanket chasing to pin their opponents in their own half. But in the semi-final, Loffreda decided to try to catch the Springboks unawares by running the ball. It was a good idea in theory, but in practice it turned to mud as Fourie du Preez intercepted a pass by Hernández just outside the Springbok 22 and set off on a diagonal 70-metre run to the far goal line for a try in the sixth minute.

A conversion and a penalty by Montgomery and two penalties to Argentina made it 10-6 to the Boks after 30 minutes, but the Pumas, who seemed intent on perniciously trying to unsettle the South African forwards, had not made the strong start they needed.

In the 31st minute, Habana was worked free on the left, and he chipped his direct opponent Lucas Borges before winning the sprint for his first try. Nine minutes later, just on half-time, the hard toil of South Africa's loose trio paid off. Hernández could not control a back pass, and Schalk Burger swooped to claim the ball on the ground, popped it up to Juan Smith, who made some ground before sending Danie Rossouw in for a try. Montgomery kicked both conversions to put his side into a 24-6 comfort zone, and suddenly it seemed too big a hill to climb for the Pumas.

Soon after the restart, Manuel Contepomi pulled a questionable try back for the Pumas. It appeared as if he had lost control of the ball as he'd dived over the line. The Springboks, however, were content to concentrate on controlling the ball and playing in the Pumas' half, thus providing Montgomery with two more penalty opportunities. The gap built to 30-13 with just five minutes left.

The Argentines were a beaten side, and it seemed almost preordained when Bryan Habana snatched the second telling interception of the match to sprint in from long range for his second try (and eighth of the tournament, thus equalling Jonah Lomu's RWC tournament record of 1999).

It was, once again, a victory built on the superb line-out work of Victor Matfield, Bakkies Botha and Juan Smith, the thudding hits of all the tacklers, the pack of loose forwards Schalk Burger, Danie Rossouw and Smith, the poise of Butch James at flyhalf, the ability of every player to exploit the slightest chances, and the composure and control of Fourie du Preez. The Boks radiated an aura of supreme confidence. They were a team completely assured in their own abilities.

Six down. One to go.

As an aside, earlier in the afternoon Ernie Els had made it a double for South Africa over Argentina by beating Ángel Cabrera in the final of the World Match Play Championship at Wentworth, England. Els dispatched Cabrera 6 and 4 to extend his record to seven victories, and he then rushed to his personal jet to get to Paris in time for the 9 p.m. kick-off at the Stade de France!

The day before the Springbok match, England had plunged France into mourning when they won the first semi-final 14-9. In a nervy match, reserve hooker Dimitri Szarzewski made the killer mistake when he stuck out an arm and caught the low-slung Jason Robinson around the head. Jonny Wilkinson unerringly guided over the penalty to put England 11-9 ahead in the 73rd minute, the first time they had led since the 17th minute. France's worst nightmare was about to become a reality. Toby Flood and Paul Sackey dumped Sébastien Chabal into touch, allowing England to win the ensuing line-out and crawl crab-like into the French half.

And as the white pack advanced, there was an air of inevitably about the next passage. The ball came back to Wilkinson, who was standing just inside the 10-metre line within drop-goal range. His left foot connected and the ball bisected the uprights. The clock showed 77 minutes and 30 seconds, leaving France with the task of scoring a converted try to remain part of 'their' World Cup. But it was not to be. England, at times described in their media as the worst-ever squad to participate in a World Cup, had repeated their feat of 1991 by reaching the final in spite of losing in the pool stages – the only country to have done so.

With only two teams left, and one being England, the Springboks suddenly found themselves in a media scrum. They had seen off Argentina's *El Mago*, but now they had to do with The King himself: Jonny Wilkinson. In fact, England seemed to think the only way they would be able to turn a 0-36 defeat into a victory over the Springboks was the 'Jonny Factor'.

The British media's obsession with Wilkinson – who was literally described in the tabloids as the 'blond messiah' – was nauseating. Millions of words had been expended on his injuries, and now that England had defied the odds by reaching the final, the level of veneration was right back to where it was in Australia in 2003. Some claimed that the England team had rebelled against the methods of coach Brian Ashton, had done some soul-searching and changed their style of play (even though to my mind one form of pick-and-go was much like any other), but the masses were informed, ad nauseum, that if England were to retain the Webb Ellis Cup, it would be down to 'Wilko' (or the blond messiah, if you prefer).

Wilkinson had not been in the team whipped by the Boks in their pool match, but his late penalty, followed by a rare drop goal, to knock France out of the tournament had once again made him the shining knight on a white steed who would slay the Springboks.

And, it has to be said, the Springbok camp fanned the flames of Wilkomania. As the pressure mounted towards the end of the week, Jake White made constant references to the fact that Wilkinson had been absent when the Boks had thrashed England. And then Eddie Jones was quite unexpectedly pushed to the fore to face the media. Jones's Wallabies had lost to a last-gasp drop goal by Sir Jonny in Sydney in 2003, and in Paris he had the English media eating out of his hand when he skilfully ramped up the concentration on Wilkinson by speaking admiringly of the blond flyhalf's qualities.

Jones, who had been the subject of heated controversy when the South

African government had allegedly influenced SA Rugby's decision not to award him a Springbok blazer, had stayed quietly in the background for most of the tournament. In Marseille, we had had to press hard to get an interview with him, and it was odd that he suddenly faced the press conference in Paris on the Tuesday. Was this confirmation that White was beset with problems?

Then the story broke that White was set to cut ties with South African rugby following the RWC final. He claimed to have been caught unawares. Media reports in both South Africa and Britain speculated that White had already made the decision to walk away from Springbok rugby, though he tried to direct everyone's attention back to his team's bid to win the Webb Ellis Cup. SA Rugby had upset White when they decided to advertise the Bok coach's job in the week after the quarter-finals, but by then his relationship with his employers seemed to have broken down completely anyway.

White had alluded too many times to what would appear in his auto-biography, and he certainly did not seem to have any intention of staying on as coach after the World Cup. This, however, was a conviction that seemed to waver once the Webb Ellis Cup was within reach. When I read the bestselling *In Black and White* after the RWC, I formed the impression that White was intent on showing why South Africa had *not* won the World Cup in the way he described the run-up to the tournament. With everything that he'd had to put up with, it would have come as no surprise if South Africa had failed at the tournament. But at the end of the book, which came out shortly after the RWC final, he had to put a different spin on it very quickly when the Boks actually won!

In the week before the final, SA Rugby's administrators arrived in Paris in droves. While conducting an interview with White in his room, I asked him whether he was signing up with England. It transpired that he'd had a meeting with Jonathan Stones, the then MD of SA Rugby (Pty) Ltd., to discuss his contract. Stones, a close friend of SARU chairman Mpumelelo Tshume, had strong business credentials but very little rugby experience, and he would last less than two years in the job. When he was first appointed, I used to joke that if he did run into problems with SA Rugby, the headline would be: 'Dem Stones, dem Stones, dem fired Stones!'

Someone else who was spotted in the foyer of the Sofitel Paris Bercy, wearing a Springbok supporter shirt, was the man who had threatened to have the passports of the players withdrawn, which would, of course, have prevented them from travelling to France: Butana Komphela, chairman of the parliamentary portfolio committee on sport and recreation. Quite astonishingly, Komphela had asked to meet with the players and took affront when his request was rebuffed.

'Jake was very stressed out,' Fourie du Preez recalled about this time. 'He sort of lost it. He didn't want us to go and play golf on a Thursday, for instance, as we had been doing for four years,* and he was changing things on the practice field. He was wobbling. We laughed about it at the back of the bus.'

White tried his best to douse the flames of speculation surrounding him. 'My contract ends on 31 December this year, so I'm still employed by SA Rugby until the end of the year,' he said publicly. 'To be honest, the only goal I'm thinking about right now is winning the Rugby World Cup. All this talk about me leaving to coach in different countries is just speculative – in fact, there's hardly a country that doesn't have a coach that I haven't been connected to. It may be an attempt to sidetrack the focus of the team.'

Pressed on speculation that he had already made the decision to quit, White said, 'It's very difficult in the middle of the World Cup, with the team in the final, to decide whether you're staying or going. My whole focus since taking on the job has been to win the Rugby World Cup, and I think when you're in the middle of this to think about anything else would be silly.' But he added: 'I love coaching the Springboks; it's the best thing I've ever done. I really enjoy this job. It's something that's been deep inside me for a long time now and it's been part of my life for four years.'

In their last press conference before the final, the more than 20 television cameras, chirruping of myriad digital cameras and some 150 reporters crowding into the hall shocked even the seasoned Springboks. The spectacle drew a quip from John Smit that probably didn't come out quite as he had intended: 'I've had my fair share of media conferences in my couple of years as captain, and this certainly does top the list; more microphones and cameras than I've [ever] seen. I now know what it feels like to be Charlize Theron or Angelina Jolie!'

We had set ourselves the task of interviewing each one of the 22 play-

---

* *The habit of playing a game of golf two days before a match had originated with François Pienaar's 1995 team and its necessity had grown into something of a superstition.*

ers named for the final, and I had a chuckle while waiting to interview Bakkies Botha.

Scars and abrasions on the big lock's face graphically illustrated what the Pumas had got up to in the semi-final. As he explained, 'I was the only player in the last two games who went off for blood. I think the guys have been targeting me. I think they were having a go at me to try to put me off my game, and try to get me to be aggressive off the ball, but experience has taught me a lot.' A French radio reporter asked him: 'Bakkees, you and Veectorr have formed a formidable partnership. Eet ees the power of the Spreengboks, no?' To which Bakkies replied: 'Yes, definitely … Victor and I are in a relationship.'

And if the Eiffel Tower could be done up in green and gold, so could the Webb Ellis Cup when South Africa won the Rugby World Cup for the second time. It took an exceptional defensive effort to beat England 15-6 in weather that had suddenly turned bitterly cold. Just as in 1995, no tries were scored, but the Springboks did score 15 points, and their victory was built on unrelenting and deadly tackling.

Against a side with more skill the Springboks might have succumbed, but England simply did not have the nous to break down the Boks. When referee Alain Rolland's final whistle sounded, it was John Smit who stepped up to receive the trophy from Nicolas Sarkozy, the French president calling his South African counterpart Thabo Mbeki into the circle to share in the Boks' triumph.

It was a win built on the wonderful line-out work of Victor Matfield, Bakkies Botha and Juan Smith; the concentration and application in the scrums of CJ van der Linde, John Smit and Os du Randt, who stayed on the field for all of the 80 minutes of his swansong; the relentless pressure of loose forwards Smith, Schalk Burger and Danie Rossouw; and the kicking under severe pressure of Percy Montgomery, Butch James and Fourie du Preez. But most of all, it was the TACKLE.

There were times one felt England must surely break through, especially when they started to move the ball around in the final quarter, but somehow one of the Boks was always able to pull off a crucial stop, giving his teammates the time to swarm back into position and start the unyielding process all over again.

One piece of sloppy defence by the Boks provided the only stutter and a lot of copy for the English press. Moments after the restart, miscommunication between South Africa's centres François Steyn and Jaque Fourie allowed England centre Mathew Tait to break clear, and when Percy Montgomery also missed him, the Boks were scrambling. Victor Matfield (destined to be named the Man of the Match) somehow got back to pull down Tait, but England were able to move the ball to Mark Cueto on the left, and the winger appeared to smash past Danie Rossouw's desperate lunge as he hurtled for the corner.

Referee Rolland called in the assistance of TMO Stuart Dickinson to decide whether Cueto had been in touch. After what seemed too long a break, the ruling was given that the England wing had touched the chalk. It later transpired that the reason for the long delay had been because Dickinson had struggled to make it clear to the French director that he wanted the footage of Cueto's foot on the line. Rolland thus denied the English a try but awarded them a penalty, which Wilkinson goaled to make the score 9-6 to South Africa after 44 minutes.

Tait's break, after Steyn and Jaque Fourie had got in each other's way, had swung the momentum, and from then on it appeared as if the Boks did nothing but defend and scramble the ball back for one of the kickers to hoof into touch. A spectator invaded the field and had himself a good look at the back of an England maul, Montgomery was sent hurtling into a TV camera behind the advertising hoardings when he was shoved in the back by Toby Flood (an infringement that went unpunished), and the threat of a Wilkinson drop was ever present. Britain's most talked-about sportsman tried two drops but neither found their mark, and the Boks, much like their predecessors had done against the All Blacks at Ellis Park in 1995, were able to tackle their way to victory.

Montgomery opened the scoring with a penalty in the seventh minute, which was cancelled out by Wilkinson in the 13th. 'Monty' slotted his second in the 16th minute, his third on the stroke of half-time, and then Wilkinson made it 9-6 in the 44th minute. It was nip and tuck from then on, but Montgomery knocked over his fourth penalty in the 51st minute (12-6) after Martin Corry was penalised for hands-in, and François Steyn, from just inside the England half, gave the Boks a crucial nine-point buffer in the 62nd minute.

The statistics told the real story. In the line-outs, the Springboks stole seven balls off the English, while in three outings at the Stade de France during the tournament, Montgomery achieved a remarkable record of being successful with all 18 place kicks he attempted at the stadium.

It was the crowning glory on a remarkable partnership between John

Smit and Jake White, which had started with winning the Under-21 World Cup in Buenos Aires in 1999 and culminated in world champion status in France. White had delivered on his plan and Smit, who had to be injured before his true worth was recognised, stood out as arguably the outstanding captain of the tournament.

Seven down. Seven won. Mission accomplished.

Fourie du Preez, a man with a double French Huguenot name, was arguably the Boks' key play-maker, and his recollections some years later provided a fascinating insight into the quest for the Holy Grail. 'In four years leading up to France, there was always talk in the team that "Listen, our main goal is to win the World Cup." When we arrived in Paris, it was like, this is now *it*, it is finally happening. Jake spoke of winning the World Cup when he selected his first team; he said, "Listen, I'll back you guys to get there." We knew we were probably one of the four top teams, so our chances were pretty good. Obviously some guys didn't make it, but there was a core of us who went the whole way through those four years.

'Arriving in France, we just got a sense that this was probably our time to win the World Cup. We actually went to the opening game, [watching from] a box. Being at the Stade de France was just unbelievable: the opening, Argentina beating France … And we knew then that if we beat England, we would in all probability play the Pumas rather than France. Sitting there, taking in the atmosphere, being part of it, seeing France go down, it was just brilliant and set us on our way.

'There had been a lot of focus [on] and talk about the England pool game. We knew we had to win that game to have the best chance of winning the World Cup. So when that game came, they were obviously in a bit of disarray and we were quite confident. It was just one of those games in which everything came together, and after that we knew that we were going to have a great chance of winning the cup. That was probably the best game we played in Jake's time – especially given how we'd talked about it and built it up as the crucial hurdle. It was a high-pressure game, probably more so than the semi-final, and the team coming together really showed that we could deal with the pressure and do what was necessary.

'The whole organisation of the World Cup was unbelievable. It was the first time I felt like a professional soccer team must feel – everything was just laid on. We got off the plane, they took us straight into the bus, no passport control, no luggage hassles, just straight into the bus and a police escort to the hotel. That whole seven weeks was just unbelievable the way we were treated. Our police escorts were the same guys who looked after France in the Soccer World Cup in 1998.

'The metro was right by our hotel and everyone was so welcoming. We were treated like royalty. We were not used to that, and I think it also helped to raise our confidence and self-belief.

'Schalk Burger's citing could have unsettled us. Stuff like that is always disruptive, but it's something you just have to take on the chin and not let it affect you. Luckily we were a team who had been together for quite a while; we'd been through other such moments, and we knew how to get on with it. Often you can turn that kind of thing in your favour. In the team we didn't complain too much about it. We just said to ourselves, "Leave it where it is and just go and make amends on the field."

'The Fiji game got a little hectic. I don't think people realise how big and fast they were. The whole thing about that game was that on the Saturday afternoon New Zealand played France, so the whole team watched it on television. We felt the All Blacks were our biggest threat, so we were obviously very pleased that they lost ... Then that night, Australia lost to England.

'The guys couldn't get to sleep because they were really excited and then the next day we had to play Fiji. We actually started well, but they really started to play unbelievable rugby with the crowd behind them. I think they caught us by surprise a bit. They played a game we were not used to. With 20 minutes to go, it was level; JP made a great tackle and they were on our line for a couple of phases. Those were nervous moments. At that stage you start to have doubts in your mind. Everything was against us, the crowd, it was really humid and hot, some referee calls were wrong. There were two high tackles on Danie Rossouw and Schalk Burger that should have been carded but the ref let it go.

'But John [Smit] calmed us. "Listen guys, we've still got 20 minutes to go, it's still 20-all. Just relax and do what you have to do. Keep the ball and do what we do well." I'll be honest, at that stage I had doubts in my mind – it suddenly started to look as though all three of the Tri Nations teams were going home! To get through that game gave us a big lift and made us more confident for the last two games, because they would be against more conventional teams. We were busy losing that game but we got out of it and that makes you stronger.

'At the end of the day it was a World Cup quarter-final played against a team that was immensely hyped up and really had nothing to lose. They played unbelievable rugby, we were a little off our game, things were stacked against us and we still managed to win. It gave us an enormous lift going back to Paris. When the pressure was on, New Zealand and Australia folded.

'We did our homework for the semi-final against Argentina. When they played France in the opening game, we saw their main tactic was the high ball by Hernández, with runners converging on the catcher. So we made a plan to support Percy at the back with numbers and then to use the ball against them. I think we scored two tries off that situation.

'I remember waking up on the Monday after the semi-final and the people in the office block opposite our hotel had hung out a banner saying, "Go Springboks!" Everywhere we went, the French people would stop us and say: "Don't let the Roastbeefs beat you!" For the final we just maintained the attitude we had had all along – just win this game. Winning is what counts, and it doesn't matter how you do it. Sometimes playing that way might be entertaining and sometimes it won't be.

'We were in control that whole game. They really only had that one moment, when Cueto nearly scored, which came about because of a slip in the backline, but we really felt in control. I felt that if they had scored it would not really have mattered, we would have still got through, such was our control. I felt we could turn it on quite easily and go harder for tries. We just felt we had the game to do it, whichever way we needed to.'

Du Preez was fulsome in his praise of Eddie Jones. 'He was definitely one of the biggest reasons why we won the World Cup. Suddenly there was a guy with us who had looked at us from the outside, who had studied us for a few years and had pinpointed some of our weaknesses. He is one of the few coaches of whom I can really say, "He took my game to the next level." [He did the same] for Butch James. One of the key things Eddie brought to us was to be more aware of what's going on, of the guys around you, and to have more runners rather than the one-off man we tended to employ. But he didn't want to change anything. Whatever our strengths were, he just wanted us to apply them better. He played a key role that last week keeping us calm and believing in our game. Jake was incredibly tense and not quite with it. That's when John's captaincy really came through. He just took us away from the sideshows and made sure nothing got in the way.'

Du Preez also mentioned someone else as one of the reasons for South Africa's success. 'I still believe a lot of our success at the World Cup was also because of Heyneke Meyer and the structures he put in place at the Bulls. There were a lot of us Bulls in the squad and we took a lot of that to the World Cup: decision-making, maturity, defensive and attacking plays, a winning attitude. Heyneke never got a lot of credit, but after the World Cup a lot of us sat down and discussed it and realised that the things he had put in place had played a big part in our winning. [It was] the stuff that made us competitive in the Super 14.

'The final, in fact, was very easy. Our line-out was completely dominant, our scrum was good, our defence was good, our kicking was good and our discipline was good. As I said, we felt very much in control. Our players were talented enough to outplay the opposition if they managed to pick [their game] up.

'Waking up on the morning after the final and knowing we had done it … boy, you feel good.' Du Preez had, in fact, played through the tournament suffering from an AC joint injury (or separated shoulder), which meant he had to push through the pain barrier every time he pulled on a jersey.

Rugby captains David Kirk and François Pienaar have spoken about the anticlimax they experienced after winning the World Cup, and it is the same for us journalists. Unlike the players, I had felt the final was extremely close. It had been nerve-wracking, to say the least. Just as in 1995 against New Zealand, I did not find it an enjoyable experience. It was just too tense, and when I sat down in the media centre to write my final match report, I felt flat rather than elated.

There had been a rail strike on the day of the final, so it had been hard to get to Saint-Denis, and what with the presentation of the trophy it meant that it was past midnight by the time I filed my story, saved it and packed away my laptop. I was quite worried about getting back to Paris, but fortunately I passed the SuperSport team on my way out and hitched a ride. I had to clamber into the 'dicky' with director Sean Everett and the camera equipment was then piled on top of us. So much for glamour!

We decided we would drink a toast to our team at the hotel where Russell Belter, Hugh Bladen and Kobus Wiese were staying. And 'Blades' surprised us all by hurrying to his room and returning with a few bottles of red wine he had been given by South African winemaker Beyers Truter. A glass of Beyerskloof Pinotage brought the day to a fitting conclusion.

The streets of the 17th arrondissement were deserted as I made my way back to my hotel, and it was only at lunch time on Sunday, in the company of some wonderful new French friends, that feelings of euphoria started to build. Only when I saw the images of the joyous celebrations back home and heard the corks popping out of bottles of fine French champagne did I start to be swept up in the revelry.

The English made great play of Mark Cueto's non-try (including an embarrassing faux pas by one of the tabloids that showed a photograph of Cueto's foot on the line with the banner headline proclaiming: 'It was a try!' Obviously a soccer sub got it wrong – in football 'on the line' is in; in rugby, it is out.).

One more thing remained: I wanted to know how to say a few words in French, and my host obliged with the translation.

Les Springboks sont les Champions du Monde.

I thought it had a very nice ring to it.

24

What it takes to win the World Cup

The restaurant/pub in the foyer of the InterContinental Hotel at OR Tambo International Airport is called Quills, after the big chandelier that is its centrepiece, and which is made from porcupine spines. The name immediately appealed to my journalistic senses when I arrived there for a meeting in January 2008. The quill is mightier than the sword? ... I wondered whether it might be an omen, as at the time I was trying to anticipate why SuperSport was once again trying to attach me to SA Rugby. I was there to meet with the new Springbok coach, Peter de Villiers.

The first major decision SARU took in the wake of the 2007 World Cup win was to appoint De Villiers to succeed Jake White, making him the first man of colour to be put in charge of the Springboks. He was one of two candidates, and he won the vote by 10 votes to 9 after the President's Council was unable to come to a unanimous decision. On the one hand there was Heyneke Meyer, the highly successful white coach of the Bulls, and on the other was the black coach, De Villiers.

De Villiers had played his rugby on the other side of the apartheid curtain, but in the post-unity years had built up quite an impressive portfolio coaching age-group sides, not dissimilar to what Jake White had once done. In senior professional rugby, De Villiers had only ever been in charge of the Valke (the old Eastern Transvaal) for two Currie Cup seasons in the early 2000s, but to his supporters, that was only due to the prejudice he had had to face.

In announcing De Villiers' appointment, SARU president Oregan Hoskins' attempt at candidness went horribly wrong when he volunteered that rugby had not been the only criterion applied in the process. Hoskins said that SARU's transformation ideals had also played their part, which was seized upon as evidence that De Villiers was a non-merit appointment. Rumours leaked out of the boardroom (as they always do) that the vote had been swung in De Villiers' favour after an impassioned plea from Cheeky Watson (then representing Eastern Province on the President's Council) in which he raised the spectre of government censure 'if South

African rugby is unwilling to appoint a black coach in the year 2008'. After De Villiers had been given the post, Heyneke Meyer's supporters claimed he had been knifed in the back, as he had allegedly been promised the job.

It was not the ideal way to come into a position that was already fraught with controversy, and it was hardly surprising that De Villiers' propensity for making rash and provocative statements was immediately seized upon as proof that he was not up to the job.

Unlike White, who took over at a desperate time for Springbok rugby after the embarrassment of the 2003 Rugby World Cup campaign and was able to rebuild the national team on the backs of his Under-21s, De Villiers was placed in charge of the world champions, the IRB's No. 1-ranked team, packed with some of the most senior and respected players in the world. It was a vastly different proposition to the one White had had to contend with, and the key for De Villiers was going to be winning the confidence of players who had transcended being mere Springboks – players who, quite understandably, believed that they knew a good deal more about international rugby and all it entails than the new coach. Thus the onus was on De Villiers to find a way into what had become a tight-knit family.

His appointment was not only significant because of the unavoidable racial content, but also because he was being put in charge of South Africa's rugby fortunes at the start of a momentous period. The British & Irish Lions, who had delivered a great shock by winning the series in the Republic in 1997, were due back in 2009, and in 2011 the Springboks would be defending the World Cup in New Zealand, with the added incentive of becoming the first side to successfully defend it and the first to win it three times.

My presence at OR Tambo had come about with the same lack of forethought as the other occasions. I had received a call from SuperSport's production manager Tex Teixeira the day before. 'Can you be at the airport tomorrow? I need you to meet with Peter de Villiers.'

Teixeira went on to explain that SuperSport wanted to offer my services and experience to De Villiers to help him with his PR. It was again a situation in which there had been no consultation and pretty much no choice. 'You know how important rugby is to us,' said Teixeira, 'and we think this guy is going to need help.'

That he did. The next day, Teixeira met briefly with Russell Belter and Xola Ntshinga, the duo designated to be SuperSport's news interface with the Springboks, before De Villiers made his appearance, but there was no time for me to be properly briefed. Tex explained Belter and Ntshinga's supportive roles, and then the three of them left, leaving the two of us to discuss what I thought was our proposed partnership.

However, I soon got the impression that De Villiers did not really know why I was there, so I explained that SuperSport wanted me to either be appointed as his media liaison manager or to tour with the Boks on behalf of SuperSport so that I could be available as a sounding board to guide him through the pitfalls – especially given how many coaches before him had met their Waterloos by falling foul of the press.

De Villiers seemed amenable to the suggestion, saying that 'a lot of people have told me that I should get Dan Retief on board', but I was aghast at how naive he was about the world into which he was heading. I did not know De Villiers all that well, having previously met him on one or two occasions while doing stories with the Valke, but he revealed a staggering amount of arrogance in the way he suggested he was going to approach his new position. In one breath he told me that he never read any newspapers and in the next he mentioned an issue he was having with a reporter in the Cape, whom he was intent on 'sorting out'.

His idea was to announce a 'Springbok team' at the end of every month 'so that the public and players can know what's going on'. I advised him against doing this on the basis that he might paint himself into a corner if one or two major players had poor Super 14 tournaments, or were injured, and he was then forced to include them in the Springbok side even though they had not been in the monthly teams he intended to select and announce.

De Villiers revealed a remarkable level of sensitivity to old slights that would constantly come to the fore after he stepped into the job. For in-stance, he said that he would not be driving the car provided by SA Rugby's long-time vehicle sponsor, as he wanted to stay loyal to those 'who [had] helped me when everyone looked the other way'. Unsurprisingly, I found him to be quite bristly and aggressive on the racial issues that were going to confront him. I noticed that he did not ask me for advice, although I did proffer some: get John Smit back into the Bok set-up. We ended the meeting after more than two hours, with him saying that he thought it was a good idea if there was some way I could become involved. We exchanged cell phone numbers and he promised to call me when he'd had time to think about it.

I had promised to give Teixeira some feedback after the meeting, and he seemed most keen to know the outcome of our chat. 'So what happened? Will he go for it?' he inquired eagerly. My response was not what he wanted to hear. 'Candidly, Tex, I don't think so. He said he thought it was a good idea and that he would phone me. My impression, however, was that he felt our approach was patronising and that he believes he does not need help. He is quite sensitive to the race issues and I think his attitude is that he will show us whities that he can do the job. I'm afraid, though, that he is way out of his depth and has no idea what he is getting into. But I don't think I'll be hearing from him.'

As I predicted, De Villiers never did phone. Knowing that his contract had been negotiated for him by Rian Oberholzer, who secured for him the same salary Jake White was earning when he left the job, I felt he was probably being told not to use my services. De Villiers, to employ one of the biblical idioms he is so fond of using, went forth and made plenty of errors that could have been avoided.

Being touchy to criticism, he immediately got on the wrong side of the press. Some old (and unexplained) affront had him refuse to shake the hand of Clinton van der Berg (then sports editor of the *Sunday Times*) when he tried to introduce himself, he took exception to something Simnikiwe Xabanisa (rugby writer of the *Sunday Times*) wrote, and told him, 'if you want to be white, why don't you be white,' and, when backed into a tight corner, snapped, 'They can give the job [of Springbok coach] back to the whites.'

Not clever for one prone to making oddball remarks that were grist to the media mill.

De Villiers was often his own worst enemy. As some wonderful victories accrued on his scorecard, he uttered one of his most memorable and apt statements, which was spot-on in summing up the temper of his tenure: 'If you look at the Bible and see how Joseph got out of the pit and ended up in the palace, but between the pit and the palace there was a *moerse lot of kak* (a whole lot of shit).'

The coach engineered the return of skipper John Smit from Clermont-Auvergne in France, and in 2008 achieved some notable triumphs. In July the Springboks expunged an unwanted entry from the record book when they scored their first-ever victory over the All Blacks at Carisbrook in Dunedin, the scene in 1921 of the first Test match between the two greatest rivals in rugby, and in August they ran up a record 53-8 score against the

Wallabies at Ellis Park. There was some debate as to whether De Villiers deserved all the kudos or whether the players had taken charge, but what could not be altered was that these wins did occur on his watch: 30-28 in Dunedin and a 45-point margin in Johannesburg.

Nevertheless, he was criticised in the local press, labelled a 'puppet' by former All Black prop Craig Dowd and lampooned in the Australian media. His greatest triumph, over the Wallabies, was soon sullied by allegations of the existence of a compromising video tape that would apparently be used to blackmail him. De Villiers claimed it was a racist plot to remove him, for which he got into trouble with his employers.

The massacre of the Wallabies in the last home game of the year, when it was rumoured that the Springboks had got together secretly and resolved to change their tactics, provided the perfect platform for a successful end-of-year tour. With the emphasis on looking ahead to the following year's visit by the British & Irish Lions, the team responded by beating Wales 20-15, Scotland 14-10 and then running up a record 42-6 score over England at Twickenham. The players were especially fired up because they wanted once and for all to silence those English whingers who persisted in claiming that they had been lucky to win the World Cup. Back in South Africa, there was not much the doomsayers could complain about.

In 2009 the British & Irish Lions arrived, and De Villiers and his assistants, Dick Muir and Gary Gold, switched from Jake White's long-term thinking of looking ahead to the World Cup to a short-term plan on how to win each Test match. Playing against the Lions is a rare experience for a professional rugby player, as their tours are 12 years apart, so it is mostly a once-in-a-lifetime experience, which served to spur on John Smit and his men. Also, the 'inherited psyche' of the Springboks was still smarting from the series defeat by Martin Johnson's 1997 Lions team.

And, as it turned out, the three-Test series was almost a reverse copy of the previous one. The Boks, like Johnson's Lions, narrowly won the first two internationals to claim the series before suffering a heavy defeat in the third. On the back of a massive scrummaging display by Tendai Mtawarira and with Heinrich Brüssow taking the Lions apart at the breakdown, the Springboks surged to a lead of 26-7 in the first Test, at the ABSA Stadium in Durban, but then proceeded to make a series of unnecessary and quite inexplicable substitutions that had the effect of bringing the Lions right back into it. The Boks ended up having to fight hard to win 26-21.

In the second Test, at Loftus Versfeld, the Springboks survived the sin-binning of Schalk Burger in the 32nd second, falling well behind on the scoreboard, before staging a valiant fightback in the last few minutes that got them home by the narrowest of margins.

The Springboks rode their luck in both games, at first because their coaches conspired to destroy their structure in Durban and then, at Loftus, because Burger, by being sin-binned for eye-gouging, put them under enormous pressure in what could have been a victory to savour.

The second Test provided the platform for Morné Steyn to announce himself as South Africa's next great goal-kicker. Steyn kicked a penalty from his own half after the full-time whistle had blown to secure not only victory, but also the series, for the Springboks. In one of the most extraordinary Tests I have seen, the Boks staged a quite magnificent fightback to score two great tries in the final 20 minutes, thus providing Morné Steyn with his 'the winner takes all' moment. Grasping the opportunity, he secured his place in the chronicles of a history that traces its origins back to 1891.

In a match packed full of astonishing incidents, the Springboks were able to survive not only the loss of Burger, but trailing twice by 11 points against a Lions side that dominated the first 60 minutes. The Springboks managed to mount a phenomenal comeback in the last quarter, and Steyn's kick, from 53.7 metres and right in front, gave John Smit's men a 28-25 victory that had for a long time seemed out of reach. The fightback started with a Bryan Habana try (converted by Morné Steyn just two minutes after he had replaced Ruan Pienaar), cutting the Lions' lead to 19-15. A penalty by Steyn made it 18-19, but Stephen Jones soon restored the four-point margin with his fourth penalty. That made it 22-18 to the Lions with 10 minutes left to play.

Uncontested scrums had been ordered because the Lions had suffered a run of injuries to their props, and it seemed as if the tourists might be able to tie up the ball for long enough to level the series. However, a high tackle by Simon Shaw on the 'Beast', Tendai Mtawarira, gave the Boks the chance to kick for touch near the Lions' line. Matfield won the ball, Brüssow recovered it, and the forwards drove it up … and then out it came to the right, to Jaque Fourie. The angular centre seemed hemmed in, but with sheer determination he blasted over Ronan O'Gara and then hurtled through an impossibly narrow gap, beating the despairing tackles by Mike Phillips and Luke Fitzgerald to reach out and dot the ball down just inside the corner flag.

It was touch and go whether it was a try, and how ironic that the TMO was Stu Dickinson, the same man who had made the ruling on Mark Cueto's controversial non-try in the 2007 World Cup final. He finally told referee Christophe Berdos, 'I have a decision for you. You may award the try.'

Next, Steyn slotted the touchline conversion, and suddenly, in the 76th minute, the Boks were 25-22 in front, having trailed all the way. However, the script contained more drama as Andries Bekker high-tackled Jones and the shaken flyhalf stood up, gathered himself and slotted his fifth penalty from the touchline to level the scores at 25-all, seemingly giving the Lions a chance of squaring the series in the final Test, in Johannesburg.

Unlike the Lions, though, the Boks were unwilling to settle for a draw and tried to work Steyn into the pocket to attempt a drop, but he was not steady enough and missed. Back came the Lions, and Ronan O'Gara launched an up-and-under, which he chased himself. Fourie du Preez leapt high to claim the ball, O'Gara took his legs from under him and Monsieur Berdos had no hesitation in awarding a penalty.

Thus it fell to Morné Steyn to place the ball in his own half, with time already having run out, and send it soaring over the crossbar for the three points that ensured him an indelible entry in the annals of Springbok rugby.

The Springboks were ecstatic at having pulled it off, but unfortunately a mood of triumphalism overtook the team and their management and they lost sight of how lucky they had been to claim the series; something that a more mature coach would probably have sensed and nipped in the bud. Perhaps their reaction was understandable, as Smit and the other senior players could remember how the Lions had gloated after Jeremy Guscott's drop goal had snatched it for the Lions in 1997 (in a series in which the Boks scored nine tries to three). Still, it was the first sign that a lack of focus had crept into the Bok dressing room.

Odd selections turned the third Test into a humiliating 9-28 defeat (the Lions claimed that the Springbok camp had showed them a lack of respect and had paid the price). A comprehensive loss to the Aussies followed in Brisbane, but, for the first time since 1949, there were also three successive victories over the All Blacks and a third Tri Nations title.

At that point, De Villiers' record was impressive: a first win at Carisbrook, a record win over the Wallabies, a big one at Twickers (42-6), a British Lions series *and* a Tri Nations. He'd been in charge 22 times and won on 16 occasions for an impressive win percentage of 72%. But then things began to go pear-shaped. Following the Tri Nations decider, which the Springboks won 32-29 in Hamilton in September 2009, they played 18 more Tests in what was starting to become the build-up to the 2011

Rugby World Cup, and won just nine. They lost to the All Blacks three times and the Wallabies twice, while three of their wins were against Italy and two against Wales. De Villiers' win ratio was edging alarmingly close to the 50% mark. Throw in two losses to English club sides Leicester and Saracens in 2009, and it was in the negative.

There were alarming signs that the dominion of the players, exacerbated by injuries to two members of the inner clique, John Smit and Fourie du Preez, was starting to weaken. With the players either fatigued, injured, absent overseas or out of position, the Boks were not as driven and started to slip off the pace. Although furiously denied, there were telltale signs that their physical conditioning was not what it had been under White, and there were worrying indications that the coaching collective had been found wanting when it came to responding to new law interpretations.

There were also concerns about the mounting ages of some of the key men and whether they still had the desire to do what it takes with the next World Cup hurtling ever nearer.

So what *does* it take? Although there will always be unknown factors at play, a study of the six winners (New Zealand, Australia twice, South Africa twice and England) since the first tournament in 1987 reveals certain similarities, certain shared elements, that all of them possessed.

Let's call them the 10 Commandments for winning the World Cup:
1. Capabilities of the coach
There have been six World Cup–winning coaches to date: Brian Lochore (NZ), Bob Dwyer (Australia), Kitch Christie (SA), Rod Macqueen (Australia), Clive Woodward (England) and Jake White (SA). The first three came from the amateur age and the latter trio from the professional era. There were differences in their ages but striking similarities in their approaches to coaching. All were meticulous in their planning, had guided the core of their team for a good many seasons, ruled with unquestioned authority and enjoyed great respect within their team.

All had a pragmatic streak, were deep rugby thinkers, and radiated confidence and assurance in the way they wanted to play. Also, their players believed in their methods. Interestingly, only two of them were former internationals, Lochore and Woodward, with the others having not played at a particularly high level but being 'career' coaches. In all these winning teams, the coach was indisputably the man in charge.

2. A leader of men

Only six men have held up the Webb Ellis Cup in triumph – that glorious moment when the job is done – and all have possessed special qualities; some similar and some very different. They were David Kirk, Nick Farr-Jones, François Pienaar, John Eales, Martin Johnson and John Smit. Kirk was the man the All Blacks turned to in 1987 when their nominated captain, Andy Dalton, could not play (in fact, he retained the title despite not playing in a single match). In Kirk, they had recognised the intelligence and calmness under pressure required for the RWC. He was tiny by today's standards, but big on the field. He possessed a quality that stood out among the others – intelligence.

The winning captains were all quick-witted, able to handle the pressure of the media and, most of all, could cope with tense match situations. Even though they were quite different – Kirk, Eales and Smit quite shy and well-mannered, Farr-Jones and Pienaar suave and positive, and Johnson, well, gruff and strong – the mantle of captaincy sat easily on their shoulders. As with the coaches, all six winning teams possessed leaders with exceptional qualities. Some led by example, others by their words, but they led.

3. A strong quotient of *galácticos*

The word, which means 'superstars', was coined at Spanish football club Real Madrid. And if there is one thing about winning the World Cup, it's a team with a good sprinkling of *galácticos* – players who would be included in a World XV. As Morné du Plessis put it: 'The lesson we learnt from winning the World Cup in 1995 was that a nation requires a core of some 20 truly outstanding internationals to prevail. You might get one or two easier games, but in the end you need one really good team to play in and win every match.'

In South Africa's case, you could not have said that of the 1995 team going into the tournament, but by the time they'd won it, Os du Randt, Ruben Kruger, Mark Andrews (even though he played No. 8), Joost van der Westhuizen, Joel Stransky, Hennie le Roux and André Joubert were seen as world class, with some of the others not far behind.

In 2007, this was also the case. To me, John Smit was the most consistent hooker at the tournament, Victor Matfield and Bakkies Botha were supreme in the line-out, the loose-forward trio of Schalk Burger, Juan Smith and Danie Rossouw redoubtable, Fourie du Preez arguably the best player at the tournament, François Steyn the man with the X-factor, Jaque Fourie was feared by all his opponents, Bryan Habana the best finisher in the game and Percy Montgomery the most reliable goal-kicker. Eleven players, and perhaps some of the other four too, who might have made a World XV. Small wonder that we won. It follows that a team with depth is better able to cope in terms of making replacements when the inevitable injuries do occur.

4. A supreme goal-kicker

Jake White always maintained that World Cups were about defence as a means of maintaining pressure on your opponent. Pressure leads to mistakes, mistakes lead to penalties, penalties lead to points – but only if you have a kicker who can knock them over. Joel Stransky's contribution in 1995 was immense. He contributed 17 points off the boot (and also a try) in the opening 27-18 win over Australia, 10 points in the 20-0 win over Canada, 14 points in the 19-15 win over France in the semi-final, and all 15 in the 15-12 win over the All Blacks in the final.

In France, Percy Montgomery was the leading points-scorer in the tournament, with 105. Significantly, he was successful with all 18 kicks he aimed at the posts in three matches at the Stade de France. Points on the board do wonders for a team's confidence and momentum. In 1987, New Zealand had Grant Fox, in 1991 Australia had Michael Lynagh, in 1999 the Wallabies had Matt Burke, and in 2003 England had Jonny Wilkinson. The message is clear – unless you have someone to kick your goals, it is highly unlikely that you'll win the cup.

5. A perfect 10

This could well be Rugby 101, the oldest fundamental in the game. Every great team needs a flyhalf who can do the job. He need not be the flashiest player around, but he should be the most consistent and the most reliable … the one who sticks to the game plan and takes pressure off his pack. Many would argue that Joel Stransky and Butch James cannot be included among the *great* flyhalves, but in the tournaments they played in they did what they were expected to do to perfection. James was my nomination as the most valuable Springbok of France 2007.

Going into the tournament, No. 10 was considered South Africa's Achilles heel, but James accepted the job, did not put a foot wrong, defended his channel with all his might (without being penalised) and kept the Boks playing in the comfort zone with his judicious kicking out of hand. A classy flyhalf can't do it all on his own (see Hugo Porta in 1987,

Andrew Mehrtens in 1995 and Carlos Spencer in 2003), but without one, you can forget it. In most cases the kicker and the flyhalf are the same man, so the position carries enormous responsibility.

6. A deep well of experience
When Jake White was guiding the Springboks to World Cup glory in 2007, it became an in-joke among the press corps to predict at which juncture he would point out that his team was the most capped in green-and-gold history. White loved trotting out stats to emphasise a point, often referring to one or other record – thank goodness he never read out all Percy Montgomery's stats or the conference might have overrun by an hour! – and as the Boks ticked off one assignment after another on their triumphal march through France, he would say something like, 'It gives me a feeling of comfort to know that I am sending out the most-capped Springbok ever.'

The press guys would catch each other's eyes and smile at their private joke: if they were the most capped last week, Jake, and you're picking the same side this week, then they still are! However, Jake proved his point. Get your selection right, trust in the players you pick and, as their experience grows, they will become stronger mentally and be better able to cope with the pressures. The team who won South Africa's second World Cup thus came out of the tunnel at the Stade de France boasting a record 668 caps among them. The team who won for England in Australia in 2003 were dubbed 'Dad's Army'. But they had the last laugh.

7. Unwavering discipline
More important than you might think. World Cups, as many have pointed out, are not about winning, but about *not losing*. In play-off games, most teams will try to force you to play in your own half, and will try to hold onto the ball to force you into making errors, which can be turned into points. Others, like Argentina in the 2007 semi-final, will try to unsettle your hotheads with nefarious tactics. The Springboks survived some hairy moments with the judiciary in France, but it's not the kind of thing you want to carry on doing, for having a player carded is a massive handicap, while attending hearings can be most disruptive to the campaign.

8. Brilliant back-up staff
Rassie Erasmus's odd decision to withdraw as technical coach of the 2007 World Cup squad after he'd been appointed as the Stormers' coach – I

mean, who doesn't want to go to a World Cup? – turned into gold for the Boks, as it brought former Wallaby coach Eddie Jones into the set-up. Never underestimate the role Eddie Jones played in South Africa's victory. Australia had developed a method whereby their coaches and players would view an opposition team as a castle that had to be sacked and everyone had to come up with suggestions of where the team's weak points might be. Jones had been in charge of the Brumbies, followed by the Wallabies, for a number of seasons, and he had taken the Aussies to the World Cup final against England in 2003. His team had only gone down in extra time, to Jonny Wilkinson's drop.

Now all this knowledge was available to the Boks, and the players responded to a new voice and different ideas. Jones primarily pointed out that the Boks often 'telegraphed' which of their players was to be the receiver, and he made them more aware of space, communication and being in position to receive the ball, and to play the blind side more.

Towards the end, when White was wrestling with his own demons, Jones was also a great calming influence. Allister Coetzee and Gert Smal, backs and forwards coaches respectively, did a superb job. Quiet and unobtrusive, they got on with it and enjoyed great respect from the players. Dr Sherylle Calder, with her world-rated expertise in the value of developing dynamic eyesight, added an extra dimension, while the rest of the crew, doctors Yusuf Hassan and Clint Readhead, physio Vivian Verwant, baggage master Phillip Malakoane, logistics manager Mac Hendricks, strength and conditioning coach Derik Coetzee, match analyst Willem Maree and psychologist Henning Gericke were a tight-knit, always supportive crew who worked hard at giving meaning to the word 'back-up'.

The 1995 side (as explained in Chapter 3) also had the benefit of a strong auxiliary component, as did all the winning sides. John Eales' 1999 Wallaby side, for instance, had three former Wallabies – Tim Lane, Jeff Miller and Cameron Lillicrap – in their management group, as well as the hugely respected Alex Evans in the role of the wise old head. Clive Woodward took it to extremes with the British Lions in New Zealand in 2005, and got it wrong, but in 2003 when England won the World Cup, he was spot-on with experts in every field.

9. *Esprit de corps*
Alexandre Dumas put it best with the pledge of the four musketeers: 'All for one, one for all.' It's that common spirit of comradeship, enthusiasm,

honour and devotion to the cause among the members of a group. Winning teams have it in heaps, and it is evident in the way top players, who might be the captain of their provinces, sublimate their own egos to support the captain in the best interests of the team. However, the greatest example of this selflessness comes from the players who are part of the squad but know they are not going to get much game time.

In 2007, Gary Botha was such a player. He went to France as John Smit's understudy but found himself eclipsed by the younger, heavier and stronger Bismarck du Plessis. Botha saw little more than 40 minutes of action, but he never let his disappointment show. He ran at the front in training, hit the tackle bags, hammered the scrum machine and constantly encouraged the others.

André Pretorius' key contribution, apart from that involuntarily lifted elbow that pole-axed Brian Lima, could well have been running into a melee near the end of the semi-final, jumping as he did onto Schalk Burger's chest and pinning his arms at a time when it seemed the flanker had had quite enough of the Pumas' harassment and was about to take matters into his own hands.

10. Extreme fitness

There are other elements that have to be factored in, such as a brute pack, home-ground advantage, having a winning momentum going into the tournament, a well-drilled style of play and being favoured by the rub of the green, but exceptional fitness is more important. The 1995 Springboks were driven into the ground by Kitch Christie, but they will tell you that at the end of extra time in the final, they gained an advantage because they sensed that the All Blacks were out on their feet. The 2007 side said that their reserves of energy pulled them through against Fiji, and at no stage did they feel they would lose to England in the final.

A strong body makes for a calm mind. The Boks let their usual top levels of fitness slip in 2010 and paid the price. As Gary Player was fond of saying: 'The more I practise, the luckier I get.'

So there they are, the key ingredients to winning the Rugby World Cup. Home advantage could be very important, as studies have shown that upward of 70% of penalties are awarded to the home side. Of the six finals, two have been won by the home side (New Zealand 1987 and South Africa 1995); and the home side has been the losing finalist in two other finals (England 1991 and Australia 2003). Only Wales in 1999 and

France in 2007 did not progress to the final, but *Les Tricolores* did make the last four.

Luck obviously plays a role. Abdel Benazzi coming up just short in the swimming pool that was King's Park in the 1995 semi-final, for instance. In 2007, France's shock defeat to Argentina in the opening game resulted in a more favourable course for the Springboks, but it might still have gone wrong, for there were three 'corner-flag' moments that went the Springboks' way.

But for the bounce of the ball against Tonga in Lens, tackles by JP Pietersen in the quarter-final against Fiji in Marseille and Danie Rossouw in the final, we might now be telling a very different story. On such minuscule things do World Cups turn. Without JP Pietersen's tackle or Danie Rossouw's collision with Mark Cueto, it might have been Phil Vickery and not John Smit receiving rugby's golden grail from Nicolas Sarkozy.

But could it be that the World Cup also works on some cosmic level that we don't understand? That sometimes victory is preordained; that the stars are aligned? Consider the following similarities between the 1995 and 2007 Rugby World Cup–winning teams, dear reader, and you tell me.

BOTH TEAMS:

- Scored 15 points in the final but did not score a try.
- Were coached by English-speaking coaches who themselves were not Springboks (Kitch Christie and Jake White).
- Played in the same pool as the defending champions and beat them comfortably (Australia and England).
- Had highly charged and controversial matches against Samoa.
- Had flyhalves who went to Maritzburg College (Joel Stransky and Butch James).
- Had No. 8s who normally played lock (Mark Andrews and Danie Rossouw).
- Had tighthead props who were more comfortable at loosehead (Balie Swart and CJ van der Linde).
- Had Natal/Sharks fullbacks who had previously played for other provinces (André Joubert (FS) and Percy Montgomery (WP)).
- Had Northern Transvaal/Bulls scrumhalves (Joost van der Westhuizen and Fourie du Preez).
- Had Transvaal/Lions outside centres (Japie Mulder and Jaque Fourie).

- Had a (so-called) player of colour and national hero in the No. 11 jersey (Chester Williams and Bryan Habana).
- Had a left wing who scored four tries against Samoa (Williams and Habana).
- Had provincial lock mates in the No. 4 and 5 jerseys (Kobus Wiese/Hannes Strydom (Transvaal) and Victor Matfield/Bakkies Botha (Blue Bulls)).
- Had a born-and-bred Free Stater in the No. 7 jersey (Ruben Kruger and Juan Smith).
- Had a Pienaar from Bloemfontein in their squad, father and son Gysie and Ruan. (Gysie was the backline coach in 1995 and in 2007 Ruan was on the bench for the final.)
- Contained seven Afrikaans-speaking forwards and a single English-speaker.
- Had Os du Randt at loosehead.
- Played in a green-and-gold jersey with a leaping Springbok on the left breast!

Can South Africa retain the Webb Ellis Cup in New Zealand in 2011? Of course they can. The Springboks have a tough draw, with pool matches against Wales, Fiji, Samoa (the islands again!) plus a stroll in the park against Namibia, and if all goes according to plan, they'll meet Ireland in their quarter-final and then meet up with their arch-enemies, the All Blacks, in one of the semi-finals.

As shown by France in 2007, a shock defeat can throw things out of kilter, but those are impossible to plan for. One can but consider the constants, and they point to a semi-final between South Africa, the champions, and New Zealand. And if South Africa beat New Zealand, the team waiting on the other side of the draw will be one of Australia, England or France.

Can the Springboks beat the All Blacks? Of course they can. They know how, as they have done so before, and they will again. I've staked quite a lot on it!

Appendices

Appendix A: Springbok matches, teams and results in the Rugby World Cup

1995 South Africa

MATCH ONE:

South Africa (14) 27 Australia (13) 18
25 May: Newlands (Cape Town)
Referee: Mr Derek Bevan (Wales)

South Africa: André Joubert, James Small, Japie Mulder, Hennie le Roux, Pieter Hendriks, Joel Stransky, Joost van der Westhuizen, Rudolf Straeuli, Ruben Kruger, François Pienaar (c), Hannes Strydom, Mark Andrews, Balie Swart (Garry Pagel, 65), James Dalton & Os du Randt. Unused subs: Gavin Johnson, Brendan Venter, Johan Roux, Krynauw Otto & Chris Rossouw.

Australia: Matt Pini, David Campese, Daniel Herbert, Jason Little, Damian Smith, Michael Lynagh (c), George Gregan, Tim Gavin, David Wilson, Willie Ofahengaue, John Eales, Rod McCall, Ewen McKenzie, Phil Kearns & Dan Crowley. Unused subs: Matt Burke, Scott Bowen, Peter Slattery, Troy Coker, Mark Hartill & Michael Foley.

Scorers were:
South Africa – Tries: Hendriks, Stransky. Con: Stransky. Pens: Stransky (4). DG: Stransky.
Australia – Tries: Lynagh, Kearns. Con: Lynagh. Pens: Lynagh (2).

MATCH TWO:

South Africa (8) 21 Romania (0) 8
30 May: Newlands (Cape Town)
Referee: Mr Ken McCartney (Scotland)

South Africa: Gavin Johnson, James Small, Christiaan Scholtz, Brendan Venter (Joel Stransky, 33-36), Pieter Hendriks, Hennie le Roux, Johan Roux, Adriaan Richter (c), Robbie Brink, Ruben Kruger, Krynauw Otto, Kobus Wiese, Marius Hurter, Chris Rossouw & Garry Pagel. Unused subs: André Joubert, Joost van der Westhuizen, Rudolf Straeuli, Os du Randt & James Dalton.

Romania: Vasile Brici, Lucian Colceriu, Nicolae Racean, Romeo Gontineac, Gheorge Solomie, Ilie Ivanciuc, Vasile Flutur, Tiberiu Brinza (c), Adrian Gealapu, Andrei Guranescu, Constantin Cojocariu, Sandu Ciorascu, Gabriel Vlad, Ionel Negreci (Vaiere Tufa, 62) & Gheorge Leonte. Unused subs: Nicolae Nichitean, Adrian Lungu, Daniel Neaga, Ovidiu Slusariuc & Leodor Costea.

Scorers were:
South Africa – Tries: Richter (2). Con: Johnson. Pens: Johnson (2).
Romania – Try: Guranescu. Pen: Ivanciuc.

MATCH THREE:

South Africa (17) 20 Canada (0) 0
3 June: Boet Erasmus Stadium (Port Elizabeth)
Referee: Mr Dave McHugh (Ireland)

South Africa: André Joubert, Gavin Johnson (Joost van der Westhuizen, 17), Christiaan Scholtz, Brendan Venter, Pieter Hendriks, Joel Stransky (Hennie le Roux, 59), Johan Roux, Adriaan Richter, Robbie Brink, François Pienaar (c), Hannes Strydom (Krynauw Otto, 73), Kobus Wiese, Marius Hurter, James Dalton & Garry Pagel. Unused subs: Japie Mulder, Os du Randt & Chris Rossouw.

Canada: Scott Stewart, Winston Stanley, Christian Stewart, Steve Gray, David Lougheed, Gareth Rees (c), John Graf, Colin McKenzie (Chris Michaluk, 80), Gord McKinnon, Ian Gordon, Glenn Ennis (John Hutchison, 65), Al Charron, Rod Snow, Mark Cardinal & Eddie Evans. Unused subs: Ron Toews, Alan Tynan, Paul Le Blanc & Karl Svoboda.

Scorers were:
South Africa – Tries: Richter (2). Cons: Stransky (2). Pens: Stransky (2).
Canada – none
Cards: James Dalton (SA – red card, 70), Gareth Rees (Canada – red card, 70) & Rod Snow (Canada – red card, 70) Pieter Hendriks (SA) cited, found guilty and suspended for 90 days.
Scott Stewart (Canada) cited, found guilty and suspended for 60 days.

MATCH FOUR:

QUARTER-FINAL:
South Africa (23) 42 Western Samoa (0) 14
10 June: Ellis Park (Johannesburg)
Referee: Mr Jim Fleming (Scotland)

South Africa: André Joubert (Brendan Venter,18), Gavin Johnson, Christiaan Scholz, Japie Mulder, Chester Williams, Hennie le Roux, Joost van der Westhuizen, Rudolf Straeuli, Ruben Kruger (Adriaan Richter, 48), François Pienaar (c), Mark Andrews (Krynauw Otto, 71), Kobus Wiese (Naka Drotské, 78), Balie Swart, Chris Rossouw & Os du Randt. Unused subs: Joel Stransky & Johan Roux.

Western Samoa: Mike Umaga, Brian Lima, To'o Vaega, Tupo Fa'amasino, George Harder, Fata Sini, Tu Nu'uali'itia, Pat Lam (c), Junior Paramore, Shem Tatupu, Saini Lemamea, Lio Falaniko, George Latu, Talu Leiasamaivao & Mike Mika. Unused subs: Fereti Tuilagi, Va'a Vitale, Sila Vaifale, Sam Kaleta, Brendan Reidy & Peter Fatialofa.

Scorers were:
South Africa – Tries: Williams (4), Rossouw, Andrews. Cons: Johnson (3).
Pens: Johnson (2).
Western Samoa – Tries: Nu'uali'itia, Tatupu. Cons: Fa'amasino (2).

MATCH FIVE:

SEMI-FINAL:
South Africa (10) 19 France (6) 15
17 June: The Stadium, King's Park (Durban)
Referee: Mr Derek Bevan (Wales)

South Africa: André Joubert, James Small, Japie Mulder, Hennie le Roux, Chester Williams, Joel Stransky, Joost van der Westhuizen (Johan Roux, 62), Mark Andrews, Ruben Kruger, François Pienaar (c), Hannes Strydom, Kobus Wiese, Balie Swart, Chris Rossouw & Os du Randt. Unused subs: Gavin Johnson, Christiaan Scholtz, Rudolf Straeuli, Garry Pagel & Naka Drotské.

France: Jean-Luc Sadourny, Emile Ntamack, Philippe Sella, Thierry Lacroix, Philippe Saint-André (c), Christophe Deylaud, Fabien Galthie, Marc Cecillon, Laurent Cabannes, Abdelatif Benazzi, Olivier Roumat, Olivier Merle, Christian Califano, Jean-Michel Gonzales & Louis Armary. Unused subs: Frank Mesnel, Yann Delaigue, Aubin Heuber, Albert Cigagna, Philippe Galart & Laurent Benezech.

Scorers were:
South Africa – Try: Kruger. Con: Stransky. Pens: Stransky (4).
France – Pens: Lacroix (5).

MATCH SIX:

FINAL:
South Africa (9) (9) 15 New Zealand (6) (9) 12 – after extra time (9-all after 80 minutes)
24 June: Ellis Park (Johannesburg)
Referee: Mr Ed Morrison (England)

South Africa: André Joubert, James Small (Brendan Venter, 97), Japie Mulder, Hennie le Roux, Chester Williams, Joel Stransky, Joost van der Westhuizen, Mark Andrews (Rudolf Straeuli, 90), Ruben Kruger, François Pienaar (c), Hannes Strydom, Kobus Wiese, Balie

Swart (Garry Pagel, 68), Chris Rossouw & Os du Randt. Unused subs: Gavin Johnson, Johan Roux & Naka Drotské.

New Zealand: Glen Osborne, Jeff Wilson (Marc Ellis, 55), Frank Bunce, Walter Little, Jonah Lomu, Andrew Mehrtens, Graeme Bachop (Ant Strachan, 66-70), Zinzan Brooke, Josh Kronfeld, Mike Brewer (Jamie Joseph, 40), Robin Brooke, Ian Jones, Olo Brown, Sean Fitzpatrick (c) & Craig Dowd (Richard Loe, 83). Unused subs: Simon Culhane & Norm Hewitt.

Scorers were:
South Africa – Pens: Stransky (3). DG: Stransky (2).
New Zealand – Pens: Mehrtens (3). DG: Mehrtens.

1999 Wales
MATCH ONE:

South Africa (13) 46 Scotland (16) 29
3 October: Murrayfield (Edinburgh)
Referee: Mr Colin Hawke (New Zealand)

South Africa: Percy Montgomery, Deon Kayser (Breyton Paulse, 70), Robbie Fleck, Brendan Venter, Pieter Rossouw, Jannie de Beer, Joost van der Westhuizen (c), Bob Skinstad, André Venter, Johan Erasmus (André Vos, 80), Mark Andrews (Krynauw Otto, 48), Albert van den Berg, Cobus Visagie, Naka Drotské & Os du Randt (Ollie le Roux, 48). Unused subs: Chris Rossouw, Werner Swanepoel & Pieter Müller.

Scotland: Glenn Metcalfe, Cameron Murray, Alan Tait, John Leslie (Jamie Mayer, 54), Kenny Logan, Gregor Townsend, Gary Armstrong (c), Gordon Simpson (Peter Walton, 61), Budge Pountney, Martin Leslie, Stuart Grimes, Scott Murray (Doddie Weir, 72), George Graham (David Hilton, 73), Gordon Bulloch & Tom Smith. Unused subs: Duncan Hodge, Bryan Redpath & Robbie Russell.

Scorers were:
South Africa – Tries: B Venter, A Venter, Fleck, Le Roux, Kayser,
Van der Westhuizen. Cons: De Beer (5). Pens: De Beer (2).
Scotland – Tries: M Leslie, Tait. Cons: Logan (2). Pens: Logan (4).
DG: Townsend.

MATCH TWO:

South Africa (21) 47 Spain (0) 3
10 October: Murrayfield (Edinburgh)
Referee: Mr Paul Honiss (New Zealand)

South Africa: Breyton Paulse, Stefan Terblanche, Wayne Julies (Deon
Kayser, 22), Pieter Muller, Kaya Malotana, Jannie de Beer, Werner
Swanepoel (Joost van der Westhuizen, 62), André Vos (c), Anton Leonard
(Bob Skinstad, 62), Ruben Kruger, Krynauw Otto, Fritz van Heerden,
Adrian Garvey, Chris Rossouw (Naka Drotské, 65) & Ollie le Roux
(Os du Randt, 65). Unused subs: Percy Montgomery & Mark Andrews.

Spain: Francisco Puertas, Jose Inchausti, Alberto Socias, Fernando Diez,
Miguel Frechilla, Aitor Etxeberria (Ferran Velazco, 47), Aratz Gallastegui,
Alberto Malo (c) (Alfonso Mata, 40), Carlos Souto (Luis Javier
Martinez, 67), Jose Diaz, Oskar Astarloa, Jose Miguel Villau, Jose
Ignacio Zapatero, Diego Zarzosa (Fernando de la Calle, 63) & Jordi
Camps (Victor Torres, 20). Unused sub: Jaime Alonso.

Scorers were:
South Africa – Tries: Vos (2), Swanepoel, Leonard, Muller, Skinstad,
Pen try. Cons: De Beer (6).
Spain – Pen: Velazco.

MATCH THREE:

South Africa (27) 39 Uruguay (3) 3
15 October: Hampden Park (Glasgow)
Referee: Mr Peter Marshall (Australia)

South Africa: Percy Montgomery, Deon Kayser, Robbie Fleck, Brendan Venter, Pieter Rossouw, Jannie de Beer, Joost van der Westhuizen (c), Bob Skinstad, André Venter, Johan Erasmus, Mark Andrews (Albert van den Berg, 67), Krynauw Otto, Cobus Visagie, Naka Drotské & Os du Randt. (Ollie le Roux, 51). Unused subs: Stefan Terblanche, Pieter Müller, Werner Swanepoel, André Vos & Chris Rossouw.

Uruguay: Alfonso Cardosa, Juan Menchaca (Jose Viana, 78), Pedro Vecino, Fernando Paullier (Sebastian Aguirre, 22), Pablo Costabile, Diego Aguiar (Sebastian Aguirre, 13-20), Fernando Sosa Diaz, Diego Ormachea (c), Martin Panizza, Nicolas Grille (Nicolas Brignoni, 58), Mario Lame (Juan Alzueta, 78), Juan Carlos Bado, Pablo Lemoine (Guillermo Storace, 69), Diego Lamelas, Rodrigo Sanchez (Francisco de los Santos, 69). Unused sub: Eduardo Berruti.

Scorers were:
South Africa – Tries: Van den Berg (2), Fleck, Van der Westhuizen, Kayser. Cons: De Beer (4). Pens: De Beer (2).
Uruguay – Pen: Aguiar.
Card: Brendan Venter (SA) – red card, 41 (of first half), cited, found guilty and suspended for 21 days.

MATCH FOUR:

QUARTER-FINAL:
South Africa (16) 44 England (12) 21
24 October: Stade de France (Saint-Denis)
Referee: Mr Jim Fleming (Scotland)

South Africa: Percy Montgomery, Deon Kayser (Stefan Terblanche, 62-64), Robbie Fleck, Pieter Müller, Pieter Rossouw, Jannie de Beer, Joost van der Westhuizen (c), Bob Skinstad (André Vos, 75), André Venter, Johan Erasmus, Mark Andrews (Albert van den Berg, 67), Krynauw Otto, Cobus Visagie, Naka Drotské & Os du Randt. (Ollie le Roux, 62). Unused subs: Henry Honiball, Werner Swanepoel & Chris Rossouw.

England: Matt Perry, Nick Beal (Austin Healey, 55), Will Greenwood, Phil de Glanville (Mike Catt, 75), Dan Luger, Paul Grayson (Jonny Wilkinson, 55), Matt Dawson (Martin Corry, 73), Lawrence Dallaglio, Neil Back, Richard Hill, Danny Grewcock, Martin Johnson (c), Phil Vickery, Phil Greening & Jason Leonard. Unused subs: Tim Rodber, Darren Garforth & Richard Cockerill.

Scorers were:
South Africa – Tries: Van der Westhuizen, Rossouw. Cons: De Beer (2). Pen: De Beer (5). DG: De Beer (5)
England – Pens: Grayson (6), Wilkinson.

MATCH FIVE:

SEMI-FINAL:
South Africa (6) 21 Australia (12) 27 – after extra time
(18-all after 80 minutes)
30 October: Twickenham (London)
Referee: Mr Derek Bevan (Wales)

South Africa: Percy Montgomery, Deon Kayser (Stefan Terblanche, 72), Robbie Fleck, Pieter Muller (Henry Honiball, 80), Pieter Rossouw, Jannie de Beer, Joost van der Westhuizen (c), Bob Skinstad (André Vos, 71), André Venter, Johan Erasmus, Mark Andrews (Albert van den Berg, 59), Krynauw Otto, Cobus Visagie, Naka Drotské & Os du Randt. (Ollie le Roux, 60). Unused subs: Werner Swanepoel & Chris Rossouw.

Australia: Matt Burke, Ben Tune (Jason Little, 61), Daniel Herbert, Tim Horan (Nathan Grey, 74), Joe Roff, Stephen Larkham, George Gregan, Toutai Kefu, David Wilson, Matt Cockbain (Owen Finegan, 58), John Eales (c), David Giffin (Mark Connors, 92), Andrew Blades, Michael Foley & Richard Harry. Unused subs: Chris Whitaker, Rod Moore & Jeremy Paul.

Scorers were:
South Africa – Pens: De Beer (6). DG: De Beer.
Australia – Pens: Burke (8). DG: Larkham.

THIRD AND FOURTH PLACE PLAY-OFF
South Africa (16) 22 New Zealand (12) 18
4 November: Millennium Stadium (Cardiff)
Referee: Mr Peter Marshall (Australia)

South Africa: Percy Montgomery, Breyton Paulse, Robbie Fleck, Pieter Müller, Stefan Terblanche, Henry Honiball, Joost van der Westhuizen (c) (Werner Swanepoel, 56-66), André Vos (Ruben Kruger, 70), André Venter, Johan Erasmus, Mark Andrews (Albert van den Berg, 65), Krynauw Otto, Cobus Visagie, Naka Drotské (Chris Rossouw, 74) & Os du Randt (Ollie le Roux, 48). Unused subs: Wayne Julies & Jannie de Beer.

New Zealand: Jeff Wilson, Tana Umaga (Pita Alatini, 40), Christian Cullen, Alama Ieremia, Jonah Lomu, Andrew Mehrtens, Justin Marshall, Tane Randell (c), Josh Kronfeld, Reuben Thorne (Dylan Mika, 64), Royce Willis, Norm Maxwell, Kees Meeuws, Mark Hammet (Anton Oliver, 69) & Craig Dowd (Carl Hoeft, 49). Unused subs: Tony Brown, Rhys Duggan & Ian Jones.

Scorers were:
South Africa – Try: Paulse. Con: Honiball. Pens: Honiball (3).
DG: Montgomery (2)
New Zealand – Pens: Mehrtens (6).

Australia (12) 35 France (6) 12
6 November: Millennium Stadium (Cardiff)
Referee: Mr André Watson (South Africa)

Australia: Matt Burke, Ben Tune, Daniel Herbert (Jason Little, 46), Tim Horan (Nathan Grey, 86), Joe Roff, Stephen Larkham, George Gregan (Chris Whitaker, 86), Toutai Kefu, David Wilson (Mark Connors, 73-84), Matt Cockbain (Owen Finegan, 52), John Eales (c), David Giffin,

Andrew Blades, Michael Foley (Jeremy Paul, 85) & Richard Harry (Dan Crowley, 75).

France: Xavier Garbajosa (Ugo Mola, 67), Philippe Bernat-Salles, Richard Dourthe (Stephane Glas, 49-55, 74), Emile Ntamack, Christophe Dominici, Christophe Lamaison, Fabien Galthié (Stephane Castaignède, 76), Christophe Juillet (Olivier Brouzet, 41), Olivier Magne (Arnaud Costes, 19-22), Marc Lièvremont (Arnaud Costes, 67), Fabien Pelous, Abdelatif Benazzi, Franck Tournaire, Raphael Ibañez (c) (Marc Dal Maso, 79) & Cedric Soulette (Pieter de Villiers, 47).

Scorers were:
Australia – Tries: Tune, Finegan. Cons: Burke (2). Pens: Burke (7).
France – Pens: Lamaison (4).

2003 Australia
MATCH ONE:

South Africa (36) 72 Uruguay (6) 6
11 October: Subiaco Oval (Perth)
Referee: Mr Paddy O'Brien (New Zealand)

South Africa: Werner Greeff, Ashwin Willemse, Jaque Fourie, De Wet Barry, Thinus Delport (Ricardo Loubscher, 67), Louis Koen (Derick Hougaard, 60), Joost van der Westhuizen (c) (Neil de Kock, 60), Juan Smith, Danie Rossouw (Hendro Scholtz, 72), Joe van Niekerk, Victor Matfield (Selborne Boome, 67), Bakkies Botha, Richard Bands (Faan Rautenbach, 57), Danie Coetzee (John Smit, 57) & Lawrence Sephaka.

Uruguay: Joaquin Pastore, Alfonso Cardosa (Juan Menchaca, 45), Diego Aguirre (c), Martin Mendaro, Emiliano Ibarra, Sebastian Aguirre, Emiliano Caffera (Bernardo Amarillo, 60), Rodrigo Capo, Marcelo Gutierrez (Nicolas Grille, 45), Nicolas Brignoni (Herman Ponti, 58), Juan-Carlos Bado, Juan Alzueta, Pablo Lemoine (Guillermo Storace, 73), Diego Lemelas (Juan-Andres Perez, 68) & Rodrigo Sanchez (Eduardo Berruti, 35-37, 68).

Scorers were:
South Africa – Tries: Van der Westhuizen (3), Botha (2), Van Niekerk, Delport, Fourie, Bands, Rossouw, Scholtz, Greeff. Cons: Koen (5), Hougaard.
Uruguay – Pens: D Aguirre (2).

MATCH TWO:

South Africa (6) 6 England (6) 25
18 October: Subiaco Oval (Perth)
Referee: Mr Peter Marshall (Australia)

South Africa: Jaco van der Westhuyzen, Ashwin Willemse, Jorrie Müller, De Wet Barry, Thinus Delport, Louis Koen (Derick Hougaard, 69), Joost van der Westhuizen, Juan Smith, Joe van Niekerk, Corné Krige (c), Victor Matfield, Bakkies Botha, Richard Bands (Lawrence Sephaka, 7-14, 69), Danie Coetzee (John Smit, 45-52, 58) & Christo Bezuidenhout. Unused subs: Selborne Boome, Danie Rossouw, Neil de Kock & Werner Greeff.

England: Jason Robinson, Josh Lewsey, Will Greenwood, Mike Tindall (Dan Luger, 71), Ben Cohen, Jonny Wilkinson, Kyran Bracken, Lawrence Dallaglio, Neil Back (Joe Worsley, 47-52), Lewis Moody, Ben Kay, Martin Johnson (c), Phil Vickery, Steve Thompson & Trevor Woodman (Jason Leonard, 74). Unused subs: Dorian West, Martin Corry, Andy Gomarsall & Paul Grayson.

Scorers were:
South Africa – Pens: Koen (2).
England – Try: Greenwood. Con: Wilkinson. Pens: Wilkinson (4). DG: Wilkinson (2).

MATCH THREE:

South Africa (24) 46 Georgia (6) 19
24 October: Aussie Stadium (Sydney)
Referee: Mr Stuart Dickinson (Australia)

South Africa: Ricardo Loubscher, Stefan Terblanche, Jaque Fourie, Werner Greeff (Jorrie Müller, 77), Breyton Paulse, Derick Hougaard, Neil de Kock, Joe van Niekerk (Schalk Burger, 63), Danie Rossouw, Hendro Scholtz, Selborne Boome, Bakkies Botha, Faan Rautenbach, John Smit (c) & Lawrence Sephaka (Dale Santon, 68). Unused subs: Christo Bezuidenhout, Victor Matfield, Joost van der Westhuizen & Louis Koen.

Georgia: Irakli Kavtarashvili (Besiki Khamashuridze, 61), Gocha Khonelidze, Otar Eloshivili, Vasil Katsadze (c), Archil Kavtarashvili, Pavle Jimsheladze (Merab Kvirikashvili, 59), Irakli Mobebadaze, George Chkaidze (Ilia Zedginidze, 77), David Bolgashvili (Irakli Abuseridze, 75), George Tsiklauri, Victor Didebulidze, Sergo Gujaraidze, Alexandre Margvelashvili (Soso Nikolaenko, 75), David Dadunashvili (Akvsenti Giorgadze, 75), Avtandil Kopaliani. Unused sub: Gregoire Yachvili.

Scorers were:
South Africa – Tries: Rossouw (2), Hougaard, Van Niekerk, Fourie, Botha, Burger. Cons: Hougaard (4). Pen: Hougaard.
Georgia – Try: Dadunashvili. Con: Jimsheladze. Pens: Jimsheladze (3), Kvirikashvili.
Cards: Hendro Scholtz (SA – yellow card, 58-68), Merab Kvirikashvili (Georgia – yellow card, 82).

MATCH FOUR:

South Africa (31) 60 Samoa (3) 10
1 November: Suncorp Stadium (Brisbane)
Referee: Mr Chris White (England)

South Africa: Jaco van der Westhuyzen, Ashwin Willemse, Jorrie Müller, De Wet Barry (Jaque Fourie, 71), Thinus Delport, Derick Hougaard (Louis Koen, 69), Joost van der Westhuizen (Neil de Kock, 75), Juan Smith, Joe van Niekerk (Danie Rossouw, 41), Corné Krige (c) (Schalk Burger, 69), Victor Matfield, Bakkies Botha, Faan Rautenbach (Richard Bands, 56), John Smit (Danie Coetzee, 56) & Christo Bezuidenhout.

Samoa: Tanner Vili, Lome Fa'atau, Romi Ropati (Dale Rasmussen, 63), Brian Lima, Sailosi Tagicakibau, Earl Va'a (Dominic Feaunati, 58), Steven So'oialo (Denning Tyrell, 72), Semo Sititi (c), Maurie Fa'asavlu, Peter Poulos (Kitiona Viliamu, 50), Leo Lafaiali'i, Opeta Palepoi (Des Tuiavi'i, 69), Jeremy Tomuli (Tamato Leupolu, 40), Jonathan Meredith & Kas Lealamanua. Unused sub: Mahonri Schwalger.

Scorers were:
South Africa – Tries: Van Niekerk, Müller, Hougaard, Smith, Willemse, Fourie, Van der Westhuyzen, De Kock. Cons: Hougaard (5), Koen (2). Pen: Hougaard. DG: Hougaard.
Samoa – Try: Palepoi. Con: Va'a. Pen: Va'a.

MATCH FIVE:

QUARTER-FINAL:
South Africa (6) 9 New Zealand (13) 29
8 November: Telstra Dome (Melbourne)
Referee: Mr Tony Spreadbury (England)

South Africa: Jaco van der Westhuyzen, Ashwin Willemse, Jorrie Müller, De Wet Barry, Thinus Delport (Jaque Fourie, 41), Derick Hougaard (Louis Koen, 73), Joost van der Westhuizen (Neil de Kock, 76), Juan Smith, Danie Rossouw (Schalk Burger, 61), Corné Krige (c), Victor Matfield (Selborne Boome, 76), Bakkies Botha, Faan Rautenbach (Richard Bands, 60), John Smit (Danie Coetzee, 73) & Christo Bezuidenhout.

New Zealand: Mils Muliaina, Doug Howlett, Leon MacDonald, Aaron Mauger (Dan Carter, 76), Joe Rokocoko (Caleb Ralph, 77), Carlos Spencer, Justin Marshall (Steve Devine, 76), Jerry Collins, Richie McCaw (Marty Holah, 60-63, 73), Reuben Thorne (c), Ali Williams, Chris Jack (Brad Thorn, 50), Greg Somerville, Keven Mealamu (Mark Hammet, 73) & Dave Hewett (Kees Meeuws, 49).

Scorers were:
South Africa – Pens: Hougaard (3).

New Zealand – Tries: MacDonald, Mealamu, Rokocoko.
Con: MacDonald. Pens: MacDonald (3). DG: Mauger.

FINAL

***England (14) (14) 20 Australia (5) (14) 17 – after extra time
(14-all after 80 minutes)***
22 November: Telstra Sadium (Sydney)
Referee: Mr André Watson (South Africa)

England: Josh Lewsey (Iain Balshaw, 85), Jason Robinson,
Will Greenwood, Mike Tindall (Mike Catt, 78), Ben Cohen, Jonny
Wilkinson, Matt Dawson, Lawrence Dallaglio, Neil Back, Richard Hill
(Lewis Moody, 93), Ben Kay, Martin Johnson (c), Phil Vickery (Jason
Leonard, 80), Steve Thompson & Trevor Woodman. Unused subs:
Dorian West, Martin Corry & Kyran Bracken.

Australia: Matt Rogers, Wendell Sailor (Joe Roff, 70), Stirling Mortlock,
Elton Flatley, Lote Tuqiri, Stephen Larkham (Matt Giteau, 18-30, 55-63
& 85-93) George Gregan (c), David Lyons (Matt Cockbain, 56), Phil
Waugh, George Smith, Nathan Sharpe (David Giffin, 48), Justin
Harrison, Al Baxter, Brendan Cannon (Jeremy Paul, 56) & Bill Young
(Matt Dunning, 92). Unused subs: Chris Whitaker.

Scorers were:
England – Try: Robinson. Pens: Wilkinson (4). DG: Wilkinson.
Australia – Try: Tuqiri. Pens: Flatley (4).

2007 France
MATCH ONE:

South Africa (21) 59 Samoa (7) 7
9 September: Parc des Princes (Paris)
Referee: Mr Paul Honiss (New Zealand)

South Africa: Percy Montgomery, JP Pietersen, Jaque Fourie,
Jean de Villiers (François Steyn, 44), Bryan Habana, Butch James (André

Pretorius, 58), Fourie du Preez (Ricky Januarie, 65), Danie Rossouw
(Wikus van Heerden, 58), Juan Smith, Schalk Burger, Victor Matfield,
Bakkies Botha (Johann Muller, 65), CJ van der Linde, John Smit (c)
(Bismarck du Plessis, 63) & Os du Randt (BJ Botha, 52).

Samoa: David Lemi, Lome Fa'atau, Gavin Williams, Jerry Meafou
(Brian Lima, 59) (Taniela Fuga, 65), Alesana Tuilagi, Eliota Fuimaona,
Aukusitino Poluleuligaga (Elvis Seveali'li, 59), Henry Tuilagi (Alfie
Vaeluaga, 57), Semo Sititi (c), Daniel Leo (Justin Purdie, 57), Kane
Thompson, Iosefa Tekori, Census Johnston, Mahonri Schwalger &
Justin Va'a (Kas Lealamanua, 63).

Scorers were:
South Africa – Tries: Habana (4), Montgomery (2), Fourie, Pietersen.
Cons: Montgomery (5). Pens: Montgomery (3).
Samoa – Try: Williams. Con: Williams.
Citing: Schalk Burger (SA) cited, found guilty and suspended for four
weeks, reduced to two after an appeal.

MATCH TWO:

South Africa (20) 36 England (0) 0
14 September: Stade de France (Saint-Denis)
Referee: Mr Joël Jutge (France)

South Africa: Percy Montgomery, JP Pietersen, Jaque Fourie, François
Steyn (Wynand Olivier, 76), Bryan Habana (Ruan Pienaar, 56-60),
Butch James (André Pretorius, 71), Fourie du Preez (Ruan Pienaar, 67),
Danie Rossouw, Juan Smith (Bob Skinstad, 71), Wikus van Heerden,
Victor Matfield, Bakkies Botha (Johann Muller, 52), BJ Botha
(CJ van der Linde, 61), John Smit (c) (Bismarck du Plessis, 71)
& Os du Randt.

England: Jason Robinson (Matthew Tait, 57), Josh Lewsey, Jamie Noon
(Peter Richards, 80), Andy Farrell, Paul Sackey, Mike Catt, Shaun Perry
(Andy Gomarsall, 41), Nick Easter, Tom Rees (Lewis Moody, 53),
Martin Corry (c), Ben Kay, Simon Shaw (Steve Borthwick, 55-59, 78),

Matt Stevens, Mark Regan (George Chuter, 56) & Andrew Sheridan (Perry Freshwater, 78).

Scorers were:
South Africa – Tries: Pietersen (2), Smith. Cons: Montgomery (3). Pens: Montgomery (4), Steyn.
England – none

MATCH THREE:

South Africa (7) 30 Tonga (3) 25
22 September: Félix-Bollaert Stadium (Lens)
Referee: Mr Wayne Barnes (England)

South Africa: Ruan Pienaar, Ashwin Willemse (Bryan Habana, 46), Wynand Olivier, Wayne Julies (François Steyn, 46), JP Pietersen, André Pretorius (Percy Montgomery, 60), Ricky Januarie, Bob Skinstad (c), Danie Rossouw (Juan Smith, 25-31, 50), Wikus van Heerden, Albert van den Berg (Victor Matfield, 46), Bakkies Botha, CJ van der Linde, Gary Botha (John Smit, 46) & Gurthrö Steenkamp (BJ Botha, 46).

Tonga: Vunggakoto Lilo (Aisea Havili, 79), Tevita Tu'ifua, Sukanaivalu Hufanga, Epeli Taione (Isileli Tupou, 76), Joseph Vaka, Pierre Hola, Sione Tu'ipulotu (Soane Havea, 67), Finau Maka, Nili Latu (c) (Lotu Filipine, 67), Viliami Vaki, Emosi Kauhenga (Inoke Afeaki, 51-67), Paino Hehea (Inoke Afeaki, 67), Kisi Palu, Aleki Lutui (Ephraim Taukafa, 67) & Soane Tonga'uiha. Unused sub: Toma Toke.

Scorers were:
South Africa – Tries: Pienaar (2), Smith, Skinstad. Cons: Pretorius, Montgomery. Pens: Steyn, Montgomery.
Tonga – Tries: Pulu, Hufanga, Vaki. Cons: Hola (2). Pens: Hola (2).
Cards: François Steyn (SA – yellow card, 63-73), Joseph Vaka (Tonga – yellow card, 63-73) & Bryan Habana (SA – yellow card, 69-79).

South Africa (24) 64 USA (10) 15
30 September: Stade de la Mosson (Montpellier)
Referee: Mr Tony Spreadbury (England)

South Africa: Percy Montgomery (Ruan Pienaar, 67), Akona Ndungane,
Jaque Fourie, François Steyn (André Pretorius, 67), Bryan Habana
(JP Pietersen, 53), Butch James, Fourie du Preez, Schalk Burger,
Juan Smith, Wikus van Heerden (Bob Skinstad, 71), Victor Matfield
(Albert van den Berg, 75), Albert van den Berg (Bakkies Botha, 56),
BJ Botha (CJ van der Linde, 25), John Smit (c) & Os du Randt
(Bismarck du Plessis, 71).

USA: Chris Wyles (Valanese Mailfa, 74), Takudzwa Ngwenya, Phillip
Eloff, Vaha Esikia, Salesi Sika (Thretton Palamo, 74), Mike Hercus (c),
Chad Erskine, Dan Payne (Mark Aylor, 74), Todd Clever (Mark Aylor,
43-55) (Mike Petri, 74), Louis Stanfill (Henry Bloomfield, 74), Mike
Magan, Alec Parker, Chris Osentowski, Owen Lentz (Blake Burdette,
74) & Mike McDonald (Matekitonga Moeakiola, 40).

Scorers were:
South Africa – Tries: Habana (2), Fourie (2), Burger, Steyn,
Van der Linde, Du Preez, Smith. Cons: Montgomery (6), James (2).
Pen: Montgomery.
USA – Tries: Ngwenya, Wyles. Con: Hercus. Pen: Hercus.
Card: Todd Clever (USA – yellow card, 23-33).

QUARTER-FINAL:
South Africa (13) 37 Fiji (3) 20
7 October: Stade Vélodrome (Marseille)
Referee: Mr Alan Lewis (Ireland)

South Africa: Percy Montgomery, JP Pietersen, Jaque Fourie, François
Steyn, Bryan Habana, Butch James, Fourie du Preez, Danie Rossouw

(Wikus van Heerden, 50), Juan Smith, Schalk Burger, Victor Matfield, Bakkies Botha (Johann Muller, 55-58, 75), Jannie du Plessis, John Smit (c) & Os du Randt (Gurthrö Steenkamp, 53). Unused subs: Gary Botha, Ruan Pienaar, André Pretorius & Wynand Olivier.

Fiji: Norman Ligairi, Vilimone Delasau, Kameli Ratuvou (Gabiriele Lovobalavu, 63), Seru Rabeni, Sereli Bobo, Seremaia Bai, Mosese Raulini (c), Sisa Koyamaibole, Akapusi Qera (Aca Ratavu, 71), Semisi Naevo, Ifereimi Rawaqa, Kelemete Leawere (Wame Lewaravu, 73), Henry Qiodravu (Jone Railomo, 55), Sunia Koto (Viliame Gadolo, 71) & Graham Dewes. Unused subs: Jone Daunivucu & Waisea Luveniyali.

Scorers were:
South Africa – Tries: Fourie, Smit, Pietersen, Smith, James.
Cons: Montgomery (3). Pens: Steyn, Montgomery.
Fiji – Tries: Delasau, Bobo. Cons: Bai (2). Pens: Bai (2).
Card: Seru Rabeni (Fiji – yellow card, 51-61).

MATCH SIX:

SEMI-FINAL:
South Africa (24) 37 Argentina (6) 13
14 October: Stade de France (Saint-Denis)
Referee: Mr Steve Walsh (New Zealand)

South Africa: Percy Montgomery, JP Pietersen (Ruan Pienaar, 77), Jaque Fourie, François Steyn (Wynand Olivier, 77), Bryan Habana, Butch James (André Pretorius, 77), Fourie du Preez, Danie Rossouw (Bob Skinstad, 75), Juan Smith, Schalk Burger, Victor Matfield, Bakkies Botha (Johann Muller, 21-29, 77), CJ van der Linde, John Smit (c) (Bismarck du Plessis, 77) & Os du Randt (Jannie du Plessis, 44-49, 72).

Argentina: Ignacio Corleto, Lucas Borges, Manuel Contepomi (Gonzalo Tiesi, 65), Felipe Contepomi, Horacio Agulla, Juan-Martin Hernández, Augustin Pichot (c), Gonzalo Longo, Juan-Martin Fernández Lobbe, Lucas Ostiglia (Juan-Manuel Leguizamón, 65), Patricio Albacete, Ignacio Fernández Lobbe (Rimas Alvarez Kairelis, 54), Martin Scelzo

(Omar Hasan, 34), Mario Ledesma & Rodrigo Roncero. Unused sub: Alberto Basualdo, Nicolas Fernández Miranda & Frederico Todeschini.

Scorers were:
South Africa – Tries: Habana (2), Du Preez, Rossouw.
Cons: Montgomery (4). Pens: Montgomery (3).
Argentina – Try: M Contepomi. Con: F Contepomi.
Pens: F Contepomi (2).
Cards: Juan Smith (SA – yellow card, 78), Felipe Contepomi (Argentina – yellow card, 79).

MATCH SEVEN:

FINAL:
South Africa (9) 15 England (3) 6
20 October: Stade de France (Saint-Denis)
Referee: Mr Alain Rolland (Ireland)

South Africa: Percy Montgomery, JP Pietersen, Jaque Fourie, François Steyn, Bryan Habana, Butch James, Fourie du Preez, Danie Rossouw (Wikus van Heerden, 72), Juan Smith, Schalk Burger, Victor Matfield, Bakkies Botha, CJ van der Linde, John Smit (c) (Bismarck du Plessis, 72-77) & Os du Randt. Unused subs: Jannie du Plessis, Johann Muller, Ruan Pienaar, André Pretorius & Wynand Olivier.

England: Jason Robinson (Dan Hipkiss, 47), Paul Sackey, Matthew Tait, Mike Catt (Toby Flood, 51), Mark Cueto, Jonny Wilkinson, Andy Gomarsall, Nick Easter (Lawrence Dallaglio, 65), Lewis Moody (Joe Worsley, 63) (Peter Richards, 71), Martin Corry, Ben Kay, Simon Shaw, Phil Vickery (c) (Matt Stevens, 41), Mark Regan (George Chuter, 63) & Andrew Sheridan.

Scorers were:
South Africa – Pens: Montgomery (4), Steyn.
England – Pens: Wilkinson (2).

Appendix B: RWC 2011 pools and match schedule

The Vodacom Super Rugby season kicked off on 18 February and runs until the final on 9 July. The Springboks play their first Tri Nations Test against the Wallabies in Sydney two weeks later, and the series concludes for the Boks just three weeks before the first match of Rugby World Cup 2011.

The Springboks are due to name their first squad of the year on 9 July and have to submit their final World Cup squad to the International Rugby Board on 22 August.

The opening game of Rugby World Cup 2011 (NZ vs Tonga) is on Friday 9 September.

Pool A	Pool B
New Zealand	Argentina
France	England
Tonga	Scotland
Canada	Georgia
Japan	Romania
Pool C	**Pool D**
Australia	South Africa
Ireland	Wales
Italy	Fiji
Russia	Samoa
USA	Namibia

DATE	NO	POOL	MATCH DETAILS	LOCATION	STADIUM
Fri 9 Sept	1	A	New Zealand v Tonga	Auckland	Eden Park
Sat 10 Sept	2	B	Scotland v Romania	Invercargill	Rugby Park Stadium
Sat 10 Sept	3	D	Fiji v Namibia	Rotorua	Rotorua International Stadium
Sat 10 Sept	4	A	France v Japan	Auckland	North Harbour Stadium
Sat 10 Sept	5	B	Argentina v England	Dunedin	Otago Stadium
Sun 11 Sept	6	C	Australia v Italy	Auckland	North Harbour Stadium
Sun 11 Sept	7	C	Ireland v USA	New Plymouth	Stadium Taranaki
Sun 11 Sept	8	D	**South Africa** v Wales	Wellington	Wellington Regional Stadium
Wed 14 Sept	9	D	Samoa v Namibia	Rotorua	Rotorua International Stadium
Wed 14 Sept	10	A	Tonga v Canada	Whangarei	Northland Events Centre
Wed 14 Sept	11	B	Scotland v Georgia	Invercargill	Rugby Park Stadium
Thurs 15 Sept	12	C	Russia v USA	New Plymouth	Stadium Taranaki
Fri 16 Sept	13	A	New Zealand v Japan	Hamilton	Waikato Stadium
Sat 17 Sept	14	B	Argentina v Romania	Invercargill	Rugby Park Stadium
Sat 17 Sept	15	D	**South Africa** v Fiji	Wellington	Wellington Regional Stadium
Sat 17 Sept	16	C	Australia v Ireland	Auckland	Eden Park
Sun 18 Sept	17	D	Wales v Samoa	Hamilton	Waikato Stadium
Sun 18 Sept	18	B	England v Georgia	Dunedin	Otago Stadium
Sun 18 Sept	19	A	France v Canada	Napier	McLean Park
Tues 20 Sept	20	C	Italy v Russia	Nelson	Trafalgar Park

DATE	NO	POOL	MATCH DETAILS	LOCATION	STADIUM
Wed 21 Sept	21	A	Tonga v Japan	Whangarei	Northland Events Centre
Thurs 22 Sept	22	D	**South Africa** v Namibia	Auckland	North Harbour Stadium
Fri 23 Sept	23	C	Australia v USA	Wellington	Wellington Regional Stadium
Sat 24 Sept	24	B	England v Romania	Dunedin	Carisbrook
Sat 24 Sept	25	A	New Zealand v France	Auckland	Eden Park
Sun 25 Sept	26	D	Fiji v Samoa	Auckland	Eden Park
Sun 25 Sept	27	C	Ireland v Russia	Rotorua	Rotorua International Stadium
Sun 25 Sept	28	B	Argentina v Scotland	Wellington	Wellington Regional Stadium
Mon 26 Sept	29	D	Wales v Namibia	New Plymouth	Stadium Taranaki
Tues 27 Sept	30	A	Canada v Japan	Napier	McLean Park
Tues 27 Sept	31	C	Italy v USA	Nelson	Trafalgar Park
Wed 28 Sept	32	B	Georgia v Romania	Palmerston North	Arena Manawatu
Fri 30 Sept	33	D	**South Africa** v Samoa	Auckland	North Harbour Stadium
Sat 1 Oct	34	C	Australia v Russia	Nelson	Trafalgar Park
Sat 1 Oct	35	A	France v Tonga	Wellington	Wellington Regional Stadium
Sat 1 Oct	36	B	England v Scotland	Auckland	Eden Park
Sun 2 Oct	37	B	Argentina v Georgia	Palmerston North	Arena Manawatu
Sun 2 Oct	38	A	New Zealand v Canada	Wellington	Wellington Regional Stadium
Sun 2 Oct	39	D	Wales v Fiji	Hamilton	Waikato Stadium
Sun 2 Oct	40	C	Ireland v Italy	Dunedin	Carisbrook

DATE	NO	POOL	MATCH DETAILS	LOCATION	STADIUM
Sat 8 Oct	41		QF1: W Pool C v RU Pool D	Wellington	Wellington Regional Stadium
Sat 8 Oct	42		QF2: W Pool B v RU Pool A	Auckland	Eden Park
Sun 9 Oct	43		QF3: W Pool D v RU Pool C	Wellington	Wellington Regional Stadium
Sun 9 Oct	44		QF4: W Pool A v RU Pool B	Auckland	Eden Park
Sat 15 Oct	45		SF1: W QF1 v W QF2	Auckland	Eden Park
Sun 16 Oct	46		SF2: W QF3 v W QF4	Auckland	Eden Park
Fri 21 Oct	47		Bronze Medal Final	Auckland	Eden Park
Sun 23 Oct	48		Final	Auckland	Eden Park

Bibliography

Dobson, Paul, et al (eds.). *The Badge: A Centenary of the Springbok Emblem.* Cape Town: SA Rugby, 2006

FitzSimons, Peter. *The Rugby War.* Sydney: Harper Sports, 1996

Griffiths, Edward. *Kitch – Triumph of a Decent Man.* Johannesburg: CAB, 1997

Guides and Publications Produced for the Rugby World Cups, 1995, 1999, 2003 and 2007. International Rugby Board (IRB)

Kay, Laurie. *Flight for a Nation – DVD on SAA fly-pasts.* Johannesburg: SA Guide-Dogs Association, 2000

Keohane, Mark. *Springbok Rugby Uncovered.* Cape Town: Zebra Press, 2004

Kervin, Alison. *Thirty Bullies: A History of the Rugby World Cup.* London: Simon & Schuster, 2007

Krige, Corné (with Peter Bills). *The Right Place at the Wrong Time.* Cape Town: Zebra Press, 2005

Luyt, Louis. *Walking Proud: The Louis Luyt Autobiography.* Cape Town: Don Nelson, 2003

McLean, Sir TP 'Terry'. *The All Blacks.* London: Sidgwick & Jackson Ltd., 1991

Pienaar, François (with Edward Griffiths). *Rainbow Warrior.* London: Collins Willow, 1999

Robertson, Ian (ed.). *The Complete Book of the Rugby World Cup 1995.* London: Hodder & Stoughton, 1995

Smit, John (with Mike Greenaway). *Captain in the Cauldron.* Cape Town: Safika, 2009

Smit, Kobus. *The Complete book of Springbok Rugby Records.* Cape Town: Don Nelson, 2007

Steyn, Rory (with Debora Patta). *One Step Behind Mandela: The Story of Rory Steyn, Nelson Mandela's Chief Bodyguard.* Cape Town: New Holland Books, 2001

Van der Valk, Rob (with Andy Colquhoun). *Nick & I – An adventure in rugby.* Cape Town: Don Nelson, 2002

Van Rooyen, Quintus, Andy Colquhoun, and Duane Heath (eds.).
   SA Rugby Annuals (from 1991 to 2010). Pretoria and Cape Town:
   Bankfin, Sasol, SA Rugby
White, Jake (with Craig Ray). *In Black and White – The Jake White Story.*
   Cape Town: Zebra Press, 2007
Zavos, Spiro. *Watching the Rugby World Cup.* Sydney: Allen & Unwin, 2007

Index